College Nicknames
The Ultimate Guide

Cullen Vane & Jim Gragnola

Strike Three Publishing

COLLEGE NICKNAMES
The Ultimate Guide

Strike Three Publishing
Roseville-San Jose

Printed in the United States of America

To learn more, or for information on ordering additional copies of this book, please visit:
www.thecollegenicknames.com or **www.amazon.com**

Contact the authors at
strike3publishing@yahoo.com

ISBN-13: 978-1463735630
ISBN-10: 1463735634

For my sons, Tyler and Zachary
and my brother, Terry

To my son Dominic, my daughter Giada
and my wife Yvonne,
without them it would have taken
much less time to write this book

Contents

About This Book

We started writing this book to answer the question, "What the *heck* is a Billiken?" in reference to the St. Louis University Billikens (and for a long time the title of this book was to be, *What's a Billiken?)* but also because we had no idea where schools like Xavier, Stetson and Canisius are located. Now we know.

Whatever the name, be it Aggies, Eagles or Zips, college nicknames are a rallying cry or a derisive antagonist. However, almost all schools have played under the mantle of a different name than the one used today. Even the famed "Fighting Irish" were known as the "Ramblers" throughout the Knute Rockne era. Nicknames come and go, and in the end, we root for or against a school and not the nickname.

Although a school's nickname and its mascot are invariably linked, the main impetus of this book is on nicknames. Some mascots are discussed in Chapter 4, but we're most concerned with nicknames only.

In Chapter 4 we answer the question of how over 600 schools got their nickname and we've recorded almost all of the unusual names, while most of those that remain are of the "common" sort. We apologize to those "Bulldogs," "Eagles," "Hawks" and "Tigers" (as well as all the others) for not being included.

Although NCAA Division I schools are the ones most often seen on TV and get the most reportage, it would have been unfair (and made for a very short book) to have left out the hundreds of others schools that compete intercollegiately.

Most of these schools are hardly known outside the region in which they reside but get a modicum of recognition here.

The schools listed in this book are derived from those that take part in all divisions of the:

NCAA	National Collegiate Association of Athletics (Div. I, II and III)
NAIA	National Association of Intercollegiate Athletics
ACAC	Alberta Colleges Athletic Conference
ACAL	Alberta Colleges Athletic League
ACCA	Association of Christian College Athletics
BCCAA	British Columbia Colleges Athletic Association
CIS	Canadian Interuniversity Sports
HVAC	Hudson Valley Athletic Conference
NCCAA	National Christian College Athletic Association
ORCC	Ohio Regional Campus Conference
OUA	Ontario University Athletics
USCAA	United States Collegiate Athletic Association
IND	Two schools compete as complete independents—Bryn Athyn and Bethany Bible College)

Only four-year colleges and universities are listed and only if they belong to and compete in any of the associations listed above.

Many Canadian schools regularly compete against American schools so we added those that compete in major conferences. Several Puerto Rican schools compete in the NCAA and we've added those schools as well.

We believe this to be the most comprehensive look at college nicknames ever put together in the history of mankind, and we're proud of our creation.

Cullen Vane (Marquette Warriors)
Jim Gragnola (San Jose State Spartans)

College Nicknames

The Ultimate Guide

Chapter 1

The Nicknames, A to Z

From the 49ers to Zips, they're all here. Big schools, little schools, the famous and many you've never even heard of, they all get the same fair treatment and at least a moment in the sun.

Many institutions have different names for their women's teams but we've listed only those that are *significantly* different from the men's teams. When two nicknames are shown the first is the men's (proceeded by a /) and the second is for the women. Also, "Fighting" is a popular antecedent to many names and we have only shown those schools that are "officially" known as such.

NICKNAME	SCHOOL	LOCATION	DIVISION
49ers	Charlotte, Univ. of N. Carolina at	Charlotte, NC	I
49ers	Long Beach, Calif. State Univ.	Long Beach, CA	I
Aggies	Cameron Univ.	Lawton, OK	II
Aggies	Davis, Univ. of Calif.	Davis, CA	I
Aggies	Delaware Valley College	Doylestown, PA	III
Aggies	N. Carolina Ag. and Tech. St. Univ.	Greensboro, NC	I
Aggies	Nebraska College of Tech. Agric.	Curtis, NE	USCCA
Aggies	New Mexico State Univ.	Las Cruces, NM	I
Aggies	Oklahoma Panhandle State Univ.	Goodwell, OK	II
Aggies	Texas A&M Univ.	College Station, TX	I
Aggies	Utah State Univ.	Logan, UT	I
Aigles Bleus/ Aigles Bleues	Moncton, Universite de	Moncton, NB	CIS
Ambassadors	Oakwood Univ.	Huntsville, AL	USCCA
Ambassadors	Ozark Christian College	Joplin, MO	NCCAA
AMCats	Anna Maria College	Paxton, MA	III
Anchormen	Rhode Island College	Providence, RI	III
Anteaters	Calif., Irvine, Univ. of	Irvine, CA	I
Antelopes	Grand Canyon Univ.	Phoenix, AZ	II
Archers	Moody Bible Institute	Chicago, IL	NCCAA
Argonauts	West Florida, Univ. of	Pensacola, FL	II
Argos	Great Falls, Univ. of	Great Falls, MT	NAIA
Argos	Notre Dame de Namur Univ.	Belmont, CA	II
Arrows	Ursuline College	Pepper Pike, OH	NAIA
Auggies	Augsburg College	Minneapolis, MN	III
Aurora	Canadian Univ. College	Lacombe, AB	ACAL
Avalanche	College of the Rockies	Cranbrook, BC	BCCAA
Avenging Angels	Meredith College	Raleigh, NC	III
Axemen/ Axewomen	Acadia Univ.	Wolfville, AUS	CIS
Aztecs	San Diego State Univ.	San Diego, SD	I
Badgers	Brock Univ.	St. Catharines, ON	OUA
Badgers	Johnson State College	Johnson, VT	III

Badgers	Spring Hill College	Mobile, AL	NAIA
Badgers	Wisconsin–Madison, Univ. of	Madison, WI	I
Bald Eagles	Lock Haven Univ. of Pennsylvania	Lock Haven, PA	II
ℓ **Banana Slugs**	Santa Cruz, Univ. of Calif.	Santa Cruz, CA	III
Bantams	Trinity College	Hartford, CT	III
Barons	Brewton-Parker College	Mount Vernon, GA	NAIA
Barons	Franciscan Univ. of Steubenville	Steubenville, OH	III
Barons	Ohio State Univ., Lima	Lima, OH	ORCC
Battlers	Alderson–Broaddus College	Philippi, WV	II
Battlers	Medicine Hat College	Medicine Hat, AB	ACAC
Battlin' Bears	Rocky Mountain College	Billings, MT	NAIA
Battling Bishops	N. Carolina Wesleyan College	Rocky Mount, NC	III
Battling Bishops	Ohio Wesleyan Univ.	Delaware, OH	III
Beacons	Massachusetts Boston, Univ. of	Boston, MA	III
Beacons	Northwest Christian Univ.	Eugene, OR	NAIA
Bearcats	Baruch College	New York, NY	III
Bearcats	Binghamton, State U. New York at	Vestal, NY	I
Bearcats	Brescia Univ.	Owensboro, KY	NAIA
Bearcats	Cincinnati, Univ. of	Cincinnati, OH	I
Bearcats	Lander Univ.	Greenwood, SC	II
Bearcats	McKendree Univ.	Lebanon, IL	NAIA
Bearcats	Northwest Missouri State Univ.	Maryville, MO	II
Bearcats	Rust College	Holly Springs, MS	III
Bearcats	Saint Vincent College	Latrobe, PA	III
Bearcats	Southwest Baptist Univ.	Bolivar, MO	II
Bearcats	Willamette Univ.	Salem, OR	III
Bearkats	Sam Houston State Univ.	Huntsville, TX	I
Bears	Barclay College	Haviland, KS	ACCA
Bears	Baylor Univ.	Waco, TX	I
Bears	Bridgewater State Univ.	Bridgewater, MA	III
Bears	Brown Univ.	Providence, RI	I
Bears	Golden State Baptist College	Santa Clara, CA	USCAA
Bears	Lenoir–Rhyne Univ.	Hickory, NC	II
Bears	Mercer Univ.	Macon, GA	I

Bears	Missouri State Univ.	Springfield, MO	I
Bears	Morgan State Univ.	Baltimore, MD	I
Bears	New York at Potsdam, State Univ. of	Potsdam, NY	III
Bears	New York Institute of Tech.	Old Westbury, NY	II
Bears	Northern Colorado, Univ. of	Greeley, CO	I
Bears	Pikeville College	Pikeville, KY	NAIA
Bears	Saint Joseph's College	Brooklyn, NY	USCCA
Bears	Shaw Univ.	Raleigh, NC	II
Bears	Shawnee State Univ.	Portsmouth, OH	NAIA
Bears	Truett-McConnell College	Cleveland, GA	NAIA
Bears	United States Coast Guard Acad.	New London, CT	III
Bears	Ursinus College	Collegeville, PA	III
Bears	Washington Univ. in Saint Louis	Saint Louis, MO	III
Bears/ Sugar Bears	Central Arkansas, Univ. of	Conway, AR	I
Beavers	Babson College	Wellesley, MA	III
Beavers	Bemidji State Univ.	Bemidji, MN	II
Beavers	Blackburn College	Carlinville, IL	III
Beavers	Bluffton Univ.	Bluffton, OH	III
Beavers	Buena Vista Univ.	Storm Lake, IA	III
Beavers	Calif. Institute of Tech.	Pasadena, CA	III
Beavers	City College of New York	New York, NY	III
Beavers	Maine at Farmington, Univ. of	Farmington, ME	III
Beavers	Minot State Univ.	Minot, ND	NAIA
Beavers	Oregon State Univ.	Corvallis, OR	I
Bees	Savannah Coll. of Art & Design	Savannah, GA	NAIA
Behrend Lions	Pennsylvania State Univ., Erie	Erie, PA	III
Belles	Bennett College	Greensboro, NC	USCAA
Belles	Saint Mary's College	Notre Dame, IN	III
Bengals	Buffalo State College	Buffalo, NY	III
Bengals	Idaho State Univ.	Pocatello, ID	I
Bengals	Maine at Fort Kent, Univ. of	Fort Kent, ME	NAIA
Big Blue	Millikin Univ.	Decatur, IL	III
Big Blues	Bluefield State College	Bluefield, WV	II
Big Green	Dartmouth College	Hanover, NH	I
Big Red	Cornell Univ.	Ithaca, NY	I

Big Red	Denison Univ.	Granville, OH	III
Billikens	Saint Louis Univ.	St. Louis, MO	I
Bison	Bethany College	Bethany, WV	III
Bison	Bucknell Univ.	Lewisburg, PA	I
Bison	Gallaudet Univ.	Washington, DC	III
Bison	Harding Univ.	Searcy, AR	II
Bison	Howard Univ.	Washington, DC	I
Bison	Nichols College	Dudley, MA	III
Bison	North Dakota State Univ.	Fargo, ND	I
Bison	Oklahoma Baptist Univ.	Shawnee, OK	NAIA
Bisons	Lipscomb Univ.	Nashville, TN	I
Bisons	Manitoba, Univ. of	Winnipeg, MT	CIS
Black Bears	Maine, Univ. of	Orono, ME	I
Black Knights	United States Military Academy	West Point, NY	I
Blackbirds	Long Island Univ.-Brooklyn	Brooklyn, NY	I
Blazers	Belhaven College	Jackson, MS	NAIA
Blazers	Bethany Bible College	Sussex, NB	IND
Blazers	Birmingham, Univ. of Alabama at	Birmingham, AL	I
Blazers	Canadian Mennonite Univ.	Winnipeg, MT	MCAC
Blazers	Elms College	Chicopee, MA	III
Blazers	Hood College	Frederick, MD	III
Blazers	Saint Benedict's Univ.	St. Joseph, MN	III
Blazers	Valdosta State Univ.	Valdosta, GA	II
Bloodhounds	John Jay Coll. of Criminal Justice	New York, NY	III
Blue	Wellesley College	Wellesley, MA	III
Blue Angels	Mount Mary College	Milwaukee, WI	III
Blue Angels	New Rochelle, College of	New Rochelle, NY	III
Blue Bears	Livingstone College	Salisbury, NC	II
Blue Demons	DePaul Univ.	Chicago, IL	I
Blue Devils	Central Connecticut State Univ.	New Britain, CT	I
Blue Devils	Dickinson College	Carlisle, PA	III
Blue Devils	Dillard Univ.	New Orleans, LA	NAIA
Blue Devils	Duke Univ.	Durham, NC	I
Blue Devils	King's College, Univ. of	Halifax, NS	ACAA
Blue Devils	New York at Fredonia, State Univ. of	Fredonia, NY	III

Blue Devils	Wisconsin–Stout, Univ. of	Menomonie, WI	III
Blue Hawks	Dickinson State Univ.	Dickinson, ND	NAIA
Blue Hens	Delaware, Univ. of	Newark, DE	I
Blue Hose	Presbyterian College	Clinton, SC	I
Blue Jays	Elizabethtown College	Elizabethtown, PA	III
Blue Jays	Johns Hopkins Univ.	Baltimore, MD	III
Blue Jays	Saint Joseph College	West Hartford, CT	III
Blue Jays	Westminster College	Fulton, MO	III
Blue Knights	New York at Geneseo, State Univ. of	Genesco, NY	III
Blue Knights	Urbana Univ.	Urbana, OH	II
Blue Raiders	Lindsey Wilson College	Columbia, KY	NAIA
Blue Raiders	Middle Tennessee State Univ.	Murfreesboro, TN	I
Blue Streaks	John Carroll Univ.	Univ. Heights, OH	III
Blue Tigers	Lincoln Univ. of Missouri	Jefferson City, MO	II
Blueboys	Illinois College	Jacksonville, IL	III
Bluejays	Creighton Univ.	Omaha, NE	I
Bluejays	Elmhurst College	Elmhurst, IL	III
Bluejays	Polytechnic Inst. of New York Univ.	Brooklyn, NY	III
Bluejays	Tabor College	Hillsboro, KS	NAIA
Blues	Capilano Univ.	N. Vancouver, BC	BCCAA
Blugolds	Wisconsin–Eau Claire, Univ. of	Eau Claire, WI	III
Bobcats	Bates College	Lewiston, ME	III
Bobcats	Brandon, Univ. of	Brandon, AB	CIS
Bobcats	College of the Ozarks	Point Lookout, MO	NAIA
Bobcats	Frostburg State Univ.	Frostburg, MD	III
Bobcats	Georgia College & State Univ.	Milledgeville, GA	II
Bobcats	Lees–McRae College	Banner Elk, NC	II
Bobcats	Montana State Univ. – Bozeman	Bozeman, MT	I
Bobcats	Ohio Univ.	Athens, OH	I
Bobcats	Paul Smith's College	Paul Smith, NY	NAIA
Bobcats	Peru State College	Peru, NE	NAIA
Bobcats	Pittsburgh at Greensburg, Univ. of	Greensburg, PA	III
Bobcats	Quinnipiac Univ.	Hamden, CT	I
Bobcats	Saint Thomas Univ. Florida	Miami Gardens, FL	NAIA
Bobcats	Texas State Univ.–San Marcos	San Marcos, TX	I

Bobcats	West Virginia Wesleyan College	Buckhannon, WV	II
Boilermakers	Purdue Univ.	West Lafayette, IN	I
Boll Weevils/ Cotton Blossoms	Arkansas at Monticello, Univ. of	Monticello, AR	II
Bombers	Ithaca College	Ithaca, NY	III
Bonnies	Saint Bonaventure Univ.	St. Bonaventure, NY	I
Boxers	Pacific Univ.	Forest Grove, OR	III
Braves	Alcorn State Univ.	Lorman, MS	I
Braves	Bradley Univ.	Peoria, IL	I
Braves	North Carolina-Pembroke, Univ. of	Pembroke, NC	II
Braves	Ottawa Univ.	Ottawa, KS	NAIA
Brewers	Vassar College	Poughkeepsie, NY	III
Britons	Albion College	Albion, MI	III
Bronchos	Central Oklahoma, Univ. of	Edmond, OK	II
Broncos	Boise State Univ.	Boise, ID	I
Broncos	Calif. State Polytechnic, Pomona	Pomona, CA	II
Broncos	Delhi, State Univ. of New York at	Delhi, NY	NAIA
Broncos	Fayetteville State Univ.	Fayetteville, NC	II
Broncos	Hastings College	Hastings, NE	NAIA
Broncos	Olds College	Olds, AB	ACAC
Broncos	Santa Clara Univ.	Santa Clara, CA	I
Broncos	Western Michigan Univ.	Kalamazoo, MI	I
Broncs	Rider Univ.	Lawrenceville, NJ	I
Broncs	Texas–Pan American, Univ. of	Edinburg, TX	I
Bruins	Bellevue Univ.	Bellevue, NE	NAIA
Bruins	Belmont Univ.	Nashville, TN	I
Bruins	Bethany Univ.	Scotts Valley, CA	NAIA
Bruins	Calif., Los Angeles, Univ. of	Los Angeles, CA	I
Bruins	George Fox Univ.	Newberg, OR	III
Bruins	Sheridan College	Oakville, ON	CIS
Buccaneers	Barry Univ.	Miami Shores, FL	II
Buccaneers	Beloit College	Beloit, WI	III
Buccaneers	Charleston Southern Univ.	Charleston, SC	I
Buccaneers	Christian Brothers Univ.	Memphis, TN	II
Buccaneers	East Tennessee State Univ.	Johnson City, TN	I

Buccaneers	Massachusetts Maritime Acad.	Buzzards Bay, MA	III
Buckeyes	Ohio State Univ., The	Columbus, OH	I
Buffaloes	Colorado at Boulder, Univ. of	Boulder, CO	I
Buffaloes	Milligan College	Milligan College, TN	NAIA
Buffaloes	West Texas A&M Univ.	Canyon, TX	II
Builders	Apprentice School, The	Newport News, VA	USCCA
Bulldogs	Adrian College	Adrian, MI	III
Bulldogs	Alabama A&M	Huntsville, AL	I
Bulldogs	Barton College	Wilson, NC	II
Bulldogs	Benedictine Univ. at Springfield	Springfield, IL	NAIA
Bulldogs	Bowie State Univ.	Bowie, MD	II
Bulldogs	Boyce College	Louisville, KY	NCCAA
Bulldogs	Brooklyn College	Brooklyn, NY	III
Bulldogs	Bryant Univ.	Smithfield, RI	I
Bulldogs	Butler Univ.	Indianapolis, IN	I
Bulldogs	Calif. State Univ., Fresno	Fresno, CA	I
Bulldogs	Citadel, The	Charleston, SC	I
Bulldogs	Concordia Univ., Seward	Seward, NE	NAIA
Bulldogs	Cumberland Univ.	Lebanon, TN	NAIA
Bulldogs	DeSales Univ.	Lehigh County, PA	III
Bulldogs	Drake Univ.	Des Moines, IA	I
Bulldogs	Ferris State Univ.	Big Rapids, MI	II
Bulldogs	Fisk Univ.	Nashville, TN	NAIA
Bulldogs	Georgia, Univ. of	Athens, GA	I
Bulldogs	Gonzaga Univ.	Spokane, WA	I
Bulldogs	Jarvis Christian College	Hawkins, TX	NAIA
Bulldogs	Louisiana Tech Univ.	Ruston, LA	I
Bulldogs	McPherson College	McPherson, KS	NAIA
Bulldogs	Minnesota Duluth, Univ. of	Duluth, MN	II
Bulldogs	Mississippi State Univ.	Starkville, MS	I
Bulldogs	Montana - Western, Univ. of	Dillon, MT	NAIA
Bulldogs	North Carolina-Asheville, Univ. of	Asheville, NC	I
Bulldogs	Redlands, Univ. of	Redlands, CA	III
Bulldogs	Samford	Homewood, AL	I
Bulldogs	Selma Univ.	Selma, AL	USCCA

Bulldogs	South Carolina State Univ.	Orangeburg, SC	I
Bulldogs	Southwestern Okla. State Univ.	Weatherford, OK	II
Bulldogs	Tennessee Wesleyan College	Athens, TN	NAIA
Bulldogs	Texas Lutheran Univ.	Seguin, TX	III
Bulldogs	Tougaloo College	Tougaloo, MS	NAIA
Bulldogs	Truman State Univ.	Kirksville, MO	II
Bulldogs	Union College	Barbourville, KY	NAIA
Bulldogs	Union Univ.	Jackson, TN	NAIA
Bulldogs	Wilberforce Univ.	Wilberforce, OH	NAIA
Bulldogs	Wingate Univ.	Wingate, NC	II
Bulldogs	Yale Univ.	New Haven, CT	I
Bullets	Gettysburg College	Gettysburg, PA	III
Bulls	New York at Buffalo, State Univ. of	Buffalo, NY	I
Bulls	South Florida, Univ. of	Tampa, FL	I
Cadets	Norwich Univ.	Northfield, VT	III
Camels	Campbell Univ.	Buies Creek, NC	I
Camels	Connecticut College	New London, CT	III
Cannoneers	Pratt Institute	Brooklyn, NY	III
Capers	Cape Breton Univ.	Sydney, NS	CIS
Captains	Christopher Newport Univ.	Newport News, VA	III
Carabins	Montreal, Universite de	Montreal, QC	CIS
Cardinal	Stanford Univ.	Palo Alto, CA	I
Cardinals	Andrews Univ.	Berrien Springs, MI	USCCA
Cardinals	Ball State Univ.	Muncie, IN	I
Cardinals	Catholic Univ. of America, The	Washington, DC	III
Cardinals	Concordia Univ., Ann Arbor	Ann Arbor, MI	NAIA
Cardinals	Incarnate Word, Univ. of the	San Antonio, TX	II
Cardinals	Lamar Univ.	Beaumont, TX	I
Cardinals	Louisville, Univ. of	Louisville, KY	I
Cardinals	New York at Plattsburgh, Stat U. of	Plattsburgh, NY	III
Cardinals	North Central College	Naperville, IL	III
Cardinals	Otterbein Univ.	Westerville, OH	III
Cardinals	Saginaw Valley State Univ.	Univ. Center, MI	II
Cardinals	Saint John Fisher College	Pittsford, NY	III
Cardinals	Saint Mary's Univ. of Minnesota	Winona, MN	III

Cardinals	Wesleyan Univ.	Middleton, CT	III
Cardinals	Wheeling Jesuit Univ.	Wheeling, WV	II
Cardinals	William Jewell College	Liberty, MO	NAIA
Cardinals	York College, City Univ. of NY	Jamaica, NY	III
Cascades	Fraser Valley, Univ. of the	Abbotsford, BC	BCCAA
Catamounts	Vermont, Univ. of	Burlington, VT	I
Catamounts	Western Carolina Univ.	Cullowhee, NC	I
Cavaliers	Cabrini College	Radnor, PA	III
Cavaliers	Concordia Univ., Portland	Portland, OR	NAIA
Cavaliers	Montreat College	Montreat, NC	NAIA
Cavaliers	Saint Gregory's Univ.	Shawnee, OK	NAIA
Cavaliers	Virginia, Univ. of	Charlottesville, VA	I
Cavaliers	Virginia-Wise	Wise, VA	NAIA
Cavaliers	Walsh Univ.	North Canton, OH	NAIA
Celtics	Carlow Univ.	Pittsburgh, PA	NAIA
Celts	Saint Thomas, Univ. of	Houston, TX	NAIA
Chanticleers	Coastal Carolina Univ.	Conway, SC	I
Chaparrals	Lubbock Christian Univ.	Lubbock, TX	NAIA
Chargers	Alabama in Huntsville, Univ. of	Huntsville, AL	II
Chargers	Atlanta Christian College	East Point, GA	NCCAA
Chargers	Briar Cliff Univ.	Sioux City, IA	NAIA
Chargers	Colby–Sawyer College	New London, NH	III
Chargers	Crandall Univ.	Moncton, NB	ACAA
Chargers	Dominican College	Orangeburg, NY	II
Chargers	Hillsdale College	Hillsdale, MI	II
Chargers	Lancaster Bible College	Lancaster, PA	III
Chargers	New Haven, Univ. of	West Haven, CT	II
Chippewas	Central Michigan Univ.	Mt. Pleasant, MI	I
Choctaws	Mississippi College	Clinton, MS	III
Citadins	Quebec a Montreal, Universite du	Montreal, QC	CIS
Clan	Simon Fraser Univ.	Burnaby, BC	NAIA
Clippers	Briercrest College	Caronport, SK	ACAC
Clippers	Concordia College	Bronxville, NY	II
Clippers	Maine at Machias, Univ. of	Machias, ME	NAIA
Cobbers	Concordia College	Moorhead, MN	III

Cobras	Coker College	Hartsville, SC	II
Cobras	Virginia Intermont College	Bristol, VA	NAIA
Colonels	Centre College	Danville, KY	III
Colonels	Curry College	Milton, MA	III
Colonels	Eastern Kentucky Univ.	Richmond, KY	I
Colonels	Nicholls State Univ.	Thibodaux, LA	I
Colonels	Wilkes Univ.	Wilkes-Barre, PA	III
Colonials	George Washington Univ., The	Washington, DC	I
Colonials	Robert Morris Univ.	Moon Twsp., PA	I
Colonials	Western Connecticut State Univ.	Danbury, CT	III
Colts	Centennial College	Scarborough, ON	CIS
Comets	Mayville State Univ.	Mayville, ND	NAIA
Comets	Olivet College	Olivet, MI	III
Comets	Texas at Dallas, Univ. of	Dallas, TX	III
Commodores	Vanderbilt Univ.	Nashville, TN	I
Condors	Conestoga College	Kitchener, ON	CIS
Conquerors	Association Free Lutheran Bible College	Plymouth, MN	ACCA
Conquerors	Piedmont Baptist College	Winston-Salem, NC	NCCAA
Continentals	Hamilton College	Clinton, NY	III
Cornhuskers	Nebraska–Lincoln, Univ. of	Lincoln, NE	I
Corsairs	Massachusetts Dartmouth, Univ. of	Dartmouth, MA	III
Cougars	Averett Univ.	Danville, VA	III
Cougars	Azusa Pacific Univ.	Azusa, CA	NAIA
Cougars	Brigham Young Univ.	Provo, UT	I
Cougars	Caldwell College	Caldwell, NJ	II
Cougars	Calif. State Univ., San Marcos	San Marcos, CA	NAIA
Cougars	Carver Bible College	Atlanta, GA	NCCAA
Cougars	Charleston, College of	Charleston, SC	I
Cougars	Chatham Univ.	Pittsburgh, PA	III
Cougars	Chicago State Univ.	Chicago, IL	I
Cougars	Clark Univ.	Worcester, MA	III
Cougars	Clearwater Christian College	Clearwater, FL	NCCAA
Cougars	Clermont College	Batavia, OH	USCCA
Cougars	Colorado Christian Univ.	Lakewood, CO	II
Cougars	Columbia College	Columbia, MO	NAIA

Cougars	Columbus State Univ.	Columbus, GA	II
Cougars	Concordia Univ. Chicago	River Forest, IL	III
Cougars	Houston, Univ. of	Houston, TX	I
Cougars	Kean Univ.	Union Twsp., NJ	III
Cougars	Kuyper College	Grand Rapids, MI	NCCAA
Cougars	Medgar Evers College	Brooklyn, NY	III
Cougars	Mid-Continent Univ.	Mayfield, KY	NAIA
Cougars	Minnesota Morris, Univ. of	Morris, MN	III
Cougars	Misericordia Univ.	Dallas, TX	III
Cougars	Mount Royal Univ.	Calgary, AB	ACAC
Cougars	Mount Vernon Nazarene Univ.	Mt. Vernon, OH	NAIA
Cougars	Mountain State Univ.	Beckley, WA	NAIA
Cougars	Ohio Univ., Lancaster	Lancaster, OH	ORCC
Cougars	Quebec a Chicoutimi, Universite du	Chicoutimi, QC	CIS
Cougars	Regina, Univ. of	Regina, SK	NAIA
Cougars	Saint Francis, Univ. of	Fort Wayne, IN	NAIA
Cougars	Saint Xavier Univ.	Chicago, IL	NAIA
Cougars	Sioux Falls, Univ. of	Sioux Falls, SD	NAIA
Cougars	Southern Ill. Univ. Edwardsville	Edwardsville, IL	I
Cougars	Spring Arbor Univ.	Spring Arbor, MI	NAIA
Cougars	Washington State Univ.	Pullman, WA	I
Cowboys	Hardin–Simmons Univ.	Abilene, TX	III
Cowboys	McNeese State Univ.	Lake Charles, LA	I
Cowboys	New Mexico Highlands Univ.	Las Vegas, NV	II
Cowboys	Oklahoma State Univ.–Stillwater	Stillwater, OK	I
Cowboys	Puerto Rico at Bayamón, Univ. of	Bayamon, PR	II
Cowboys	Wyoming, Univ. of	Laramie, WY	I
Coyotes	Calif. State Univ., San Bernardino	San Bernardino, CA	II
Coyotes	College of Idaho, The	Caldwell, ID	NAIA
Coyotes	Kansas Wesleyan Univ.	Salina, KS	NAIA
Coyotes	La Cite College	Ottawa, ON	CIS
Coyotes	South Dakota, Univ. of	Vermillion, SD	I
Crimson	Harvard Univ.	Cambridge, MA	I
Crimson Eagles	Philadelphia Biblical Univ.	Langhorne, PA	III
Crimson Hawks	Indiana Univ. of Pennsylvania	Indiana, PA	II

Crimson Storm	Southern Nazarene Univ.	Bethany, OK	NAIA
Crimson Tide	Alabama, Univ. of	Tuscaloosa, AL	I
Crimson Wave	Calumet College of Saint Joseph	Whiting, IN	NAIA
Crusaders	Alvernia Univ.	Reading, PA	III
Crusaders	Belmont Abbey College	Belmont, NC	II
Crusaders	Capital Univ.	Columbus, OH	III
Crusaders	Christendom College	Front Royal, VA	USCCA
Crusaders	Cincinnati Christian College	Cincinnati, OH	USCCA
Crusaders	Clarke College	Dubuque, IA	NAIA
Crusaders	Dallas Christian College	Dallas, TX	NCCAA
Crusaders	Dallas, Univ. of	Dallas, TX	III
Crusaders	Evangel Univ.	Springfield, MO	NAIA
Crusaders	Holy Cross, College of the	Worcester, MA	I
Crusaders	Madonna Univ.	Livonia, MI	NAIA
Crusaders	Manhattan Christian College	Manhattan, KS	NCCAA
Crusaders	Maranatha Baptist Bible College	Watertown, WI	III
Crusaders	Mary Hardin–Baylor, Univ. of	Belton, TX	III
Crusaders	North Greenville Univ.	Tigerville, SC	II
Crusaders	Northwest Nazarene Univ.	Nampa, ID	II
Crusaders	Susquehanna Univ.	Selinsgrove, PA	III
Crusaders	Tennessee Temple Univ.	Chattanooga, TN	NCCAA
Crusaders	Valparaiso Univ.	Valparaiso, IN	I
Crusaders	William Carey College	Hattiesburg, MS	NAIA
Cyclones	Centenary College	Hackettstown, NJ	III
Cyclones	Iowa State Univ.	Ames, IA	I
Cyclones	Mills College	Oakland, CA	NAIA
Deacons	Bloomfield College	Bloomfield, NJ	II
Deacons	New Hope Christian College	Eugene, OR	NCCAA
Defenders	Baptist Bible College & Seminary	Clarks Summit, PA	III
Defenders	Dordt College	Sioux Center, IA	NAIA
Delta Devils	Mississippi Valley State Univ.	Itta Bena, MS	I
Demon Deacons	Wake Forest Univ.	Winston-Salem, NC	I
Demons	Northwestern State Univ.	Natchitoches, LA	I
Devils	Fairleigh Dickinson Univ., Florham	Madison, NJ	III
Devils	Sciences in Philadelphia, Univ. of the	Philadelphia, PA	II

Dinos	Calgary, Univ. of	Calgary, AB	CIS
Diplomats	Franklin & Marshall College	Lancaster, PA	III
Dolphins	Jacksonville Univ.	Jacksonville, FL	I
Dolphins	Le Moyne College	DeWitt, NY	II
Dolphins	Mount Saint Vincent, College of	Bronx, NY	III
Dolphins	Staten Island, College of	Staten Island, NY	III
Dons	San Francisco, Univ. of	San Francisco, CA	I
Dragons	Drexel Univ.	Philadelphia, PA	I
Dragons	Lane College	Jackson, TN	II
Dragons	Minnesota State Univ. Moorhead	Moorhead, MN	II
Dragons	Sainte-Anne, Universite	Digby County, NS	ACAA
Dragons	Tiffin Univ.	Tiffin, OH	II
Drovers	Science and Arts of Okla., Univ. of	Chickasaw, OK	NAIA
Ducks	Oregon, Univ. of	Eugene, OR	I
Ducks	Stevens Institute of Tech.	Hoboken, NJ	III
Duhawks	Loras College	Dubuque, IA	III
Dukes	Duquesne Univ.	Pittsburgh, PA	I
Dukes	James Madison Univ.	Harrisonburg, VA	I
Dustdevils	Texas A&M International Univ.	Laredo, TX	II
Dutch	Central College	Pella, IA	III
Dutchmen	Union College	Schenectady, NY	III
Eagles	AIB School of Business	Des Moines, IA	NAIA
Eagles	Alice Lloyd College	Pippa Passes, KY	NAIA
Eagles	American Univ.	Washington, DC	I
Eagles	Asbury College	Wilmore, KY	NAIA
Eagles	Ashland Univ.	Ashland, OH	II
Eagles	Avila Univ.	Kansas City, MO	NAIA
Eagles	Baptist College of Florida	Graceville, FL	NCCAA
Eagles	Benedictine Univ.	Lisle, IL	III
Eagles	Bethany College	Hepburn, SK	PAC
Eagles	Biola Univ.	La Mirada, CA	NAIA
Eagles	Boston College	Chestnut Hill, MA	I
Eagles	Bridgewater College	Bridgewater, VA	III
Eagles	Carson–Newman College	Jefferson City, TN	II
Eagles	Central Methodist Univ.	Fayette, MO	NAIA

Eagles	Chadron State College	Chadron, NE	II
Eagles	Cincinnati Christian Univ.	Cincinnati, OH	NAIA
Eagles	Concordia Univ., Irvine	Irvine, CA	NAIA
Eagles	Coppin State Univ.	Baltimore, MD	I
Eagles	Daniel Webster College	Nashua, NH	III
Eagles	Eastern Michigan Univ.	Ypsilanti, MI	I
Eagles	Eastern Univ.	St. Davids, PA	III
Eagles	Eastern Washington Univ.	Cheney, WA	I
Eagles	Edgewood College	Madison, WI	III
Eagles	Embry–Riddle Aero., Daytona Beach	Daytona Beach, FL	NAIA
Eagles	Embry-Riddle Aeronautical Univ.	Prescott, AZ	NAIA
Eagles	Emmaus Bible College	Dubuque, IA	ACCA
Eagles	Emory Univ.	Atlanta, GA	III
Eagles	Faith Baptist Bible College	Ankeny, IA	NCCAA
Eagles	Faulkner Univ.	Montgomery, AL	NAIA
Eagles	Florida Gulf Coast Univ.	Fort Myers, FL	I
Eagles	Georgia Southern Univ.	Statesboro, GA	I
Eagles	Green Mountain College	Poultney, VT	III
Eagles	Husson Univ.	Bangor, ME	III
Eagles	Judson Univ.	Elgin, IL	NAIA
Eagles	Juniata College	Huntingdon, PA	III
Eagles	Kwantlen Polytechnic Univ.	Surrey, BC	BCCAA
Eagles	Lambuth Univ.	Jackson, TN	II
Eagles	Life Univ.	Marietta, GA	NAIA
Eagles	Mary Washington, Univ. of	Fredericksburg, VA	III
Eagles	Midway College	Midway, KY	NAIA
Eagles	Morehead State Univ.	Morehead, KY	I
Eagles	North Carolina Central Univ.	Durham, NC	I
Eagles	Northern New Mexico College	Espanola, NC	NAIA
Eagles	Northwest Univ.	Kirkland, WA	NAIA
Eagles	Northwestern College	Roseville, MN	III
Eagles	Oklahoma Christian Univ.	Oklahoma City, OK	NAIA
Eagles	Oklahoma Wesleyan Univ.	Bartlesville, OK	NAIA
Eagles	Ozarks, Univ. of the	Clarksville, AR	III
Eagles	Pensacola Christian College	Pensacola, FL	NCCAA

Eagles	Post Univ.	Waterbury, CT	II
Eagles	Reinhardt College	Waleska, GA	NAIA
Eagles	Rhema Bible College	Broken Arrow, OK	ACCA
Eagles	Robert Morris Univ.	Chicago, IL	NAIA
Eagles	Robert Morris Univ.-Lake County	Waukegan, IL	USCCA
Eagles	Robert Morris Univ.-Peoria	Peoria, IL	USCCA
Eagles	Robert Morris Univ.-Springfield	Springfield, IL	USCCA
Eagles	Saint Elizabeth, College of	Convent Station, NJ	III
Eagles	Shepherd Technical College	Memphis, TN	ACCA
Eagles	Southwestern Christian Univ.	Bethany, OK	NCCAA
Eagles	Southwestern College	Phoenix, AZ	NAIA
Eagles	The King's Univ. College	Edmonton, AB	ACAC
Eagles	Toccoa Falls College	Toccoa Falls, GA	NCCAA
Eagles	Trinity Lutheran College	Everett, WA	NCCAA
Eagles	Victory Univ.	Memphis, WA	NCCAA
Eagles	West Coast Baptist College	Lancaster, CA	ACCA
Eagles	Williams Baptist College	Walnut Ridge, AR	NAIA
Eagles	Winthrop Univ.	Rock Hill, SC	I
Eagles	Wisconsin–La Crosse, Univ. of	La Crosse, WI	III
Engineers	Massachusetts Institute of Tech.	Cambridge, MA	III
Engineers	Rensselaer Polytechnic Institute	Troy, NY	III
Engineers	Worcester Polytechnic Institute	Worcester, MA	III
Ephs	Williams College	Williamstown, MA	III
Eutectic	Saint Louis College of Pharmacy	St. Louis, MO	NAIA
Evangels	Johnson Bible College	Knoxville, TN	NCCAA
Evangels	Mid-America Christian Univ.	Oklahoma City, OK	NAIA
Excalibur	Trent Univ.	Peterborough, ON	OUA
Explorers	La Salle Univ.	Philadelphia, PA	I
Express	Wells College	Aurora, NY	III
Falcons	Albertus Magnus College	New Haven, CT	III
Falcons	Bentley Univ.	Waltham, MA	II
Falcons	Bowling Green State Univ.	Bowling Green, OH	I
Falcons	Cedar Crest College	Allentown, PA	III
Falcons	Concordia Univ. Wisconsin	Mequon, WI	III
Falcons	Davis College	Johnson City, NY	NCCAA

Falcons	Fairmont State Univ.	Fairmont, WV	II
Falcons	Fanshawe College	London, ON	CIS
Falcons	Fisher College	Sunrise, MA	NAIA
Falcons	Fitchburg State Univ.	Fitchburg, MA	III
Falcons	Florida College	Temple Terrace, FL	USCCA
Falcons	Friends Univ.	Wichita, KS	NAIA
Falcons	Messiah College	Grantham, PA	III
Falcons	Montevallo, Univ. of	Montevallo, AL	II
Falcons	Notre Dame College	South Euclid, OH	NAIA
Falcons	Pfeiffer Univ.	Misenheimer, NC	II
Falcons	Saint Augustine's College	Raleigh, NC	II
Falcons	Seattle Pacific Univ.	Seattle, WA	II
Falcons	Texas of the Permian Basin, Univ. of	Odessa, TX	II
Falcons	United States Air Force Academy	Col. Springs, CO	I
Falcons	Wisconsin–River Falls, Univ. of	River Falls, WI	III
Fightin' Engineers	Rose–Hulman Institute of Tech.	Terre Haute, IN	III
Fightin' Tigers	Louisiana State Univ.	Baton Rouge, LA	I
Fighting Leathernecks	Western Illinois Univ.	Macomb, IL	I
Fighting Squirrels	Mary Baldwin College	Stauton, VA	III
Fighting Illini	Illinois at Urbana–Champaign, Univ. of	Urbana–Champaign, IL	I
Fighting Bees/ Queen Bees	Saint Ambrose Univ.	Davenport, IA	NAIA
Fighting Indians	Haskell Indian Nations Univ.	Lawrence, KS	NAIA
Fighting Irish	Notre Dame, Univ. of	Notre Dame, IN	I
Fighting Knights	Lynn Univ.	Boca Raton, FL	II
Fighting Koalas	Columbia College	Columbia, SC	NAIA
Fighting Muskies	Muskingum Univ.	New Concord, OH	III
Fighting Saints	Saint Joseph, College of	Rutland, VT	NAIA
Fighting Scots	College of Wooster	Wooster, OH	III
Fighting Scots	Covenant College	Lookout Mtn., GA	NAIA
Fighting Scots	Gordon College	Wenham, MA	III
Fighting Scots	Monmouth College	Monmouth, IL	III

Fighting Scots	Ohio Valley Univ.	Vienna, WV	II
Fighting Sioux	North Dakota, Univ. of	Grand Forks, ND	I
Fighting Tigers	New York at Cobleskill, St. Univ. of	Cobleskill, NY	III
Fire	Southeastern Univ.	Lakeland, FL	NAIA
Firebirds	District of Columbia, Univ. of the	Washington, DC	II
Flames	Bethesda Christian Univ.	Anaheim, CA	NCCAA
Flames	Free Will Baptist Bible College	Nashville, TN	NCCAA
Flames	Illinois at Chicago, Univ. of	Chicago, IL	I
Flames	Lee Univ.	Cleveland, OH	NAIA
Flames	Liberty Univ.	Lynchburg, VA	I
Flames	Saint Mary, College of (women)	Omaha, NE	NAIA
Flyers	Dayton, Univ. of	Dayton, OH	I
Flyers	Lewis Univ.	Romeoville, IL	II
Flying Dutchmen	Hope College	Holland, MI	III
Flying Dutch	Lebanon Valley College	Annville, PA	III
Flying Fleet	Erskine College	Due West, SC	II
Fords	Haverford College	Haverford, PA	III
Foresters	Huntington Univ.	Huntington, IN	NAIA
Foresters	Lake Forest College	Lake Forest, IL	III
Freemen	Providence College	Otterburne, BC	NCCAA
Friars	Providence College	Providence, RI	I
Gaels	Iona College	New Rochelle, NY	I
Gaels	Queen's Univ.	Kingston, ON	OUA
Gaels	Saint Mary's College of Calif.	Moraga, CA	I
Gaillards/ Astrelles	Quebec a Abitibi-Temiscamingue, Universite du	Rouyn Noranda, QC	CIS
Gaiters	Bishop's Univ.	Sherbrooke, QC	CIS
Gamecocks	Jacksonville State Univ.	Jacksonville, AL	I
Gamecocks	South Carolina, Univ. of	Columbia, SC	I
Garnet	Swarthmore College	Swarthmore, PA	III
Gators	Allegheny College	Meadville, PA	III
Gators	Florida, Univ. of	Gainesville, FL	I
Gators	Notre Dame of Maryland, College of	Baltimore, MD	III
Gators	Pine Manor College	Chestnut Hill, MA	III
Gators	Russell Sage College	Troy, NY	III

Gators	San Francisco State Univ.	San Francisco, CA	II
Gauchos	Calif., Santa Barbara, Univ. of	Santa Barbara, CA	I
Gee Gees	Ottawa, Univ. of	Ottawa, ON	OUA
Generals	Louisiana State Univ. at Alexandria	Alexandria, LA	NAIA
Generals	Washington and Lee Univ.	Lexington, VA	III
Gents/Ladies	Centenary College of Louisiana	Shreveport, LA	I
Geoducks	Evergreen State College	Olympia, WA	NAIA
Giants	Keystone College	La Plume, PA	III
Gold Rush/ Gold Nuggets	Xavier Univ. of Louisiana	New Orleans, LA	NAIA
Golden Tornadoes	Geneva College	Beaver Falls, PA	III
Golden Hurricane	Tulsa, Univ. of	Tulsa, OK	I
Golden Gophers	Minnesota Twin Cities, Univ. of	Minneapolis and St. Paul, MN	I
Golden Grizzlies	Oakland Univ.	Rochester, MI	I
Golden Panthers	Florida International Univ.	Miami, FL	I
Golden Bears	Calif., Berkeley, Univ. of	Berkeley, CA	I
Golden Bears	Concordia Univ.	St. Paul, MN	II
Golden Bears	Kutztown Univ. of Pennsylvania	Kutztown, PA	II
Golden Bears	Miles College	Fairfield, AL	II
Golden Bears	West Virginia Tech	Montgomery, WA	NAIA
Golden Bears	Western New England College	Springfield, MA	III
Golden Bears/ Pandas	Alberta, Univ. of	Alberta, AB	NAIA
Golden Bulls	Johnson C. Smith Univ.	Charlotte, NC	II
Golden Eagles	Calif. State Univ., Los Angeles	Los Angeles, CA	II
Golden Eagles	Charleston, Univ. of	Charleston, WV	II
Golden Eagles	Clarion Univ. of Pennsylvania	Clarion, PA	II
Golden Eagles	Cornerstone Univ.	Grand Rapids, MI	NAIA
Golden Eagles	John Brown Univ.	Siloam Springs, AR	NAIA
Golden Eagles	Marquette Univ.	Milwaukee, WI	I
Golden Eagles	Minnesota Crookston, Univ. of	Crookston, MN	II
Golden Eagles	New York at Brockport, State U. of	Brockport, NY	III

Golden Eagles	Oral Roberts Univ.	Tulsa, OK	I
Golden Eagles	Saint Joseph's College	New York, NY	III
Golden Eagles	Southern Mississippi, Univ. of	Hattiesburg, MS	I
Golden Eagles	Spalding Univ.	Louisville, KY	III
Golden Eagles	Tennessee Technological Univ.	Cookeville, TN	I
Golden Falcons	Felician College	Lodi, NJ	II
Golden Flashes	Kent State Univ.	Kent, OH	I
Golden Flyers	Nazareth College	Rochester, NY	III
Golden Hawks	Wilfrid Laurier Univ.	Waterloo, ON	OUA
Golden Knights	Clarkson Univ.	Potsdam, NY	III
Golden Knights	Gannon Univ.	Erie, PA	II
Golden Knights	Saint Rose, College of	Albany, NY	II
Golden Lions	Arkansas Pine Bluff, Univ. of	Pine Bluff, AR	I
Golden Lions	Dowling College	Oakdale, NY	II
Golden Rams	Albany State Univ.	Albany, GA	II
Golden Rams	West Chester Univ. of Penn.	West Chester, PA	II
Golden Tigers	Brenau Univ.	Gainesville, GA	NAIA
Golden Tigers	Tuskegee Univ.	Tuskegee, AL	II
Gophers	Goucher College	Towson, MD	III
Gorillas	Pittsburg State Univ.	Pittsburg, KS	II
Gorloks	Webster Univ.	Webster Groves, MO	III
Gothic Knights	New Jersey City Univ.	Jersey City, NJ	III
Governors	Austin Peay State Univ.	Clarksville, TN	I
Gray Wolves	Lourdes College	Sylvania, OH	NAIA
Great Danes	New York at Albany, State Univ. of	Albany, NY	I
Green Knights	Saint Norbert College	De Pere, WI	III
Green Knights	Vermont Technical College	Randolph Ctr., VT	NAIA
Green Terror	McDaniel College	Westminster, MD	III
Green Wave	Tulane Univ.	New Orleans, LA	I
Grenadiers	Indiana Univ. Southeast	New Albany, IN	NAIA
Greyhounds	Assumption College	Worcester, MA	II
Greyhounds	Indianapolis, Univ. of	Indianapolis, IN	II
Greyhounds	Loyola Univ. Maryland	Baltimore, MD	I
Greyhounds	Moravian College	Bethlehem, PA	III

Greyhounds/ Zias	Eastern New Mexico Univ.	Portales, NM	II
Griffins	Canisius College	Buffalo, NY	I
Griffins	Chestnut Hill College	Philadelphia, PA	II
Griffins	Fontbonne Univ.	Clayton, MO	III
Griffins	Grant MacEwan Univ.	Edmonton, AB	ACAC
Griffins	Gwynedd–Mercy College	Lower Gwynedd, PA	III
Griffins	Quebec a Outaouais, Universite du	Gatineau, QC	CIS
Griffins	Seton Hill Univ.	Greensburg, UT	II
Griffins	Westminster College, Salt Lake City	Salt Lake City, UT	NAIA
Griffons	Missouri Western State Univ.	St. Joseph, MO	II
Grizzlies	Adams State College	Alamosa, CO	II
Grizzlies	Franklin College	Franklin, IN	III
Grizzlies	Georgian College	Barrie, ON	CIS
Grizzlies	Montana, Univ. of	Missoula, MT	I
Gryphons	Guelph, Univ. of	Guelph, ON	OUA
Gryphons	Sarah Lawrence College	Bronxville, NY	HVAC
Gulls	Endicott College	Beverly, MA	III
Gusties	Gustavus Adolphus College	St. Peter, MN	III
Gyrenes	Ave Maria Univ.	Ave Maria, FL	NAIA
Hardrockers	South Dak. School of Mines & Tech.	Rapid City, SD	NAIA
Harriers	Miami Univ.- Hamilton	Hamilton, OH	USCCA
Hatters	Stetson Univ.	DeLand, FL	I
Hawkeyes	Iowa, Univ. of	Iowa City, IA	I
Hawks	Becker College	Worcester, MA	III
Hawks	Chowan Univ.	Murfreesboro, NC	II
Hawks	Cooper Union	New York, NY	HVAC
Hawks	Hartford, Univ. of	West Hartford, CT	I
Hawks	Hartwick College	Oneonta, NY	III
Hawks	Hilbert College	Hamburg, NY	III
Hawks	Holy Names Univ.	Oakland, CA	NAIA
Hawks	Humber College	Etobicoke, ON	CIS
Hawks	Hunter College	New York, NY	III
Hawks	Huntingdon College	Montgomery, AL	III
Hawks	Maryland Eastern Shore, Univ. of	Princess Anne, MD	I

Hawks	Monmouth Univ.	W. Long Branch, NJ	I
Hawks	Navajo Technical College	Crownpoint, NM	USCCA
Hawks	New York at New Paltz, State U. of	New Paltz, NY	III
Hawks	Quincy Univ.	Quincy, MA	II
Hawks	Rockhurst Univ.	Kansas City, MO	II
Hawks	Roger Williams Univ.	Bristol, RI	III
Hawks	Saint Anselm College	Goffstown, NH	II
Hawks	Saint Joseph's Univ.	Philadelphia, PA	I
Hawks	San Diego Christian College	El Cajon, CA	NAIA
Hawks	Shorter Univ.	Rome, GA	NAIA
Heat	British Columbia-Okanagan, Univ. of	Kelowna, BC	BCCAA
Herons	William Smith College	Geneva, NY	III
Highlanders	Calif., Riverside, Univ. of	Riverside, CA	I
Highlanders	Houghton College	Houghton, NY	NAIA
Highlanders	MacMurray College	Jacksonville, IL	III
Highlanders	New Jersey Institute of Tech.	Newark, NJ	I
Highlanders	Radford Univ.	Radford, VA	I
Hillcats	Rogers State Univ.	Claremore, OK	NAIA
Hilltoppers	Ohio Univ., Chillicothe	Chillicothe, OH	ORCC
Hilltoppers	Saint Edward's Univ.	Austin, TX	II
Hilltoppers	West Liberty Univ.	West Liberty, WV	II
Hilltoppers	Western Kentucky Univ.	Bowling Green, KY	I
Hokies	Virginia Polytech. Inst. & State Univ.	Blacksburg, VA	I
Hoosiers	Indiana Univ.	Bloomington, IN	I
Horned Frogs	Texas Christian Univ.	Fort Worth, TX	I
Hornets	Alabama State	Montgomery, AL	I
Hornets	Calif. State Univ., Sacramento	Sacramento, CA	I
Hornets	Concordia College-Selma	Selma, AL	USCCA
Hornets	Delaware State Univ.	Dover, DE	I
Hornets	Emporia State Univ.	Emporia, KS	II
Hornets	Harris-Stowe State Univ.	St. Louis, MO	NAIA
Hornets	Kalamazoo College	Kalamazoo, MI	III
Hornets	Lynchburg College	Lynchburg, VA	III
Hornets	Lyndon State College	Lyndonville, VT	III
Hornets	Morris College	Sumter, PA	NAIA

Hornets	Shenandoah Univ.	Winchester, VA	III
Hoyas	Georgetown Univ.	Washington, DC	I
Hurricanes	Georgia Southwestern State Univ.	Americus, GA	II
Hurricanes	Miami, Univ. of	Coral Gables, FL	I
Huskies	Bloomsburg Univ. of Penn.	Bloomsburg, PA	II
Huskies	Connecticut, Univ. of	Storrs, CT	I
Huskies	George Brown College	Toronto, ON	CIS
Huskies	Houston Baptist Univ.	Houston, TX	I
Huskies	Keyano College	Ft. MacMurray, AB	ACAC
Huskies	Michigan Technological Univ.	Houghton, MI	II
Huskies	Northeastern Univ.	Boston, MA	I
Huskies	Northern Illinois Univ.	DeKalb, IL	I
Huskies	Saint Cloud State Univ.	St. Cloud, MN	II
Huskies	Saskatchewan, Univ. of	Saskatoon, SK	CIS
Huskies	Southern Maine, Univ. of	Portland, ME	III
Huskies	St. Mary's Univ.	Halifax, NS	CIS
Huskies	Washington, Univ. of	Seattle, WA	I
Hustlin' Quakers	Earlham College	Richmond, IN	III
Ichabods/ Lady Blues	Washburn Univ.	Topeka, KS	II
Indians	Catawba College	Salisbury, NC	II
Inferno	Alverno College	Milwaukee, WI	III
Islanders	Texas A&M Univ.–Corpus Christi	Corpus Christi, TX	I
Jackrabbits	South Dakota State Univ.	Brookings, SD	I
Jaguars	Augusta State Univ.	Augusta, GA	II
Jaguars	Houston-Victoria, Univ. of	Victoria, TX	NAIA
Jaguars	Indiana Univ. Purdue-Indianapolis	Indianapolis, IN	I
Jaguars	South Alabama	Mobile, AL	I
Jaguars	Southern Univ.	Baton Rouge, LA	I
Jaguars	Spelman College	Atlanta, GA	III
Jaspers	Manhattan College	Riverdale, NY	I
Javelinas	Texas A&M Univ.–Kingsville	Kingsville, TX	II
Jayhawks	Kansas, Univ. of	Lawrence, KS	I
Jets	Newman Univ.	Wichita, KS	II
Jimmies	Jamestown College	Jamestown, ND	NAIA

Johnnies	Saint John's Univ.	Collegeville, MN	III
Judges	Brandeis Univ.	Waltham, MA	III
Jumbos	Tufts Univ.	Medford, MA	III
Kangaroos	Austin College	Sherman, TX	III
Kangaroos	Missouri–Kansas City, Univ. of	Kansas City, MO	I
Kangaroos	New York at Canton, State Univ. of	Canton, NY	NAIA
Keelhaulers	Calif. Maritime Academy	Vallejo, CA	NAIA
Kermodes	Quest Univ. Canada	Squamish, BC	BCCAA
Keydets	Virginia Military Institute	Lexington, VA	I
Kings/Queens	Red Deer College	Red Deer, AB	ACAC
Kingsmen/Regals	Calif. Lutheran Univ.	Thousand Oaks, CA	III
Knights	Academy of Art Univ.	San Francisco, CA	II
Knights	Arcadia Univ.	Glenside, PA	III
Knights	Bellarmine Univ.	Louisville, KY	II
Knights	Berkeley College, NJ	Woodland Park, NJ	USCCA
Knights	Berkeley College, NY	New York, NY	USCCA
Knights	Calvin College	Grand Rapids, MI	III
Knights	Carleton College	Northfield, MN	III
Knights	Central Florida, Univ. of	Orlando, FL	I
Knights	Central Pennsylvania College	Summerdale, PA	USCCA
Knights	Crossroads College	Rochester, MN	ACCA
Knights	Fairleigh Dickinson Univ.	Hackensack, NJ	I
Knights	Fleming College	Peterborough, ON	CIS
Knights	Kentucky Christian Univ.	Grayson, KY	NAIA
Knights	Marian Univ.	Indianapolis, IN	NAIA
Knights	Martin Luther College	New Ulm, MN	III
Knights	Mount Saint Mary College	Newburgh, NY	III
Knights	Neumann Univ.	Aston, PA	III
Knights	Niagara College	Welland, ON	CIS
Knights	Northwood Univ.	Cedar Hill, TX	NAIA
Knights	Queens College	Queens, NY	II
Knights	Saint Andrews Presbyterian Coll.	Laurinburg, NC	II
Knights	Southern Univ. at New Orleans	New Orleans, LA	NAIA
Knights	Southern Virginia Univ.	Buena Vista, VA	NAIA
Knights	Warner Pacific College	Portland, OR	NAIA

Knights	Wartburg College	Waverly, IA	III
Kodiaks	Lethbridge College	Lethbridge, AB	ACAC
Kohawks	Coe College	Cedar Rapids, IA	III
Lakers	Clayton State Univ.	Morrow, GA	II
Lakers	Grand Valley State Univ.	Allendale, MI	II
Lakers	Lake Superior State Univ.	Sault Ste. Marie, MI	II
Lakers	Mercyhurst College	Erie, PA	II
Lakers	New York at Oswego, State Univ. of	Oswego, NY	III
Lakers	Nipissing Univ.	North Bay, ON	OUA
Lakers	Roosevelt Univ.	Chicago, IL	NAIA
Lakers	Silver Lake College	Manitowoc, WI	USCCA
Lakers	Wright State Univ., Lake Campus	Celina, OH	ORCC
Lancers	Calif. Baptist Univ.	Riverside, CA	II
Lancers	Grace College	Winona Lake, IN	NAIA
Lancers	Longwood Univ.	Farmville, VA	I
Lancers	Loyalist College	Belleville, ON	CIS
Lancers	Mount Marty College	Yankton, SD	NAIA
Lancers	Windsor, Univ. of	Windsor, ON	OUA
Lancers	Worcester State Univ.	Worcester, MA	III
Lasers	Lasell College	Newton, MA	III
Leopards	La Verne, Univ. of	La Verne, CA	III
Leopards	Lafayette College	Easton, PA	I
Leopards	Wentworth Institute of Tech.	Boston, MA	III
Lightning	Goldey–Beacom College	Pike Creek, DE	II
Lightning	Lehman College	Bronx, NY	III
Lightning	St. Mary's Univ. College	Calgary, AB	ACAL
Lights/ Skylights	Montana State Univ. – Northern	Havre, MT	NAIA
Lions	Albright College	Reading, PA	III
Lions	Ambrose College	Calgary, AB	ACAL
Lions	Arkansas – Fort Smith, Univ. of	Fort Smith, AR	II
Lions	Bryan College	Dayton, TN	NAIA
Lions	Bryn Athyn College	Bryn Athyn, PA	IND
Lions	Columbia Univ.	New York, NY	I
Lions	Eastern Nazarene College	Quincy, MA	III
Lions	Emerson College	Boston, MA	III

Lions	Emmanuel College, Georgia	Franklin Springs, GA	NAIA
Lions	Finlandia Univ.	Hancock, MI	III
Lions	Florida Memorial Univ.	Miami Gardens, FL	NAIA
Lions	Freed-Hardeman Univ.	Henderson, TN	NAIA
Lions	Georgian Court Univ.	Lakewood, NJ	II
Lions	Lambton College	Sarnia, ON	CIS
Lions	Langston Univ.	Langston, OK	NAIA
Lions	Lincoln Univ. of Pennsylvania	Chester County, PA	II
Lions	Lindenwood Univ.	St. Charles, MO	NAIA
Lions	Loyola Marymount Univ.	Los Angeles, CA	I
Lions	Mars Hill College	Mars Hill, NC	II
Lions	Missouri Southern State Univ.	Joplin, MO	II
Lions	Molloy College	Rockville Centre, NY	II
Lions	Mount Saint Joseph, College of	Cincinnati, OH	III
Lions	North Alabama, Univ. of	Florence, AL	II
Lions	Paine College	Augusta, GA	II
Lions	Patten Univ.	Oakland, CA	NAIA
Lions	Pennsylvania State Univ., Harrisburg	Middletown, PA	III
Lions	Piedmont College	Demorest, GA	III
Lions	Saint Leo Univ.	St. Leo, FL	II
Lions	Soka Univ. of America	Aliso Viejo, CA	NAIA
Lions	Southeastern Louisiana Univ.	Hammond, LA	I
Lions	Southwestern Assemblies of God U.	Waxahachie, TX	NAIA
Lions	Texas A&M Univ.–Commerce	Commerce, TX	II
Lions	Trinity Bible College	Ellendale, ND	NCCAA
Lions	Vanguard Univ.	Costa Mesa, CA	NAIA
Lions	York Univ.	Toronto, ON	OUA
Lions	Multnomah Univ.	Portland, OR	NCCAA
Little Giants	Wabash College	Crawfordsville, IN	III
Lobos	New Mexico, Univ. of	Albuquerque, NM	I
Lobos	Sul Ross State Univ.	Alpine, TX	III
Loggers	Puget Sound, Univ. of	Tacoma, WA	III
Longhorns	Texas at Austin, Univ. of	Austin, TX	I
Lopers	Nebraska at Kearney, Univ. of	Kearney, NB	II
Lord Jeffs	Amherst College	Amherst, MA	III

Lords	Kenyon College	Gambier, OH	III
Lumberjacks	Humboldt State Univ.	Arcata, CA	II
Lumberjacks	Northern Arizona Univ.	Flagstaff, AZ	I
Lumberjacks	Northland College	Ashland, WI	III
Lumberjacks	Stephen F. Austin State Univ.	Nacogdoches, TX	I
Lutes	Pacific Lutheran Univ.	Tacoma, WA	III
Lynx	Lesley Univ.	Boston, MA	III
Lynx	Lindenwood Univ.-Belleville	Belleville, IL	USCCA
Lynx	Rhodes College	Memphis, TN	III
Lyons	Mount Holyoke College	South Headley, MA	III
Lyons	Wheaton College	Norton, MA	III
Maccabees	Yeshiva Univ.	New York, NY	III
Magicians	LeMoyne–Owen College	Memphis, TN	II
Majors	Millsaps College	Jackson, MS	III
Maple Leafs	Goshen College	Goshen, IN	NAIA
Marauders	Central State Univ.	Wilberforce, OH	II
Marauders	Mary, Univ. of	Bismarck, ND	II
Marauders	McMaster Univ.	Hamilton, ON	OUA
Marauders	Millersville Univ. of Pennsylvania	Millersville, PA	II
Mariners	Maine Maritime Academy	Castine, ME	III
Mariners	Mitchell College	New London, CT	III
Mariners	United States Merchant Marine Acad.	Kings Point, NY	III
Mariners	Vancouver Island Univ.	Nanaimo, BC	BCCAA
Marlins	Virginia Wesleyan College	Norfolk, VA	III
Maroon Tigers	Morehouse College	Atlanta, GA	II
Maroons	Chicago, Univ. of	Chicago, IL	III
Maroons	Roanoke College	Salem, VA	III
Mastodons	Indiana Univ.-Purdue-Fort Wayne	Fort Wayne, IN	I
Matadors	Calif. State Univ., Northridge	Northridge, CA	I
Mavericks	Medaille College	Buffalo, NY	III
Mavericks	Mercy College	Dobbs Ferry, NY	II
Mavericks	Mesa State College	Grand Junction, CO	II
Mavericks	Minnesota State Univ., Mankato	Mankato, MN	II
Mavericks	Nebraska at Omaha, Univ. of	Omaha, NE	II
Mavericks	Ohio State Univ., Mansfield	Mansfield, OH	ORCC

Mavericks	Texas at Arlington, Univ. of	Arlington, TX	I
Mean Green	North Texas, Univ. of	Denton, TX	I
Midshipmen	United States Naval Academy	Annapolis, MD	I
Mighty Macs	Immaculata Univ.	Malvern, PA	III
Mighty Oaks	New York College of Science and Forestry	Syracuse, NY	NAIA
Mighty Oaks	Oakland City Univ.	Oakland City, IN	II
Miners	Missouri Univ. of Science and Technology	Rolla, MO	II
Miners	Texas at El Paso, Univ. of	El Paso, TX	I
Minutemen	Massachusetts Amherst, Univ. of	Amherst, MA	I
Missionaries	Whitman College	Walla Walla, WA	III
Moccasins	Florida Southern College	Lakeland, FL	II
Mocs	Tennessee at Chattanooga, Univ. of	Chattanooga, TN	I
Monarchs	King's College	Wilkes-Barre, PA	III
Monarchs	Methodist Univ.	Fayetteville, NC	III
Monarchs	Old Dominion Univ.	Norfolk, VA	I
Monks	Saint Joseph's College of Maine	Standish, ME	III
Moose	Maine-Augusta, Univ. of	Augusta, ME	USCCA
Moundbuilders	Southwestern College	Winfield, KS	NAIA
Mountain Hawks	Lehigh Univ.	Bethlehem, PA	I
Mountain Lions	Colorado at Colorado Springs, U. of	Colorado Springs, CO	II
Mountain Lions	Concord Univ.	Athens, WV	II
Mountain Cats	Pittsburgh at Johnstown, Univ. of	Johnstown, PA	II
Mountaineers	Appalachian State Univ.	Boone, NC	I
Mountaineers	Berea College	Berea, KY	NAIA
Mountaineers	Eastern Oregon Univ.	La Grande, OR	NAIA
Mountaineers	Mohawk College	Hamilton, ON	CIS
Mountaineers	Mount Saint Mary's Univ.	Emmitsburg, MD	I
Mountaineers	Schreiner Univ.	Kerrville, TX	III
Mountaineers	Southern Vermont College	Bennington, VT	III
Mountaineers	West Virginia Univ.	Morgantown, WV	I
Mountaineers	Western State Coll. of Colorado	Gunnison, CO	II

Mounties	Mansfield Univ. of Pennsylvania	Mansfield, PA	II
Mounties	Mount Allison Univ.	Sackville, NB	ACAA
Mounties	Mount Aloysius College	Cresson, PA	III
Muleriders	Southern Arkansas Univ.	Magnolia, AR	II
Mules	Muhlenberg College	Allentown, PA	III
Mules/Jennies	Central Missouri, Univ. of	Warrensburg, MO	II
Musketeers	Xavier Univ.	Cincinnati, OH	I
Muskies	Lakeland College	Sheboygan, WI	III
Mustangs	California Polytechnic State Univ.	San Luis Obispo, CA	I
Mustangs	Central Baptist College	Conway, AR	NAIA
Mustangs	Marygrove College	Detroit, MI	NAIA
Mustangs	Master's College, The	Santa Clarita, CA	NAIA
Mustangs	Midwestern State Univ.	Wichita Falls, TX	II
Mustangs	Morningside College	Sioux City, IA	NAIA
Mustangs	Mount Ida College	Newton, MA	III
Mustangs	Mount Mercy College	Cedar Rapids, IA	NAIA
Mustangs	New York at Morrisville, State U. at	Morrisville, NY	III
Mustangs	Southern Methodist Univ.	University Park, TX	I
Mustangs	Southwest Minnesota State Univ.	Marshall, MN	II
Mustangs	Southwest, Univ. of the	Hobbs, NM	NAIA
Mustangs	Stevenson Univ.	Stevenson, MD	III
Mustangs	Western New Mexico Univ.	Silver City, NM	II
Mustangs	Western Ontario, Univ. of	London, ON	OUA
Mystics	Mount Saint Vincent Univ.	Halifax, NS	ACAA
Nanooks	Alaska Fairbanks, Univ. of	Fairbanks, AK	II
Night Hawks	Thomas Univ.	Thomasville, GA	NAIA
Nighthawks	Newbury College	Brookline, MA	III
Nittany Lions	Penn State Brandywine	Media, PA	USCCA
Nittany Lions	Penn State Fayette, Eberly Campus	Uniontown, PA	USCCA
Nittany Lions	Penn State Greater Allegheny	McKeesport, PA	USCCA
Nittany Lions	Penn State Lehigh Valley	Fogelsville, PA	USCCA
Nittany Lions	Penn State Mont Alto	Mont Alto, PA	USCCA
Nittany Lions	Penn State Schuylkill	Schuylkill Haven, PA	USCCA
Nittany Lions	Penn State Shenango	Sharon, PA	USCCA
Nittany Lions	Penn State Univ.	State College, PA	I

Nittany Lions	Penn State Univ., Altoona	Altoona, PA	III
Nittany Lions	Penn State Univ., Berks College	Reading, PA	III
Nittany Lions	Penn State Wilkes-Barre	Lehman, PA	USCCA
Nittany Lions	Penn State Worthington Scranton	Dunmore, PA	USCCA
Nittany Lions	Penn State York	York, PA	USCCA
Nittany Lions	Penn State DuBois	DuBois, PA	USCCA
Nittany Lions	Penn State Hazelton	Hazleton, PA	USCCA
Nittany Lions	Penn State-Beaver	Monaca, PA	USCCA
Nittany Lions	Penn State-New Kensington	Upper Burrell, PA	USCCA
No Nickname	Hollins Univ.	Roanoke, VA	III
Nor'easters	New England, Univ. of	Biddeford, ME	III
Norse	Luther College	Decorah, IA	III
Norse	Northern Kentucky Univ.	Highland Hghts, IL	II
Northern Timberwolves	Northern British Columbia, Univ. of	Prince George, BC	BCCAA
Oaks	Menlo College	Atherton, CA	NAIA
Oilers	Findlay, Univ. of	Findlay, OH	II
Oles	Saint Olaf College	Northfield, MN	III
Ooks	Northern Alberta Inst. of Tech.	Edmonton, AB	ACAC
Orange	Syracuse Univ.	Syracuse, NY	I
Orediggers	Colorado School of Mines	Golden, CO	II
Orediggers	Montana Tech of The Univ. of Montana	Butte, MT	NAIA
Ospreys	North Florida, Univ. of	Jacksonville, FL	I
Ospreys	Richard Stockton College of NJ	Pomona, NJ	III
Otters	Calif. State Univ., Monterey Bay	Seaside, CA	II
Owls	Bryn Mawr College	Bryn Mawr, PA	III
Owls	Florida Atlantic Univ.	Boca Raton, FL	I
Owls	Keene State College	Keene, NH	III
Owls	Kennesaw State Univ.	Kennesaw, GA	I
Owls	Maine at Presque Isle, Univ. of	Presque Isle, ME	III
Owls	Oregon Institute of Tech.	Klamath Falls, OR	NAIA
Owls	Rice Univ.	Houston, TX	I
Owls	Southern Connecticut State Univ.	New Haven, CT	II
Owls	Temple Univ.	Philadelphia, PA	I
Owls	Warren Wilson College	Asheville, NC	NAIA

Owls	Westfield State Univ.	Westfield, MA	III
Owls	William Woods Univ.	Fulton, MO	NAIA
Pacers	Marywood Univ.	Scranton, PA	III
Pacers	Peace College	Raleigh, NC	III
Pacers	South Carolina Aiken, Univ. of	Aiken, SC	II
Paladins	Furman Univ.	Greenville, SC	I
Paladins	Royal Military College of Canada	Kingston, ON	OUA
Panthers	Adelphi Univ.	Garden City, NY	II
Panthers	Albany Coll. of Phar. & Health Sci.	Albany, NY	HVAC
Panthers	Birmingham–Southern College	Birmingham, AL	III
Panthers	Chapman Univ.	Orange, CA	III
Panthers	Claflin Univ.	Orangeburg, SC	II
Panthers	Clark Atlanta Univ.	Atlanta, GA	II
Panthers	Davenport Univ.	Grand Rapids, MI	NAIA
Panthers	Drury Univ.	Springfield, MO	II
Panthers	Eastern Illinois Univ.	Charleston, IL	I
Panthers	Ferrum College	Ferrum, VA	III
Panthers	Florida Institute of Tech.	Melbourne, FL	II
Panthers	Georgia State Univ.	Atlanta, GA	I
Panthers	Greenville College	Greenville, IL	III
Panthers	Hanover College	Hanover, IN	III
Panthers	High Point Univ.	High Point, NC	I
Panthers	Kentucky Wesleyan College	Owensboro, KY	II
Panthers	LaGrange College	La Grange, GA	III
Panthers	Middlebury College	Middlebury, VT	III
Panthers	New York at Old Westbury, State Univ. of	Old Westbury, NY	III
Panthers	New York at Purchase, State U. of	Purchase, NY	III
Panthers	Northern Iowa, Univ. of	Cedar Falls, IA	I
Panthers	Ohio Dominican Univ.	Columbus, OH	II
Panthers	Ohio Univ., Eastern	Clairsville, OH	ORCC
Panthers	Philander Smith College	Little Rock, OH	NAIA
Panthers	Pittsburgh at Bradford, Univ. of	Bradford, PA	III
Panthers	Pittsburgh at Titusville, Univ. of	Titusville, PA	USCCA
Panthers	Pittsburgh, Univ. of	Pittsburgh, PA	I
Panthers	Plymouth State Univ.	Plymouth, NH	III

Panthers	Prairie View A&M Univ.	Prairie View, TX	I
Panthers	Prince Edward Island, Univ. of	Charlottetown, PEI	CIS
Panthers	Principia College	Elsah, IL	III
Panthers	Purdue Univ. North Central	Westville, IN	NAIA
Panthers	Virginia Union Univ.	Richmond, VA	II
Panthers	Wisconsin–Milwaukee, Univ. of	Milwaukee, WI	I
Panthers	York College Nebraska	York, NE	NAIA
Parsons	Nebraska Christian College	Norfolk, NE	ACCA
Patriotes	Quebec a Trois Rivieres, Universite du	Tres Rivieres, QC	CIS
Patriots	Arlington Baptist College	Arlington, TX	ACCA
Patriots	Baptist Bible College (MO)	Springfield, MO	NCCAA
Patriots	Cumberlands, Univ. of the	Williamsburg, KY	NAIA
Patriots	Dallas Baptist Univ.	Dallas, TX	II
Patriots	Francis Marion Univ.	Florence, SC	II
Patriots	George Mason Univ.	Fairfax, VA	I
Patriots	Saint Catharine College	St. Catharine, KY	NAIA
Patriots	Texas at Tyler, Univ. of	Tyler, TX	III
Patriots	Valley Forge Christian College	Phoenixville, PA	NCCAA
Peacocks	Upper Iowa Univ.	Fayette, IA	II
Peacocks/ Peahens	Saint Peter's College	Jersey City, NJ	I
Penguins	Dominican Univ. of Calif.	San Rafael, CA	II
Penguins	Youngstown State Univ.	Youngstown, OH	I
Penmen	Southern New Hampshire Univ.	Manchester, NH	II
Peregrines	Purdue Univ. Calumet	Hammond, IN	NAIA
Petrels	Oglethorpe Univ.	Atlanta, GA	III
Phoenix	Elon Univ.	Elon, NC	I
Phoenix	Wilson College	Chambersburg, PA	III
Phoenix	Wisconsin–Green Bay, Univ. of	Green Bay, WI	I
Pilgrims	New England College	Henniker, NH	III
Pilots	Bethel College	Mishawaka, IN	NAIA
Pilots	Louisiana State Univ. in Shreveport	Shreveport, LA	NAIA
Pilots	Portland, Univ. of	Portland, OR	I
Pioneers	Calif. State Univ., East Bay	Hayward, CA	II
Pioneers	Carroll Univ.	Waukesha, WI	III

Pioneers	Crowley's Ridge College	Paragould, AR	ACCA
Pioneers	Denver, Univ. of	Denver, CO	I
Pioneers	Glenville State College	Glenville, WV	II
Pioneers	Grinnell College	Grinnell, IA	III
Pioneers	Lewis & Clark College	Portland, OR	III
Pioneers	Long Island Univ.-C.W. Post	Brookville, NY	II
Pioneers	Malone Univ.	Canton, OH	II
Pioneers	Marietta College	Marietta, OH	III
Pioneers	Mid-America Nazarene Univ.	Olathe, KS	NAIA
Pioneers	Northland International Univ.	Dunbar, WI	NCCAA
Pioneers	Pacific Union College	Angwin, WI	NAIA
Pioneers	Point Park Univ.	Pittsburgh, PA	NAIA
Pioneers	Sacred Heart Univ.	Fairfield, CT	I
Pioneers	Smith College	Northampton, MA	III
Pioneers	Texas Woman's Univ.	Denton, TX	II
Pioneers	Transylvania Univ.	Lexington, KY	III
Pioneers	Tusculum College	Tusculum, TN	II
Pioneers	Utica College	Utica, NY	III
Pioneers	Wayland Baptist Univ.	Plainview, TX	NAIA
Pioneers	Wesleyan College	Macon, GA	III
Pioneers	William Paterson Univ.	Wayne, NJ	III
Pioneers	Wisconsin–Platteville, Univ. of	Platteville, WI	III
Pionniers	Quebec a Rimouski, Universite du	Rimouski, QC	CIS
Pipers	Hamline Univ.	St. Paul, MN	III
Pirates	Armstrong Atlantic State Univ.	Savannah, GA	II
Pirates	East Carolina Univ.	Greenville, NC	I
Pirates	Hampton Univ.	Hampton, VA	I
Pirates	Park Univ.	Parkville, MO	NAIA
Pirates	Seton Hall Univ.	South Orange, NJ	I
Pirates	Southwestern Univ.	Georgetown, TX	III
Pirates	Whitworth Univ.	Spokane, WA	III
Poets	Whittier College	Whittier, CA	III
Pointers	Wisconsin–Stevens Point, Univ. of	Stevens Point, WI	III
Polar Bears	Bowdoin College	Brunswick, ME	III
Polar Bears	Ohio Northern Univ.	Ada, OH	III

Pomeroys	Saint Mary-of-the-Woods College	St. Mary-of-the-Woods, IN	USCCA
Prairie Fire	Knox College	Galesburg, IL	III
Prairie Stars	Illinois at Springfield, Univ. of	Springfield, IL	II
Prairie Wolves	Nebraska Wesleyan Univ.	Lincoln, NE	III
Preachers/ Evangels	Johnson Bible College	Knoxville, TN	NCCAA
Presidents	Washington & Jefferson College	Washington, PA	III
Pride	Greensboro College	Greensboro, NC	III
Pride	Hofstra Univ.	Hempstead, NY	I
Pride	Regis College	Weston, MA	III
Pride	Springfield College	Springfield, MA	III
Pride	Widener Univ.	Chester, PA	III
Privateers	New Orleans, Univ. of	New Orleans, LA	III
Privateers	New York Maritime Coll., State Univ. of	Bronx, NY	III
Profs	Rowan Univ.	Glassboro, NJ	III
Pronghorns	Lethbridge, Univ. of	Lethbridge, AB	CIS
Pumas	Saint Joseph's College	Rensselaer, IN	II
Purple Aces	Evansville, Univ. of	Evansville, IN	I
Purple Eagles	Niagara Univ.	Lewiston, NY	I
Purple Knights	Bridgeport, Univ. of	Bridgeport, CT	II
Purple Knights	Saint Michael's College	Colchester, VT	II
Purple Raiders	Mount Union College	Alliance, OH	III
Quakers	Guilford College	Greensboro, NC	III
Quakers	Pennsylvania, Univ. of	Philadelphia, PA	I
Quakers	Wilmington College	Wilmington, OH	III
Racers	Murray State Univ.	Murray, KY	I
Racers	Northwestern Ohio, Univ. of	Lima, OH	NAIA
Ragin' Cajuns	Louisiana at Lafayette, Univ. of	Lafayette, LA	I
Raiders	Colgate Univ.	Hamilton, NY	I
Raiders	Milwaukee School of Engineering	Milwaukee, WI	III
Raiders	Rivier College	Nashua, NH	III
Raiders	Roberts Wesleyan College	Rochester, NY	NAIA
Raiders	Shippensburg Univ. of Penn.	Shippensburg, PA	II
Raiders	Southern Oregon Univ.	Ashland, OR	NAIA

Raiders	Wright State Univ.	Fairborn, OH	I
Railsplitters	Lincoln Memorial Univ.	Harrogate, TN	II
Rainbow Warriors	Hawaii at Mānoa, Univ. of	Honolulu, HI	I
Ramblers	Loyola Univ. Chicago	Chicago, IL	I
Rams	Angelo State Univ.	San Angelo, TX	II
Rams	Bluefield College	Bluefield, VA	NAIA
Rams	Colorado State Univ.	Ft. Collins, CA	I
Rams	Cornell College	Mount Vernon, IA	III
Rams	Fordham Univ.	Bronx, NY	I
Rams	Framingham State Univ.	Framingham, MA	III
Rams	Huston-Tillotson Univ. of	Austin, TX	NAIA
Rams	Mobile, Univ. of	Mobile, AL	NAIA
Rams	New York at Farmingdale, St. U. of	Farmingdale, NY	III
Rams	North Central Univ.	Minneapolis, MN	III
Rams	Nova Scotia Agricultural College	Truro, NS	ACAA
Rams	Philadelphia Univ.	Philadelphia, PA	II
Rams	Rhode Island, Univ. of	Kingston, RI	I
Rams	Ryerson Univ.	Toronto, ON	OUA
Rams	Shepherd Univ.	Shepherdstown, WV	II
Rams	Suffolk Univ.	Boston, MA	III
Rams	Texas Wesleyan Univ.	Fort Worth, TX	NAIA
Rams	Unity College	Unity, ME	USCCA
Rams	Virginia Commonwealth Univ.	Richmond, VA	I
Rams	Winston-Salem State Univ.	Winston-Salem, NC	II
Rangers	Drew Univ.	Madison, NJ	III
Rangers	New Jersey, The College of	Ewing, NJ	III
Rangers	Northwestern Oklahoma State U.	Alva, OK	NAIA
Rangers	Regis Univ.	Denver, CO	II
Rangers	Wisconsin–Parkside, Univ. of	Kenosha, WI	II
Raptors	Bard College	Annondale-on-Hudson, NY	III
Rattlers	Florida Agricultural and Mech. U.	Tallahassee, FL	I
Rattlers	Saint Mary's Univ.	San Antonio, TX	II
Ravens	Anderson Univ.	Anderson, IN	III
Ravens	Benedictine College	Atchinson, KS	NAIA

Ravens	Carleton Univ.	Ottawa, ON	OUA
Ravens	Franklin Pierce Univ.	Rindge, NH	II
Ravens	Rosemont College	Rosemont, PA	III
Razorbacks	Arkansas, Univ. of	Fayetteville, AR	I
Rebels	Mississippi, Univ. of	Oxford, MS	I
Rebels	Nevada, Las Vegas, Univ. of	Paradise, NV	I
Red Devils	Eureka College	Eureka, IL	III
Red Dragons	New York at Cortland, State U. of	Cortland, NY	III
Red Dragons	New York at Oneonta, State U. of	Oneonta, NY	III
Red Flash	Saint Francis Univ.	Loretto, PA	I
Red Foxes	Marist College	Poughkeepsie, NY	I
Red Hawks	La Roche College	Pittsburgh, PA	III
Red Hawks	Montclair State Univ.	Montclair, NJ	III
Red Hawks	Ripon College	Ripon, WI	III
Red Hawks	Simpson Univ.	Redding, CA	NAIA
Red Lions	Lincoln Christian Univ.	Lincoln, IL	NCCAA
Red Men	Carthage College	Kenosha, WI	III
Red Raiders	Northwestern College	Orange City, IA	NAIA
Red Raiders	Texas Tech Univ.	Lubbock, TX	I
Red Storm	Dixie State College of Utah	St. George, UT	II
Red Storm	Rio Grande, Univ. of	Rio Grande, OH	NAIA
Red Storm	Saint John's Univ.	Jamaica, NY	I
Red Wolves	Arkansas State Univ.	Jonesboro, AR	I
Red Wolves	Indiana Univ. East	Richmond, IN	NAIA
Redbirds	Illinois State Univ.	Normal, IL	I
Reddies	Henderson State Univ.	Arkadelphia, AR	II
Redhawks	Indiana Univ. Northwest	Gary, IN	NAIA
Redhawks	Martin Methodist College	Pulaski, TN	NAIA
Redhawks	Miami Univ.	Oxford, OH	I
Redhawks	Seattle Univ.	Seattle, WA	I
Redhawks	Southeast Missouri State Univ.	Cape Girardeau, MO	I
Redmen/ Martlets	McGill Univ.	Montreal, QC	CIS
Regents	Rockford College	Rockford, IL	III
Retrievers	Maryland, Baltimore County, U. of	Catonsville, MD	I
Ridgebacks	Ontario Institute of Tech., Univ. of	Oshawa, ON	OUA

River Hawks	Massachusetts Lowell, Univ. of	Lowell, MA	II
RiverHawks	Northeastern State Univ.	Tahlequah, OK	II
Roadrunners	Calif. State Univ., Bakersfield	Bakersfield, CA	I
Roadrunners	Metropolitan State Coll. of Denver	Denver, CO	II
Roadrunners	Ramapo College	Mahwah, NJ	III
Roadrunners	Texas at San Antonio, Univ. of	San Antonio, TX	I
Rockets	Toledo, Univ. of	Toledo, OH	I
Rouge et Or	Laval, Universite	Quebec, QC	CIS
Royal Crusaders	Crown College, The	Powell, TN	NCCAA
Royals	Bethel Univ.	Arden Hills, MN	III
Royals	Eastern Mennonite Univ.	Harrisonburg, VA	III
Royals	Ecclesia College	Springdale, AR	NCCAA
Royals	Grace Univ.	Omaha, NE	NCCAA
Royals	Hope International Univ.	Fullerton, CA	NAIA
Royals	Queens Univ. of Charlotte	Charlotte, NC	II
Royals	Redeemer Univ. College	Ancaster, ON	CIS
Royals	Scranton, Univ. of	Scranton, PA	III
Royals	Warner Univ.	Lake Wales, FL	NAIA
Runnin' Bulldogs	Gardner–Webb Univ.	Boiling Springs, NC	I
Runnin' Hornets	Southern Polytechnic State Univ.	Marietta, GA	NAIA
Rustlers	Lakeland College	Vermillion, AB	ACAC
Sabers	Barber-Scotia	Concord, NC	NAIA
Sabers	Southeastern Bible College	Birmingham, AL	NCCAA
Sabres	Marian Univ.	Fond du Lac, WI	III
Sagehens	Pomona-Pitzer	Claremont, CA	III
Sailfish	Palm Beach Atlantic Univ.	W. Palm Beach, FL	II
Saints	Aquinas College	Grand Rapids, MI	NAIA
Saints	Ashford Univ.	Clinton, IA	NAIA
Saints	Carroll College Montana	Helena, MT	NAIA
Saints	Central Christian Coll. of the Bible	Moberly, MO	ACCA
Saints	Emmanuel College	Boston, MA	III
Saints	Flagler College	St. Augustine, FL	II
Saints	Hillsdale Free Will Baptist Coll.	Moore, OK	ACCA

Saints	Holy Cross College	Notre Dame, IN	NAIA
Saints	Limestone College	Gaffney, SC	II
Saints	Marymount Univ.	Arlington, VA	III
Saints	Maryville Univ.	St. Louis, MO	II
Saints	North Georgia College & State U.	Dahlonega, GA	II
Saints	Our Lady of the Lake Univ.	San Antonio, TX	NAIA
Saints	Presentation College	Aberdeen, SD	III
Saints	Saint Francis, Univ. of	Joliet, IL	NAIA
Saints	Saint Lawrence Univ.	Canton, NY	III
Saints	Saint Martin's Univ.	Lacey, WA	II
Saints	Saint Scholastica, The College of	Duluth, MN	III
Saints	Siena College	Loudonville, NY	I
Saints	Siena Heights Univ.	Adrian, MI	NAIA
Saints	St. Clair College	Windsor, ON	CIS
Saints	Thomas More College	Crestview Hills, KY	III
Salukis	Southern Illinois Univ. Carbondale	Carbondale, IL	I
Sand Sharks	South Carolina at Beaufort, U. of	Bluffton, PA	NAIA
Savage Storm	Southeastern Oklahoma State U.	Durant, OK	II
Saxons	Alfred Univ.	Alfred, NY	III
Scarlet Hawks	Illinois Institute of Tech.	Chicago, IL	NAIA
Scarlet Knights	Rutgers Univ.	New Brunswick, NJ	I
Scarlet Raiders	Rutgers–Newark	Newark, NJ	III
Scarlet Raptors	Rutgers–Camden	Camden, NJ	III
Scarlet Wave	Ohio State Marion	Marion, OH	USCCA
Schooners	St. Lawrence-Brockville College	Brockville, ON	CIS
Scorpions	Texas at Brownsville, Univ. of	Brownsville, TX	NAIA
Scots	Alma College	Alma, MI	III
Scots	Edinboro Univ. of Pennsylvania	Edinboro, PA	II
Scots	Lyon College	Batesville, AR	NAIA
Scots	Macalester College	St. Paul, MN	III
Scots	Maryville College	Maryville, TN	III
Scotties	Agnes Scott College	Decatur, GA	III
Screaming Eagles	Southern Indiana, Univ. of	Evansville, IN	II
Sea Gulls	Salisbury Univ.	Salisbury, MD	III
Sea Lions	Point Loma Nazarene Univ.	San Diego, CA	NAIA

Sea Warriors	Hawaii Pacific Univ.	Honolulu, HI	II
Seahawks	Briarcliffe College	Bethpage, NY	USCCA
Seahawks	North Carolina Wilmington, U. of	Wilmington, NC	I
Seahawks	Northwood Univ.	West Palm Beach, FL	NAIA
Seahawks	Saint Mary's College of Maryland	St. Mary's City, MD	III
Seahawks	Salve Regina Univ.	Newport, RI	III
Seahawks	Wagner College	Staten Island, NY	I
Sea-Hawks	Memorial Univ. of Newfoundland	St. John's, NF	CIS
Seasiders	Brigham Young Univ.–Hawaii	Lāie, HI	II
Seawolves	Alaska Anchorage, Univ. of	Anchorage, AK	II
Seawolves	New Brunswick-St. John's, Univ. of	Saint John, NB	ACAA
Seawolves	Sonoma State Univ.	Rohnert Park, CA	II
Seawolves	Stony Brook Univ.	Stony Brook, NY	I
Seminoles	Florida State Univ.	Tallahassee, FL	I
Senators	Auburn Univ. Montgomery	Montgomery, AL	NAIA
Senators	Davis & Elkins College	Elkins, WV	II
Setters	Pace Univ.	New York, NY	II
Sharks	Nova Southeastern Univ.	Davie, FL	II
Sharks	Simmons College	Boston, MA	III
Sharks	St. Lawrence-Cornwall College	Cornwall, ON	CIS
Shock	Washington Adventist Univ.	Takoma Park, MD	II
Shockers	Wichita State Univ.	Wichita, KS	I
Shoremen	Washington College	Chesterton, MD	III
Silverswords	Chaminade Univ. of Honolulu	Honolulu, HI	II
Skyhawks	Fort Lewis College	Durango, CO	II
Skyhawks	Stonehill College	North Easton, MA	II
Skyhawks	Tennessee at Martin, Univ. of	Martin, TN	I
Soaring Eagles	Elmira College	Elmira, NY	III
Soldiers	St. Louis Christian College	Florissant, MO	ACCA
Sooners	Oklahoma, Univ. of	Norman, OK	I
Spartans	Aurora Univ.	Aurora, IL	III
Spartans	Case Western Reserve Univ.	Cleveland, OH	III
Spartans	Castleton State College	Castleton, VT	III
Spartans	Central Bible College	Springfield, MO	NCCAA
Spartans	Dubuque, Univ. of	Dubuque, IA	III

Spartans	D'Youville College	Buffalo, NY	III
Spartans	Manchester College	N. Manchester, IN	III
Spartans	Michigan State Univ.	East Lansing, MI	I
Spartans	Missouri Baptist Univ.	St. Louis, MO	NAIA
Spartans	Norfolk State Univ.	Norfolk, VA	I
Spartans	North Carolina at Greensboro, Univ. of	Greensboro, NC	I
Spartans	Saint Thomas Aquinas College	Sparkhill, NY	II
Spartans	San Jose State Univ.	San Jose, CA	I
Spartans	South Carolina Upstate, Univ. of	Spartanburg, SC	I
Spartans	Tampa, Univ. of	Tampa, FL	II
Spartans	Trinity Western Univ.	Langley, BC	CIS
Spartans	York College of Pennsylvania	York, PA	III
Spiders	Richmond, Univ. of	Richmond, VA	I
Spires	Saint Mary, Univ. of	Leavenworth, KS	NAIA
Spirits	Salem College	Winston-Salem, NC	III
Stags	Fairfield Univ.	Fairfield, CT	I
Stags/Athenas	Claremont-Mudd-Scripps	Claremont, CA	III
Stars	Dominican Univ.	River Forest, IL	III
Stars	Oklahoma City Univ.	Oklahoma City, OK	NAIA
Stars	Stephens College	Columbia, MO	NAIA
Statesmen	Delta State Univ.	Cleveland, MS	II
Statesmen	Hobart College	Geneva, NY	III
Statesmen	William Penn Univ.	Oskaloosa, IA	NAIA
Steels	Culinary Institute of America	Hyde Park, NY	HVAC
Steers	Texas College	Tyler, TX	NAIA
Sting	Seneca College	North York, ON	CIS
Stingers	Concordia Univ.	Montreal, QC	CIS
Storm	Crown College	St. Bonifacius, MN	III
Storm	Eston College	Eston, SK	PAC
Storm	Keuka College	Keuka Park, NY	III
Storm	Lake Erie College	Painesville, OH	II
Storm	Simpson College	Indianola, IA	III
Student Princes	Heidelberg Univ.	Tiffin, OH	III

Sun Devils	Arizona State Univ.	Tempe, AZ	I
Sunbirds	Fresno Pacific Univ.	Fresno, CA	NAIA
Suns	Florida Christian College	Kissimmee, FL	NCCAA
Sycamores	Indiana State Univ.	Terre Haute, IN	I
Tar Heels	North Carolina at Chapel Hill, Univ. of	Chapel Hill, NC	I
Tars	Rollins College	Winter Park, FL	II
Tartans	Carnegie Mellon Univ.	Pittsburgh, PA	III
Tarzans	Puerto Rico at Mayagüez, Univ. of	Mayaguez, PR	II
Terrapins	Maryland, College Park, Univ. of	College Park, MD	I
Terrible Swedes	Bethany College	Lindsborg, KS	NAIA
Terriers	Boston Univ.	Boston, MA	I
Terriers	Hiram College	Hiram, OH	III
Terriers	Saint Francis College	Brooklyn, NY	I
Terriers	Thomas College	Waterville, ME	III
Terriers	Wofford College	Spartanburg, SC	I
Texans	Tarleton State Univ.	Stephenville, TX	II
The Rock	Slippery Rock Univ. of Penn.	Slippery Rock, PA	II
Thorobreds	Kentucky State Univ.	Frankfort, KY	II
Thoroughbreds	Skidmore College	Saratoga Springs, NY	III
Threshers	Bethel College	North Newton, KS	NAIA
Thunder	Algonquin College	Nepean, ON	CIS
Thunder	Concordia College of Alberta	Edmonton, AB	ACAC
Thunder	Trine Univ.	Angola, IN	III
Thunder	Wheaton College	Wheaton, IL	III
Thunder Hawks	Confederation College	Thunder Bay, ON	CIS
Thunderbirds	Algoma Univ.	Sault Ste. Marie, ON	CIS
Thunderbirds	British Columbia, Univ. of	Kelowna, BC	NAIA
Thunderbirds	Southern Utah Univ.	Cedar City, UT	I
Thundering Herd	Marshall Univ.	Huntington, WV	I
ThunderWolves	Colorado State Univ.–Pueblo	Pueblo, CO	II

Thunderwolves	Lakehead Univ.	Thunder Bay, ON	OUA
Tigers	Auburn Univ.	Auburn, AL	I
Tigers	Benedict College	Columbia, SC	II
Tigers	Campbellsville Univ.	Campbellsville, KY	NAIA
Tigers	Central Christian College	McPherson, KS	NAIA
Tigers	Champion Baptist College	Hot Springs, AR	ACCA
Tigers	Clemson Univ.	Clemson, SC	I
Tigers	Colorado College	Colorado Springs, CO	III
Tigers	Dakota Wesleyan Univ.	Mitchell, SD	NAIA
Tigers	Dalhousie Univ.	Halifax, NS	CIS
Tigers	DePauw Univ.	Greencastle, IN	III
Tigers	Doane College	Crete, NE	NAIA
Tigers	East Central Univ.	Ada, OK	II
Tigers	East Texas Baptist Univ.	Marshall, TX	III
Tigers	Edward Waters College	Jacksonville, FL	NAIA
Tigers	Fort Hays State Univ.	Hays, KS	II
Tigers	Georgetown College	Georgetown, KY	NAIA
Tigers	Grace Bible College	Grand Rapids, MI	NCCAA
Tigers	Grambling State Univ.	Grambling, LA	I
Tigers	Great Lakes Christian College	Lansing, MI	NCCAA
Tigers	Hampden–Sydney College	Hampden-Sydney, VA	III
Tigers	Hiwassee College	Madisonville, TN	USCCA
Tigers	Holy Family Univ.	Philadelphia, PA	II
Tigers	Iowa Wesleyan College	Mt. Pleasant, IA	NAIA
Tigers	Jackson State Univ.	Jackson, MS	I
Tigers	Memphis, Univ. of	Memphis, TN	I
Tigers	Missouri, Univ. of	Columbia, MO	I
Tigers	Occidental College	Los Angeles, CA	III
Tigers	Olivet Nazarene Univ.	Bourbonnais, IL	NAIA
Tigers	Ouachita Baptist Univ.	Arkadelphia, AR	II
Tigers	Pacific, Univ. of the	Stockton, CA	I
Tigers	Paul Quinn College	Dallas, TX	NAIA
Tigers	Princeton Univ.	Princeton, NJ	I
Tigers	Rochester Institute of Tech.	Rochester, NY	III

Tigers	Saint Paul's College, Virginia	Lawrenceville, VA	II
Tigers	Salem Univ.	Salem, WV	II
Tigers	Savannah State Univ.	Savannah, GA	I
Tigers	Sewanee: The Univ. of the South	Sewanee, TN	III
Tigers	Stillman College	Tuscaloosa, AL	II
Tigers	Tennessee State Univ.	Nashville, TN	I
Tigers	Texas Southern Univ.	Houston, TX	I
Tigers	Towson Univ.	Towson, MD	I
Tigers	Trinity College of Florida	Trinity, FL	NCCAA
Tigers	Trinity Univ.	San Antonio, TX	III
Tigers	Trinity Washington Univ.	Washington, DC	III
Tigers	Voorhees College	Denmark, PA	NAIA
Tigers	West Alabama, Univ. of	Livingston, AL	II
Tigers	Wittenberg Univ.	Springfield, OH	III
Timberwolves	Northwood Univ.	Midland, MI	II
Titans	Calif. State Univ., Fullerton	Fullerton, CA	I
Titans	Detroit Mercy, Univ. of	Detroit, MI	I
Titans	Illinois Wesleyan Univ.	Bloomington, IL	III
Titans	Indiana Univ. South Bend	South Bend, IN	NAIA
Titans	Ohio State Univ., Newark	Newark, OH	ORCC
Titans	Westminster College	New Wilmington, PA	III
Titans	Wisconsin–Oshkosh, Univ. of	Oshkosh, WI	III
Tomcats	Thiel College	Greenville, PA	III
Tommies	Saint Thomas Univ.	Fredericton, NB	ACAA
Tommies	Saint Thomas, Univ. of	St. Paul, MN	III
Toppers	Blue Mountain College	Blue Mountain, MS	NAIA
Toreros	San Diego, Univ. of	San Diego, CA	I
Tornado	King College	Bristol, TN	II
Tornadoes	Brevard College	Brevard, NC	II
Tornadoes	Talladega College	Talladega, AL	NAIA
Tornados	Concordia Univ. Texas	Austin, TX	III
Toros	Calif. State Univ., Dominguez Hills	Carson, CA	II
Tracers	Ohio Univ., Zanesville	Zanesville, OH	ORCC
Trailblazers	Massachusetts Coll. of Lib. Arts	North Adams, MA	III
Trailblazers	Ohio Christian Univ.	Circleville, OH	NCCAA

Tribe	William & Mary, The College of	Williamsburg, VA	I
Tritons	Calif., San Diego, Univ. of	La Jolla, CA	II
Tritons	Eckerd College	St. Petersburg, FL	II
Tritons	Missouri–Saint Louis, Univ. of	St. Louis, MO	II
Trojans	Anderson Univ.	Anderson, SC	II
Trojans	Arkansas at Little Rock, Univ. of	Little Rock, AR	I
Trojans	Dakota State Univ.	Madison, SD	NAIA
Trojans	Hannibal-LaGrange College	Hannibal, MO	NAIA
Trojans	Mount Olive College	Mount Olive, NC	II
Trojans	Southern Alberta Inst. of Tech.	Calgary, SB	ACAC
Trojans	Taylor Univ.	Upland, IN	NAIA
Trojans	Trevecca Nazarene Univ.	Nashville, TN	NAIA
Trojans	Trinity International Univ.	Deerfield, IL	NAIA
Trojans	Troy	Troy, AL	I
Trojans	Virginia State Univ.	Petersburg, VA	II
Trojans/ Women of Troy	Southern Calif., Univ. of	Los Angeles, CA	I
Trolls	Trinity Christian College	Palos Heights, IL	NAIA
Utes	Utah, Univ. of	Salt Lake City, UT	I
Valiants	Manhattanville College	Purchase, NY	III
Valkyries	Converse College	Spartanburg, SC	II
Vandals	Idaho, Univ. of	Moscow, ID	I
Varsity Blues	Toronto, Univ. of	Toronto, ON	OUA
Varsity Reds	New Brunswick-Fredericton, Univ. of	Fredericton, NB	CIS
Vert et Or	Sherbrooke, Universite de	Sherbrooke, QC	CIS
V-Hawks	Viterbo Univ.	La Crosse, WI	NAIA
Vikes	Victoria, Univ. of	Victoria, BC	NAIA
Vikings	Alberta-Augustana, Univ. of	Camrose, AB	ACAC
Vikings	Augustana College	Sioux Falls, SD	II
Vikings	Augustana College	Rock Island, IL	III
Vikings	Berry College	Mount Berry, GA	NAIA
Vikings	Bethany Lutheran College	Mankato, MN	III
Vikings	Cleveland State Univ.	Cleveland, OH	I
Vikings	Elizabeth City State Univ.	Elizabeth City, NC	II
Vikings	Grand View Univ.	Des Moines, IA	NAIA
Vikings	Lawrence Univ.	Appleton, WI	III

Vikings	Missouri Valley College	Marshall, MO	NAIA
Vikings	North Park Univ.	Chicago, IL	III
Vikings	Portland State Univ.	Portland, OR	I
Vikings	Salem State Univ.	Salem, MA	III
Vikings	St. Lawrence-Kingston College	Kingston, ON	CIS
Vikings	Valley City State Univ.	Valley City, ND	NAIA
Vikings	Western Washington Univ.	Bellingham, WA	II
Violets	New York Univ.	New York, NY	III
Vixens	Sweet Briar College	Sweet Briar, VA	III
Volunteers	Tennessee, Univ. of	Knoxville, TN	I
Voyageurs	Laurentian Univ.	Sudbury, ON	OUA
Voyageurs	Portage College	Lac La Biche, AB	ACAC
Vulcans	Calif. Univ. of Pennsylvania	California, PA	II
Vulcans	Hawaii at Hilo, Univ. of	Hilo, HI	II
War Hawks	McMurry Univ.	Abilene, TX	II
Warhawks	Louisiana at Monroe, Univ. of	Monroe, LA	I
Warhawks	Wisconsin–Whitewater, Univ. of	Whitewater, WI	III
Warriors	Akron Wayne, Univ. of	Orrville, OH	ORCC
Warriors	Appalachian Bible College	Mount Hope, WV	NCCAA
Warriors	Bacone College	Muskogee, OK	NAIA
Warriors	Calif. State Univ., Stanislaus	Turlock, CA	II
Warriors	Calvary Bible College	Kansas City, MO	ACCA
Warriors	Corban Univ.	Salem, OR	NAIA
Warriors	Dine College	Tsaile, AZ	USCAA
Warriors	East Stroudsburg Univ. of Penn.	E. Stroudsburg, PA	II
Warriors	Eastern Connecticut State Univ.	Willimantic, CT	III
Warriors	Hendrix College	Conway, AZ	III
Warriors	Indiana Institute of Tech.	Fort Wayne, IN	NAIA
Warriors	Lewis-Clark State College	Lewiston, ID	NAIA
Warriors	Lycoming College	Williamsport, PA	III
Warriors	Merrimack College	North Andover, MA	II
Warriors	Midland Univ.	Fremont, NE	NAIA
Warriors	Nyack College	Nyack, NY	II
Warriors	Rochester College	Rochester Hills, MI	USCCA
Warriors	Southern Wesleyan Univ.	Central, PA	NAIA

Warriors	Sterling College	Sterling, KS	NAIA
Warriors	Valor Christian College	Columbus, OH	USCCA
Warriors	Vaughn College	Flushing, NY	HVAC
Warriors	Waldorf College	Forest City, IA	NAIA
Warriors	Waterloo, Univ. of	Waterloo, ON	OUA
Warriors	Wayne State Univ.	Detroit, MI	II
Warriors	Webber International Univ.	Babson Park, FL	NAIA
Warriors	Westmont College	Santa Barbara, CA	NAIA
Warriors	William Jessup Univ.	Rocklin, CA	NAIA
Warriors	Winona State Univ.	Winona, MN	II
Warriors	Wisconsin Lutheran College	Milwaukee, WI	III
Wasps	Emory and Henry College	Emory, VA	III
Waves	Pepperdine Univ.	Malibu, CA	I
Webbies	Webb Institute	Glen Cove, NY	HVAC
Wesmen	Winnipeg, Univ. of	Winnipeg, MT	CIS
White Mules	Colby College	Waterville, ME	III
Wildcats	Abilene Christian Univ.	Abilene, TX	II
Wildcats	Arizona, Univ. of	Tucson, AZ	I
Wildcats	Baker Univ.	Baldwin City, KS	NAIA
Wildcats	Bay Path College	Longmeadow, MA	III
Wildcats	Bethel College	McKenzie, TN	NAIA
Wildcats	Bethune-Cookman Univ.	Daytona Beach, FL	I
Wildcats	Calif. State Univ., Chico	Chico, CA	II
Wildcats	Cazenovia College	Cazenovia, NY	III
Wildcats	Central Washington Univ.	Ellensburg, WA	II
Wildcats	Culver-Stockton College	Canton, MO	NAIA
Wildcats	Daemen College	Amherst, NY	NAIA
Wildcats	Davidson College	Davidson, NC	I
Wildcats	Fort Valley State Univ.	Fort Valley, GA	II
Wildcats	Indiana Wesleyan Univ.	Marion, IN	NAIA
Wildcats	Johnson & Wales Univ.	Providence, RI	III
Wildcats	Johnson & Wales Univ.- North Miami	North Miami, FL	NAIA
Wildcats	Johnson and Wales Univ.-Denver	Denver, CO	NAIA
Wildcats	Kansas State Univ.	Manhattan, KS	I
Wildcats	Kentucky, Univ. of	Lexington, KY	I

Wildcats	Linfield College	McMinnville, OR	III
Wildcats	Louisiana College	Pineville, LA	III
Wildcats	New Hampshire, Univ. of	Durham, NH	I
Wildcats	New York Institute of Technology, State Univ. of	Utica, NY	III
Wildcats	Northern Michigan Univ.	Marquette, MI	II
Wildcats	Northwestern Univ.	Evanston, IL	I
Wildcats	Pennsylvania College of Tech.	Williamsport, PA	USCCA
Wildcats	Portland Bible College	Portland, OR	NCCAA
Wildcats	Randolph College	Lynchburg, VA	III
Wildcats	Saint Catherine Univ.	St. Paul, MN	III
Wildcats	Villanova Univ.	Radnor, PA	I
Wildcats	Wayne State College	Wayne, NE	II
Wildcats	Weber State Univ.	Ogden, UT	I
Wildcats	Wheelock College	Boston, MA	III
Wildcats	Wiley College	Marshall, TX	NAIA
Wildcats	Wilmington Univ.	New Castle, DE	II
Wolf Pack	Nevada-Reno, Univ. of	Reno, NV	I
Wolfpack	Loyola Univ. New Orleans	New Orleans, LA	NAIA
Wolfpack	North Carolina State Univ.	Raleigh, NC	I
Wolfpack	Oak Hills Christian College	Bemidji, MN	ACCA
Wolfpack	Thompson Rivers Univ.	Kamloops, BC	BCCAA
Wolverines	Grove City College	Grove City, PA	III
Wolverines	Michigan, Univ. of	Ann Arbor, MI	I
Wolverines	Utah Valley Univ.	Orem, UT	I
Wolverines	Wesley College Dover	Dover, DE	III
Wolves	Cardinal Stritch Univ.	Milwaukee, WI	NAIA
Wolves	Cheyney Univ. of Pennsylvania	Cheyney, PA	II
Wolves	Grande Prairie Regional College	Grande Prairie, AB	ACAC
Wolves	Michigan–Dearborn, Univ. of	Dearborn, MI	NAIA
Wolves	Newberry College	Newberry, SC	II
Wolves	Northern State Univ.	Aberdeen, SD	II
Wolves	Walla Walla Univ.	Walla Walla, WA	NAIA
Wolves	West Georgia, Univ. of	Carrollton, GA	II
Wolves	Western Oregon Univ.	Monmouth, OR	II

Wonder Boys/ Golden Suns	Arkansas Tech Univ.	Russellville, AR	II
X-Men/ X-Women	St. Francis Xavier Univ.	Antigonish, NS	CIS
Yellow Jackets	Allen Univ.	Columbia, SC	NAIA
Yellow Jackets	American International College	Springfield, MA	II
Yellow Jackets	Black Hills State Univ.	Spearfish, SD	NAIA
Yellow Jackets	Cedarville Univ.	Cedarville, OH	II
Yellow Jackets	Defiance College	Defiance, OH	III
Yellow Jackets	Georgia Institute of Tech.	Atlanta, GA	I
Yellow Jackets	Howard Payne Univ.	Brownwood, TX	III
Yellow Jackets	LeTourneau Univ.	Longview, TX	III
Yellow Jackets	New York City College of Tech.	Brooklyn, NY	III
Yellow Jackets	Randolph–Macon College	Ashland, VA	III
Yellow Jackets	Waynesburg Univ.	Waynesburg, PA	III
Yellow Jackets	West Virginia State Univ.	Institute, WV	II
Yellow Jackets	Wisconsin–Superior, Univ. of	Superior, WI	III
Yellowjackets	Baldwin–Wallace College	Berea, OH	III
Yellowjackets	Graceland Univ.	Lamoni, IA	NAIA
Yellowjackets	Montana State Univ. Billings	Billings, MT	II
Yellowjackets	Rochester, Univ. of	Rochester, NY	III
Yeomen	Oberlin College	Oberlin, OH	III
Zips	Akron, Univ. of	Akron, OH	I

TOTAL 1,592

Chapter 2

Colleges and their Nicknames

Abilene Christian Wildcats

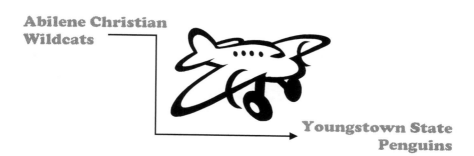

Youngstown State Penguins

For ease of use in looking up schools and their nicknames, schools in this chapter are listed alphabetically and much less formally than in Chapter 1.

SCHOOL	NICKNAME	SCHOOL	NICKNAME
Abilene Christian	Wildcats	Alma	Scots
Academy of Art	Knights	Alvernia	Crusaders
Acadia	Axemen/ Axewomen	Alverno	Inferno
		Ambrose	Lions
Adams State	Grizzlies	American	Eagles
Adelphi	Panthers	American Int'l	Yellow Jackets
Adrian	Bulldogs	Amherst	Lord Jeffs
Agnes Scott	Scotties	Anderson	Ravens
AIB School of Business	Eagles	Anderson	Trojans
Air Force	Falcons	Andrews	Cardinals
Akron	Zips	Angelo State	Rams
Akron Wayne	Warriors	Anna Maria	AMCats
Alabama	Crimson Tide	Appalachian Bible	Warriors
Alabama A&M	Bulldogs	Appalachian State	Mountaineers
Alabama in Huntsville	Chargers	Apprentice School, The	Builders
Alabama State	Hornets	Aquinas	Saints
Alaska Anchorage	Seawolves	Arcadia	Knights
Alaska Fairbanks	Nanooks	Arizona	Wildcats
Albany Phar. & Health	Panthers	Arizona State	Sun Devils
Albany State	Golden Rams	Arkansas	Razorbacks
Alberta	Golden Bears/ Pandas	Arkansas – Fort Smith	Lions
		Arkansas State	Red Wolves
Alberta-Augustana	Vikings	Arkansas Tech	Wonder Boys/ Golden Suns
Albertus Magnus	Falcons		
Albion	Britons	Arkansas-Little Rock	Trojans
Albright	Lions	Arkansas-Monticello	Boll Weevils/ Cotton Blossoms
Alcorn State	Braves		
Alderson–Broaddus	Battlers	Arkansas-Pine Bluff	Golden Lions
Alfred	Saxons	Arlington Baptist	Patriots
Algoma	Thunderbirds	Armstrong Atlantic	Pirates
Algonquin	Thunder	Army	Black Knights
Alice Lloyd	Eagles	Asbury	Eagles
Allegheny	Gators	Ashford	Saints
Allen	Yellow Jackets	Ashland	Eagles

Association Free	**Conquerors**	Bellarmine	**Knights**
Assumption	**Greyhounds**	Bellevue	**Bruins**
Atlanta Christian	**Chargers**	Belmont	**Bruins**
Auburn	**Tigers**	Belmont Abbey	**Crusaders**
Auburn-Montgomery	**Senators**	Beloit	**Buccaneers**
Augsburg	**Auggies**	Bemidji State	**Beavers**
Augusta State	**Jaguars**	Benedict	**Tigers**
Augustana	**Vikings**	Benedictine	**Ravens**
Augustana-S.D.	**Vikings**	Benedictine	**Eagles**
Aurora	**Spartans**	Benedictine-Springfield	**Bulldogs**
Austin	**Kangaroos**	Bennett	**Belles**
Austin Peay State	**Governors**	Bentley	**Falcons**
Ave Maria	**Gyrenes**	Berea	**Mountaineers**
Averett	**Cougars**	Berkeley , NJ	**Knights**
Avila	**Eagles**	Berkeley , NY	**Knights**
Azusa Pacific	**Cougars**	Berry	**Vikings**
Babson	**Beavers**	Bethany	**Bison**
Bacone	**Warriors**	Bethany	**Eagles**
Baker	**Wildcats**	Bethany	**Terrible Swedes**
Baldwin–Wallace	**Yellowjackets**	Bethany	**Bruins**
Ball State	**Cardinals**	Bethany Bible	**Blazers**
Baptist of Florida	**Eagles**	Bethany Lutheran	**Vikings**
Baptist Bible & Sem.	**Defenders**	Bethel College (IN)	**Pilots**
Baptist Bible (MO)	**Patriots**	Bethel College (KS)	**Threshers**
Barber-Scotia	**Sabers**	Bethel College (TN)	**Wildcats**
Barclay	**Bears**	Bethel Univ.	**Royals**
Bard	**Raptors**	Bethesda Christian	**Flames**
Barry	**Buccaneers**	Bethune-Cookman	**Wildcats**
Barton	**Bulldogs**	Binghamton	**Bearcats**
Baruch	**Bearcats**	Biola	**Eagles**
Bates	**Bobcats**	Birmingham	**Blazers**
Bay Path	**Wildcats**	Birmingham–Southern	**Panthers**
Baylor	**Bears**	Bishop's	**Gaiters**
Becker	**Hawks**	Black Hills State	**Yellow Jackets**
Belhaven	**Blazers**		

Dan Henige
1301 Millsboro Rd. Apt. 134
Mansfield, OH 44906

Blackburn	**Beavers**	Bryant	**Bulldogs**
Bloomfield	**Deacons**	Bryn Athyn	**Lions**
Bloomsburg	**Huskies**	Bryn Mawr	**Owls**
Blue Mountain	**Toppers**	Bucknell	**Bison**
Bluefield	**Rams**	Buena Vista	**Beavers**
Bluefield State	**Big Blues**	Buffalo State	**Bengals**
Bluffton	**Beavers**	Butler	**Bulldogs**
Boise State	**Broncos**	Cabrini	**Cavaliers**
Boston College	**Eagles**	Caldwell	**Cougars**
Boston Univ.	**Terriers**	Calgary	**Dinos**
Bowdoin	**Polar Bears**	Calif. of Pennsylvania	**Vulcans**
Bowie State	**Bulldogs**	Calif. Institute of Tech.	**Beavers**
Bowling Green State	**Falcons**		
Boyce	**Bulldogs**	Calif. Lutheran	**Kingsmen/ Regals**
Bradley	**Braves**	Calif. Maritime Acad.	**Keelhaulers**
Brandeis	**Judges**	Calif. Poly, Pomona	**Broncos**
Brandon	**Bobcats**	Calif. Poly, SLO	**Mustangs**
Brenau	**Golden Tigers**	Calif. St. Dominguez Hills	**Toros**
Brescia	**Bearcats**		
Brevard	**Tornadoes**	Calif. St.-Bakersfield	**Roadrunners**
Brewton-Parker	**Barons**	Calif. St.-Chico	**Wildcats**
Briar Cliff	**Chargers**	Calif. St.-East Bay	**Pioneers**
Briarcliffe	**Seahawks**	Calif. St.-Fresno	**Bulldogs**
Bridgeport	**Purple Knights**	Calif. St.-Fullerton	**Titans**
Bridgewater	**Eagles**	Calif. St.-Los Angeles	**Golden Eagles**
Bridgewater State	**Bears**	Calif. St.-Monterey Bay	**Otters**
Briercrest	**Clippers**	Calif. St.-Northridge	**Matadors**
Brigham Young	**Cougars**	Calif. St.-Sacramento	**Hornets**
Brigham Young –HI	**Seasiders**	Calif. St.-San Bernardino	**Coyotes**
British Columbia	**Thunderbirds**		
British Columbia-Ok.	**Heat**	Calif. St.-San Marcos	**Cougars**
Brock	**Badgers**	Calif. St.-Stanislaus	**Warriors**
Brooklyn	**Bulldogs**	Calif., Berkeley	**Golden Bears**
Brown	**Bears**	Calif., Davis	**Aggies**
Bryan	**Lions**	Calif., Irvine	**Anteaters**
		Calif., Riverside	**Highlanders**

Calif., San Diego	**Tritons**	Central	**Dutch**
Calif., Santa Barbara	**Gauchos**	Central Arkansas	**Bears/**
California Baptist	**Lancers**		**Sugar Bears**
Calumet-Saint Joseph	**Crimson Wave**	Central Baptist	**Mustangs**
Calvary Bible	**Warriors**	Central Bible	**Spartans**
Calvin	**Knights**	Central Christian	**Saints**
Cameron	**Aggies**	Central Christian	**Tigers**
Campbell	**Camels**	Central Connecticut	**Blue Devils**
Campbellsville	**Tigers**	Central Florida	**Knights**
Canadian	**Aurora**	Central Methodist	**Eagles**
Canadian Mennonite	**Blazers**	Central Michigan	**Chippewas**
Canisius	**Griffins**	Central Missouri	**Mules/Jennies**
Cape Breton	**Capers**	Central Oklahoma	**Bronchos**
Capilano	**Blues**	Central Pennsylvania	**Knights**
Capital	**Crusaders**	Central State	**Marauders**
Cardinal Stritch	**Wolves**	Central Washington	**Wildcats**
Carleton College	**Knights**	Centre	**Colonels**
Carleton Univ.	**Ravens**	Chadron State	**Eagles**
Carlow	**Celtics**	Chaminade	**Silverswords**
Carnegie Mellon	**Tartans**	Champion Baptist	**Tigers**
Carroll	**Pioneers**	Chapman	**Panthers**
Carroll Montana	**Saints**	Charleston College	**Cougars**
Carson–Newman	**Eagles**	Charleston Southern	**Buccaneers**
Carthage	**Red Men**	Charleston Univ.	**Golden Eagles**
Carver Bible	**Cougars**	Charlotte	**49ers**
Case Western	**Spartans**	Chatham	**Cougars**
Reserve		Chestnut Hill	**Griffins**
Castleton State	**Spartans**	Cheyney	**Wolves**
Catawba	**Indians**	Chicago	**Maroons**
Catholic of America	**Cardinals**	Chicago State	**Cougars**
Cazenovia	**Wildcats**	Chowan	**Hawks**
Cedar Crest	**Falcons**	Christendom	**Crusaders**
Cedarville	**Yellow Jackets**	Christian Brothers	**Buccaneers**
Centenary	**Cyclones**	Christopher Newport	**Captains**
Centenary-Louisiana	**Gents/Ladies**	Cincinnati	**Bearcats**
Centennial	**Colts**	Cincinnati Christian	**Eagles**

Cincinnati Christian Coll.	Crusaders	Columbus State	Cougars
Citadel, The	Bulldogs	Concord	Mountain Lions
City of New York	Beavers	Concordia	Clippers
City College of NY	Cardinals	Concordia	Golden Bears
Claflin	Panthers	Concordia	Stingers
Claremont-Mudd-Scripps	Stags/Athenas	Concordia College	Cobbers
Clarion-Pennsylvania	Golden Eagles	Concordia, Chicago	Cougars
Clark	Cougars	Concordia, Alberta	Thunder
Clark Atlanta	Panthers	Concordia, Ann Arbor	Cardinals
Clarke	Crusaders	Concordia, Irvine	Eagles
Clarkson	Golden Knights	Concordia, Portland	Cavaliers
Clayton State	Lakers	Concordia, Selma	Hornets
Clearwater Christian	Cougars	Concordia, Seward	Bulldogs
Clemson	Tigers	Concordia, Texas	Tornados
Clermont	Cougars	Concordia, Wisconsin	Falcons
Cleveland State	Vikings	Conestoga	Condors
Coast Guard	Bears	Confederation	Thunder Hawks
Coastal Carolina	Chanticleers	Connecticut	Huskies
Coe	Kohawks	Connecticut	Camels
Coker	Cobras	Converse	Valkyries
Colby	White Mules	Cooper Union	Hawks
Colby–Sawyer	Chargers	Coppin State	Eagles
Colgate	Raiders	Corban	Warriors
Colorado	Tigers	Cornell College	Rams
Colorado Christian	Cougars	Cornell Univ.	Big Red
Colorado Sch. of Mines	Orediggers	Cornerstone	Golden Eagles
Colorado State	Rams	Covenant	Fighting Scots
Colorado State–Pueblo	ThunderWolves	Crandall	Chargers
Colorado-Boulder	Buffaloes	Creighton	Bluejays
Colorado-Colo. Springs	Mountain Lions	Crossroads	Knights
		Crowley's Ridge	Pioneers
Columbia	Cougars	Crown	Storm
Columbia	Fighting Koalas	Crown , The	Royal Crusaders
Columbia	Lions	Culinary Inst.	Steels

54

Culver-Stockton	Wildcats	Dixie State of Utah	Red Storm
Cumberland	Bulldogs	Doane	Tigers
Cumberlands	Patriots	Dominican	Stars
Curry	Colonels	Dominican Coll.	Chargers
Daemen	Wildcats	Dominican-Calif.	Penguins
Dakota State	Trojans	Dordt	Defenders
Dakota Wesleyan	Tigers	Dowling	Golden Lions
Dalhousie	Tigers	Drake	Bulldogs
Dallas	Crusaders	Drew	Rangers
Dallas Baptist	Patriots	Drexel	Dragons
Dallas Christian	Crusaders	Drury	Panthers
Daniel Webster	Eagles	Dubuque	Spartans
Dartmouth	Big Green	Duke	Blue Devils
Davenport	Panthers	Duquesne	Dukes
Davidson	Wildcats	D'Youville	Spartans
Davis	Falcons	Earlham	Hustlin' Quakers
Davis & Elkins	Senators		
Dayton	Flyers	East Carolina	Pirates
Defiance	Yellow Jackets	East Central	Tigers
Delaware	Blue Hens	East Stroudsburg	Warriors
Delaware State	Hornets	East Tennessee State	Buccaneers
Delaware Valley	Aggies	East Texas Baptist	Tigers
Delhi, State NY	Broncos	Eastern	Eagles
Delta State	Statesmen	Eastern Connecticut	Warriors
Denison	Big Red	Eastern Illinois	Panthers
Denver	Pioneers	Eastern Kentucky	Colonels
DePaul	Blue Demons	Eastern Mennonite	Royals
DePauw	Tigers	Eastern Michigan	Eagles
DeSales	Bulldogs	Eastern Nazarene	Lions
Detroit Mercy	Titans	Eastern New Mexico	Greyhounds/ Zias
Dickinson	Blue Devils	Eastern Oregon	Mountaineers
Dickinson State	Blue Hawks	Eastern Washington	Eagles
Dillard	Blue Devils	Ecclesia	Royals
Dine	Warriors	Eckerd	Tritons
District of Columbia	Firebirds	Edgewood	Eagles

Edinboro	**Scots**	Findlay	**Oilers**
Edward Waters	**Tigers**	Finlandia	**Lions**
Elizabeth City State	**Vikings**	Fisher	**Falcons**
Elizabethtown	**Blue Jays**	Fisk	**Bulldogs**
Elmhurst	**Bluejays**	Fitchburg State	**Falcons**
Elmira	**Soaring Eagles**	Flagler	**Saints**
Elms	**Blazers**	Fleming	**Knights**
Elon	**Phoenix**	Florida	**Gators**
Embry-Riddle	**Eagles**	Florida	**Falcons**
Embry–Riddle, D.B.	**Eagles**	Florida A & M	**Rattlers**
Emerson	**Lions**	Florida Atlantic	**Owls**
Emmanuel	**Saints**	Florida Christian	**Suns**
Emmanuel-Georgia	**Lions**	Florida Gulf Coast	**Eagles**
Emmaus Bible	**Eagles**	Florida Inst. of Tech.	**Panthers**
Emory	**Eagles**	Florida Int'l	**Golden Panthers**
Emory and Henry	**Wasps**	Florida Memorial	**Lions**
Emporia State	**Hornets**	Florida Southern	**Moccasins**
Endicott	**Gulls**	Florida State	**Seminoles**
Erskine	**Flying Fleet**	Fontbonne	**Griffins**
Eston	**Storm**	Fordham	**Rams**
Eureka	**Red Devils**	Fort Hays State	**Tigers**
Evangel	**Crusaders**	Fort Lewis	**Skyhawks**
Evansville	**Purple Aces**	Fort Valley State	**Wildcats**
Evergreen State	**Geoducks**	Framingham State	**Rams**
Fairfield	**Stags**	Francis Marion	**Patriots**
Fairleigh Dickinson	**Knights**	Franciscan	**Barons**
Fairleigh Dickinson, F.	**Devils**	Franklin	**Grizzlies**
Fairmont State	**Falcons**	Franklin & Marshall	**Diplomats**
Faith Baptist Bible	**Eagles**	Franklin Pierce	**Ravens**
Fanshawe	**Falcons**	Fraser Valley	**Cascades**
Faulkner	**Eagles**	Free Will Baptist Bible	**Flames**
Fayetteville	**Broncos**	Freed-Hardeman	**Lions**
Felician	**Golden Falcons**	Fresno Pacific	**Sunbirds**
Ferris State	**Bulldogs**	Friends	**Falcons**
Ferrum	**Panthers**	Frostburg State	**Bobcats**

Furman	**Paladins**
Gallaudet	**Bison**
Gannon	**Golden Knights**
Gardner–Webb	**Runnin' Bulldogs**
Geneva	**Golden Tornadoes**
George Brown	**Huskies**
George Fox	**Bruins**
George Mason	**Patriots**
George Washington	**Colonials**
Georgetown College	**Tigers**
Georgetown Univ.	**Hoyas**
Georgia	**Bulldogs**
Georgia & State	**Bobcats**
Georgia Inst. of Tech.	**Yellow Jackets**
Georgia Southern	**Eagles**
Georgia Southwestern	**Hurricanes**
Georgia State	**Panthers**
Georgian	**Grizzlies**
Georgian Court	**Lions**
Gettysburg	**Bullets**
Glenville State	**Pioneers**
Golden State Baptist	**Bears**
Goldey–Beacom	**Lightning**
Gonzaga	**Bulldogs**
Gordon	**Fighting Scots**
Goshen	**Maple Leafs**
Goucher	**Gophers**
Grace Bible	**Tigers**
Grace College	**Lancers**
Grace Univ.	**Royals**
Graceland	**Yellowjackets**
Grambling State	**Tigers**
Grand Canyon	**Antelopes**
Grand Valley State	**Lakers**
Grand View	**Vikings**
Grande Prarie	**Wolves**
Grant MacEwan	**Griffins**
Great Falls	**Argos**
Great Lakes Christian	**Tigers**
Green Mountain	**Eagles**
Greensboro	**Pride**
Greenville	**Panthers**
Grinnell	**Pioneers**
Grove City	**Wolverines**
Guelph	**Gryphons**
Guilford	**Quakers**
Gustavus Adolphus	**Gusties**
Gwynedd–Mercy	**Griffins**
Hamilton	**Continentals**
Hamline	**Pipers**
Hampden–Sydney	**Tigers**
Hampton	**Pirates**
Hannibal-LaGrange	**Trojans**
Hanover	**Panthers**
Harding	**Bison**
Hardin–Simmons	**Cowboys**
Harris-Stowe	**Hornets**
Hartford	**Hawks**
Hartwick	**Hawks**
Harvard	**Crimson**
Haskell Indian Nations	**Fighting Indians**
Hastings	**Broncos**
Haverford	**Fords**
Hawaii at Mānoa	**Rainbow Warriors**
Hawaii Pacific	**Sea Warriors**
Hawaii-Hilo	**Vulcans**
Heidelberg	**Student Princes**
Henderson State	**Reddies**

Hendrix	**Warriors**	Illinois Inst. of Tech.	**Scarlet Hawks**
High Point	**Panthers**	Illinois State	**Redbirds**
Hilbert	**Hawks**	Illinois Wesleyan	**Titans**
Hillsdale	**Chargers**	Illinois-Chicago	**Flames**
Hillsdale Free Will	**Saints**	Illinois-Springfield	**Prairie Stars**
Hiram	**Terriers**	Illinois-Urbana–Champaign	**Fighting Illini**
Hiwassee	**Tigers**		
Hobart	**Statesmen**	Immaculata	**Mighty Macs**
Hofstra	**Pride**	Incarnate Word	**Cardinals**
Hollins	***No Nickname***	Indiana	**Hoosiers**
Holy Cross College	**Saints**	Indiana -Fort Wayne	**Mastodons**
Holy Cross, The College	**Crusaders**	Indiana Inst. of Tech.	**Warriors**
		Indiana State	**Sycamores**
Holy Family	**Tigers**	Indiana Wesleyan	**Wildcats**
Holy Names	**Hawks**	Indiana-East	**Red Wolves**
Hood	**Blazers**	Indiana-Northwest	**Redhawks**
Hope	**Flying Dutchmen**	Indiana-Pennsylvania	**Crimson Hawks**
		Indianapolis	**Greyhounds**
Hope International	**Royals**	Indiana-Purdue	**Jaguars**
Houghton	**Highlanders**	Indiana-South Bend	**Titans**
Houston	**Cougars**	Indiana-Southeast	**Grenadiers**
Houston Baptist	**Huskies**	Iona	**Gaels**
Houston-Victoria	**Jaguars**	Iowa	**Hawkeyes**
Howard	**Bison**	Iowa State	**Cyclones**
Howard Payne	**Yellow Jackets**	Iowa Wesleyan	**Tigers**
Humber	**Hawks**	Ithaca	**Bombers**
Humboldt State	**Lumberjacks**	Jackson State	**Tigers**
Hunter	**Hawks**	Jacksonville	**Dolphins**
Huntingdon	**Hawks**	Jacksonville State	**Gamecocks**
Huntington	**Foresters**	James Madison	**Dukes**
Husson	**Eagles**	Jamestown	**Jimmies**
Huston-Tillotson	**Rams**	Jarvis Christian	**Bulldogs**
Idaho State	**Bengals**	John Brown	**Golden Eagles**
Idaho, Univ. of	**Vandals**	John Carroll	**Blue Streaks**
Idaho,College of	**Coyotes**	John Jay	**Bloodhounds**
Illinois	**Blueboys**	Johns Hopkins	**Blue Jays**

Johnson & Wales	**Wildcats**	La Verne	**Leopards**
Johnson & Wales - N. M.	**Wildcats**	Lafayette	**Leopards**
Johnson and Wales -D	**Wildcats**	LaGrange	**Panthers**
Johnson Bible	**Preachers/ Evangels**	Lake Erie	**Storm**
		Lake Forest	**Foresters**
Johnson C. Smith	**Golden Bulls**	Lake Superior State	**Lakers**
Johnson State	**Badgers**	Lakehead	**Thunderwolves**
Judson	**Eagles**	Lakeland (AB)	**Rustlers**
Juniata	**Eagles**	Lakeland College (WI)	**Muskies**
Kalamazoo	**Hornets**	Lamar	**Cardinals**
Kansas	**Jayhawks**	Lambton	**Lions**
Kansas State	**Wildcats**	Lambuth	**Eagles**
Kansas Wesleyan	**Coyotes**	Lancaster Bible	**Chargers**
Kean	**Cougars**	Lander	**Bearcats**
Keene State	**Owls**	Lane	**Dragons**
Kennesaw State	**Owls**	Langston	**Lions**
Kent State	**Golden Flashes**	Lasell	**Lasers**
Kentucky	**Wildcats**	Laurentian	**Voyageurs**
Kentucky Christian	**Knights**	Laval	**Rouge et Or**
Kentucky State	**Thorobreds**	Lawrence	**Vikings**
Kentucky Wesleyan	**Panthers**	Le Moyne	**Dolphins**
Kenyon	**Lords**	Lebanon Valley	**Flying Dutch**
Keuka	**Storm**	Lee	**Flames**
Keyano	**Huskies**	Lees–McRae	**Bobcats**
Keystone	**Giants**	Lehigh	**Mountain Hawks**
King	**Tornado**		
King's College	**Monarchs**	Lehman	**Lightning**
King's College, Univ. of	**Blue Devils**	LeMoyne–Owen	**Magicians**
		Lenoir–Rhyne	**Bears**
Knox	**Prairie Fire**	Lesley	**Lynx**
Kutztown	**Golden Bears**	Lethbridge College	**Kodiaks**
Kuyper	**Cougars**	Lethbridge, Univ. of	**Pronghorns**
Kwantlen Polytechnic	**Eagles**	LeTourneau	**Yellow Jackets**
La Cite	**Coyotes**	Lewis	**Flyers**
La Roche	**Red Hawks**	Lewis & Clark	**Pioneers**
La Salle	**Explorers**	Lewis-Clark State	**Warriors**

Liberty	**Flames**	Luther	**Norse**
Life	**Eagles**	Lycoming	**Warriors**
Limestone	**Saints**	Lynchburg	**Hornets**
Lincoln Christian	**Red Lions**	Lyndon State	**Hornets**
Lincoln Memorial	**Railsplitters**	Lynn	**Fighting Knights**
Lincoln-Missouri	**Blue Tigers**	Lyon	**Scots**
Lincoln-Pennsylvania	**Lions**	Macalester	**Scots**
Lindenwood	**Lions**	MacMurray	**Highlanders**
Lindenwood - Belleville	**Lynx**	Madonna	**Crusaders**
Lindsey Wilson	**Blue Raiders**	Maine	**Black Bears**
Linfield	**Wildcats**	Maine at Augusta	**Moose**
Lipscomb	**Bisons**	Maine at Farmington	**Beavers**
Livingstone	**Blue Bears**	Maine at Fort Kent	**Bengals**
Lock Haven	**Bald Eagles**	Maine at Machias	**Clippers**
Long Beach	**49ers**	Maine at Presque Isle	**Owls**
Long Island -Brooklyn	**Blackbirds**	Maine Maritime Acad.	**Mariners**
Long Island -C.W. Post	**Pioneers**	Malone	**Pioneers**
Longwood	**Lancers**	Manchester	**Spartans**
Loras	**Duhawks**	Manhattan	**Jaspers**
Louisiana	**Wildcats**	Manhattan Christian	**Crusaders**
Louisiana St.-Alexandria	**Generals**	Manhattanville	**Valiants**
Louisiana State	**Fightin' Tigers**	Manitoba	**Bisons**
Louisiana Tech	**Bulldogs**	Mansfield	**Mounties**
Louisiana-Lafayette	**Ragin' Cajuns**	Maranatha Baptist	**Crusaders**
Louisiana-Monroe	**Warhawks**	Marian	**Knights**
Louisiana-Shreveport	**Pilots**	Marian (WI)	**Sabres**
Louisville	**Cardinals**	Marietta	**Pioneers**
Lourdes	**Gray Wolves**	Marist	**Red Foxes**
Loyalist	**Lancers**	Marquette	**Golden Eagles**
Loyola Marymount	**Lions**	Mars Hill	**Lions**
Loyola-Chicago	**Ramblers**	Marshall	**Thundering Herd**
Loyola-Maryland	**Greyhounds**	Martin Luther	**Knights**
Loyola-New Orleans	**Wolfpack**	Martin Methodist	**Redhawks**
Lubbock Christian	**Chaparrals**	Mary	**Marauders**

Mary Baldwin	**Fighting Squirrels**	Menlo	**Oaks**
Mary Hardin–Baylor	**Crusaders**	Mercer	**Bears**
Mary Washington	**Eagles**	Merchant Marine	**Mariners**
Marygrove	**Mustangs**	Mercy	**Mavericks**
Maryland-Baltimore	**Retrievers**	Mercyhurst	**Lakers**
Maryland-Eastern Shore	**Hawks**	Meredith	**Avenging Angels**
Maryland-Park	**Terrapins**	Merrimack	**Warriors**
Marymount	**Saints**	Mesa State	**Mavericks**
Maryville College	**Scots**	Messiah	**Falcons**
Maryville Univ.	**Saints**	Methodist	**Monarchs**
Marywood	**Pacers**	Metropolitan State	**Roadrunners**
Mass. Inst. Of Tech	**Engineers**	Miami - Hamilton	**Harriers**
Massachusetts Amherst	**Minutemen**	Miami Univ.	**Redhawks**
Massachusetts Boston	**Beacons**	Miami, The Univ. of	**Hurricanes**
Massachusetts-Dartmouth	**Corsairs**	Michigan	**Wolverines**
		Michigan State	**Spartans**
Massachusetts Maritime	**Buccaneers**	Michigan Tech.	**Huskies**
Massachusetts-Lib. Arts	**Trailblazers**	Michigan–Dearborn	**Wolves**
Massachusetts-Lowell	**River Hawks**	Mid-America Christian	**Evangels**
Master's , The	**Mustangs**	Mid-America Nazarene	**Pioneers**
Mayville State	**Comets**	Mid-Continent	**Cougars**
McDaniel	**Green Terror**	Middle Tennessee	**Blue Raiders**
McGill	**Redmen/ Martlets**	Middlebury	**Panthers**
		Midland	**Warriors**
McKendree	**Bearcats**	Midway	**Eagles**
McMaster	**Marauders**	Midwestern	**Mustangs**
McMurry	**War Hawks**	Miles	**Golden Bears**
McNeese State	**Cowboys**	Millersville	**Marauders**
McPherson	**Bulldogs**	Milligan	**Buffaloes**
Medaille	**Mavericks**	Millikin	**Big Blue**
Medgar Evers	**Cougars**	Mills	**Cyclones**
Medicine Hat	**Battlers**	Millsaps	**Majors**
Memorial	**Sea-Hawks**	Milw. School of Eng.	**Raiders**
Memphis	**Tigers**		

Minnesota	Golden Gophers	Montana-Western	Bulldogs
Minnesota Crookston	Golden Eagles	Montclair State	Red Hawks
Minnesota Duluth	Bulldogs	Montevallo	Falcons
Minnesota Mankato	Mavericks	Montreal	Carabins
Minnesota Moorhead	Dragons	Montreat	Cavaliers
Minnesota Morris	Cougars	Moody Bible Institute	Archers
Minot State	Beavers	Moravian	Greyhounds
Misericordia	Cougars	Morehead State	Eagles
Mississippi	Rebels	Morehouse	Maroon Tigers
Mississippi College	Choctaws	Morgan State	Bears
Mississippi State	Bulldogs	Morningside	Mustangs
Mississippi Valley State	Delta Devils	Morris	Hornets
Missouri	Tigers	Mount Allison	Mounties
Missouri of Science and Technology	Miners	Mount Aloysius	Mounties
		Mount Holyoke	Lyons
Missouri Baptist	Spartans	Mount Ida	Mustangs
Missouri Southern	Lions	Mount Marty	Lancers
Missouri State	Bears	Mount Mary	Blue Angels
Missouri Valley	Vikings	Mount Mercy	Mustangs
Missouri Western	Griffons	Mount Olive	Trojans
Missouri–Kansas City	Kangaroos	Mount Royal	Cougars
Missouri–Saint Louis	Tritons	Mount Saint Joseph	Lions
Mitchell	Mariners	Mount Saint Mary	Knights
Mobile	Rams	Mount Saint Mary's	Mountaineers
Mohawk	Mountaineers	Mount St. Vincent	Dolphins
Molloy	Lions	Mount St. Vincent Coll.	Mystics
Moncton	Aigles Bleus/ Aigles Bleues	Mount Union	Purple Raiders
Monmouth College	Fighting Scots	Mount Vernon	Cougars
Monmouth Univ.	Hawks	Mountain State	Cougars
Montana	Grizzlies	Muhlenberg	Mules
Montana St.-Billings	Yellowjackets	Multnomah	Lions
Montana Tech.	Orediggers	Murray State	Racers
Montana–Bozeman	Bobcats	Muskingum	Fighting Muskies
Montana-Northern	Lights/ Skylights	N. Car. Ag. and Tech.	Aggies

N. Carolina Wesleyan	**Battling Bishops**	New York Maritime	**Privateers**
Navajo Technical	**Hawks**	New York Science and Forestry	**Mighty Oaks**
Navy	**Midshipmen**	New York-Albany	**Great Danes**
Nazareth	**Golden Flyers**	New York-Brockport	**Golden Eagles**
Nebraska at Kearney	**Lopers**	New York-Buffalo	**Bulls**
Nebraska at Omaha	**Mavericks**	New York-Canton	**Kangaroos**
Nebraska Christian	**Parsons**	New York=Cobleskill	**Fighting Tigers**
Nebraska -Tech. Agric.	**Aggies**	New York-Cortland	**Red Dragons**
Nebraska Wesleyan	**Prairie Wolves**	New York-Farmingdale	**Rams**
Nebraska–Lincoln	**Cornhuskers**	New York-Fredonia	**Blue Devils**
Neumann	**Knights**	New York-Geneseo	**Blue Knights**
Nevada, Las Vegas	**Rebels**	New York-Morrisville	**Mustangs**
Nevada, Reno	**Wolf Pack**	New York-New Paltz	**Hawks**
New Brunswick-St. John's	**Seawolves**	New York-Old Westbury	**Panthers**
New Brunswick-Fredericton	**Varsity Reds**	New York-Oneonta	**Red Dragons**
New England	**Nor'easters**	New York-Oswego	**Lakers**
New England College	**Pilgrims**	New York-Plattsburgh	**Cardinals**
New Hampshire	**Wildcats**	New York-Potsdam	**Bears**
New Haven	**Chargers**	New York-Purchase	**Panthers**
New Hope Christian	**Deacons**	Newberry	**Wolves**
New Jersey	**Rangers**	Newbury	**Nighthawks**
New Jersey City	**Gothic Knights**	Newman	**Jets**
New Jersey Tech.	**Highlanders**	Niagara	**Purple Eagles**
New Mexico	**Lobos**	Niagra	**Knights**
New Mexico Highlands	**Cowboys**	Nicholls State	**Colonels**
New Mexico State	**Aggies**	Nichols	**Bison**
New Orleans	**Privateers**	Nipissing	**Lakers**
New Rochelle	**Blue Angels**	Norfolk State	**Spartans**
New York	**Violets**	North Alabama	**Lions**
New York City Tech.	**Yellow Jackets**	North Car.-Pembroke	**Braves**
New York Inst. of Tech.	**Bears**	North Carolina Central	**Eagles**
New York Institute of Technology	**Wildcats**	North Carolina State	**Wolfpack**
		North Carolina-Wilmington	**Seahawks**

North Carolina-Asheville	Bulldogs	Northwestern Ohio	Racers
North Carolina-Chapel Hill	Tar Heels	Northwestern Okla.	Rangers
		Northwestern State	Demons
North Carolina-Greensboro	Spartans	Northwood Univ. (FL)	Seahawks
		Northwood Univ. (MI)	Timberwolves
North Central	Rams	Northwood Univ. (TX)	Knights
North Central College	Cardinals	Norwich	Cadets
North Dakota	Fighting Sioux	Notre Dame College	Falcons
North Dakota State	Bison	Notre Dame de Namur	Argos
North Florida	Ospreys		
North Georga	Saints	Notre Dame, Univ. of	Fighting Irish
North Greenville	Crusaders	Notre Dame-MD	Gators
North Park	Vikings	Nova Scotia Agric.	Rams
North Texas	Mean Green	Nova Southeastern	Sharks
Northeastern	Huskies	Nyack	Warriors
Northeastern State	RiverHawks	Oak Hills Christian	Wolfpack
Northern Alberta	Ooks	Oakland	Golden Grizzlies
Northern Arizona	Lumberjacks	Oakland City	Mighty Oaks
Northern British Columbia	Northern Timberwolves	Oakwood	Ambassadors
Northern Colorado	Bears	Oberlin	Yeomen
Northern Illinois	Huskies	Occidental	Tigers
Northern Iowa	Panthers	Oglethorpe	Petrels
Northern Kentucky	Norse	Ohio	Bobcats
Northern Michigan	Wildcats	Ohio Christian	Trailblazers
Northern New Mexico	Eagles	Ohio Dominican	Panthers
		Ohio Northern	Polar Bears
Northern State	Wolves	Ohio State Marion	Scarlet Wave
Northland	Lumberjacks	Ohio State, Lima	Barons
Northland Int'l	Pioneers	Ohio State, Mansfield	Mavericks
Northwest	Eagles	Ohio State, Newark	Titans
Northwest Christian	Beacons	Ohio State, The	Buckeyes
Northwest Missouri	Bearcats	Ohio Valley	Fighting Scots
Northwest Nazarene	Crusaders	Ohio Wesleyan	Battling Bishops
Northwestern	Wildcats		
Northwestern College	Eagles	Ohio, Chillicothe	Hilltoppers
Northwestern College	Red Raiders	Ohio, Eastern	Panthers

64

Ohio, Lancaster	**Cougars**	Paul Quinn	**Tigers**
Ohio, Zanesville	**Tracers**	Paul Smith's	**Bobcats**
Oklahoma	**Sooners**	Peace	**Pacers**
Oklahoma Baptist	**Bison**	Penn State	**Nittany Lions**
Oklahoma Christian	**Eagles**	Penn State Allegheny	**Nittany Lions**
Oklahoma City	**Stars**	Penn State Altoona	**Nittany Lions**
Oklahoma Panhandle	**Aggies**	Penn State Beaver	**Nittany Lions**
Oklahoma State – Stillwater	**Cowboys**	Penn State Berks	**Nittany Lions**
Oklahoma Wesleyan	**Eagles**	Penn State Brandywine	**Nittany Lions**
Old Dominion	**Monarchs**	Penn State Fayette	**Nittany Lions**
Olds	**Broncos**	Penn State Lehigh V.	**Nittany Lions**
Olivet	**Comets**	Penn State Mont Alto	**Nittany Lions**
Olivet Nazarene	**Tigers**	Penn State New Kens.	**Nittany Lions**
Ontario Inst. of Tech.	**Ridgebacks**	Penn State Schuylkill	**Nittany Lions**
Oral Roberts	**Golden Eagles**	Penn State Shenango	**Nittany Lions**
Oregon	**Ducks**	Penn State Wilkes-Barre	**Nittany Lions**
Oregon Inst. of Tech.	**Owls**	Penn State Worthington	**Nittany Lions**
Oregon State	**Beavers**	Penn State York	**Nittany Lions**
Ottawa Univ.	**Braves**	Penn State DuBois	**Nittany Lions**
Ottawa, Univ. of	**Gee Gees**	Penn State Hazelton	**Nittany Lions**
Otterbein	**Cardinals**	Pennsylvania	**Quakers**
Ouachita Baptist	**Tigers**	Pennsylvania of Tech.	**Wildcats**
Our Lady of the Lake	**Saints**	Pennsylvania State , Erie	**Behrend Lions**
Ozark Christian	**Ambassadors**	Pennsylvania State, Harrisburg	**Lions**
Ozarks, College of the	**Bobcats**	Pensacola Christian	**Eagles**
Ozarks, Univ. of the	**Eagles**	Pepperdine	**Waves**
Pace	**Setters**	Peru State	**Bobcats**
Pacific	**Boxers**	Pfeiffer	**Falcons**
Pacific Lutheran	**Lutes**	Philadelphia	**Rams**
Pacific, Univ. of the	**Tigers**	Philadelphia Biblical	**Crimson Eagles**
Pacific Union	**Pioneers**	Philander Smith	**Panthers**
Paine	**Lions**	Piedmont	**Lions**
Palm Beach Atlantic	**Sailfish**	Piedmont Baptist	**Conquerors**
Park	**Pirates**	Pikeville	**Bears**
Patten	**Lions**		

Pine Manor	Gators	Quebec a Outaouais, Universite du	Griffins
Pittsburg State	Gorillas	Quebec-Abitibi	Gaillards/ Astrelles
Pittsburgh	Panthers		
Pittsburgh-Bradford	Panthers	Quebec-Montreal	Citadins
Pittsburgh-Greensburg	Bobcats	Quebec-Rimouski	Pionniers
Pittsburgh-Johnstown	Mountain Cats	Quebec-Trois Rivieres	Patriotes
Pittsburgh-Titusville	Panthers	Queens	Knights
Plymouth State	Panthers	Queen's	Gaels
Point Loma Nazarene	Sea Lions	Queens-Charlotte	Royals
Point Park	Pioneers	Quest Canada	Kermodes
Polytechnic-New York	Bluejays	Quincy	Hawks
Pomona-Pitzer	Sagehens	Quinnipiac	Bobcats
Portage	Voyageurs	Radford	Highlanders
Portland	Pilots	Ramapo	Roadrunners
Portland Bible	Wildcats	Randolph	Wildcats
Portland State	Vikings	Randolph–Macon	Yellow Jackets
Post	Eagles	Red Deer	Kings/Queens
Prairie View A&M	Panthers	Redeemer	Royals
Pratt Institute	Cannoneers	Redlands	Bulldogs
Presbyterian	Blue Hose	Regina	Cougars
Presentation	Saints	Regis College	Pride
Prince Edward Island	Panthers	Regis Univ.	Rangers
Princeton	Tigers	Reinhardt	Eagles
Principia	Panthers	Rensselaer	Engineers
Providence College	Freemen	Rhema Bible	Eagles
Providence College (RI)	Friars	Rhode Island College	Anchormen
		Rhode Island, Univ. of	Rams
Puerto Rico-Bayamón	Cowboys	Rhodes	Lynx
Puerto Rico-Mayagüez	Tarzans	Rice	Owls
Puget Sound	Loggers	Richard Stockton	Ospreys
Purdue	Boilermakers	Richmond	Spiders
Purdue Calumet	Peregrines	Rider	Broncs
Purdue North Central	Panthers	Rio Grande	Red Storm
Quebec a Chicoutimi, Universite du	Cougars	Ripon	Red Hawks
		Rivier	Raiders

Roanoke	Maroons	Saint Benedict's	Blazers
Robert Morris	Eagles	Saint Bonaventure	Bonnies
Robert Morris-PA	Colonials	Saint Catharine	Patriots
Robert Morris-Chi.	Eagles	Saint Catherine	Wildcats
Robert Morris -Lake C.	Eagles	Saint Cloud	Huskies
Robert Morris -Peoria	Eagles	Saint Edward's	Hilltoppers
Roberts Wesleyan	Raiders	Saint Elizabeth	Eagles
Rochester, Univ. of	Yellowjackets	Saint Francis, Univ. of	Cougars
Rochester College	Warriors	Saint Francis-Ill.	Saints
Rochester Inst. of Tech.	Tigers	Saint Francis College	Terriers
		Saint Francis Univ.	Red Flash
Rockford	Regents	Saint Gregory's	Cavaliers
Rockhurst	Hawks	Saint John Fisher	Cardinals
Rocky Mountain	Battlin' Bears	Saint John's (MN)	Johnnies
Roger Williams	Hawks	Saint John's (NY)	Red Storm
Rogers State	Hillcats	Saint Joseph, College of	Fighting Saints
Rollins	Tars		
Roosevelt	Lakers	Saint Joseph	Blue Jays
Rose–Hulman	Fightin' Engineers	Saint Joseph's (NY)	Bears
		Saint Joseph's College	Golden Eagles
Rosemont	Ravens	Saint Joseph's Coll. (IN)	Pumas
Rowan	Profs		
Royal Military-Canada	Paladins	Saint Joseph's Univ.	Hawks
Russell Sage	Gators	Saint Joseph's-Maine	Monks
Rust	Bearcats	Saint Lawrence	Saints
Rutgers	Scarlet Knights	Saint Leo	Lions
Rutgers–Camden	Scarlet Raptors	Saint Louis	Billikens
Rutgers–Newark	Scarlet Raiders	Saint Louis Pharmacy	Eutectic
Ryerson	Rams	Saint Martin's	Saints
Sacred Heart	Pioneers	Saint Mary, College of	Flames
Saginaw Valley State	Cardinals	Saint Mary	Spires
Saint Ambrose	Fighting Bees/ Queen Bees	Saint Mary's Coll. (IN)	Belles
		Saint Mary's	Rattlers
Saint Andrews	Knights	Saint Mary's-Calif.	Gaels
Saint Anselm	Hawks	Saint Mary's-Maryland	Seahawks
Saint Augustine's	Falcons		
		Saint Mary's-Minn.	Cardinals

Saint Mary-Woods	**Pomeroys**	Savannah State	**Tigers**
Saint Michael's	**Purple Knights**	Schreiner	**Mountaineers**
Saint Norbert	**Green Knights**	Science and Arts-Okla.	**Drovers**
Saint Olaf	**Oles**	Sciences in Phil.	**Devils**
Saint Paul's	**Tigers**	Scranton	**Royals**
Saint Peter's	**Peacocks/ Peahens**	Seattle	**Redhawks**
Saint Rose, of	**Golden Knights**	Seattle Pacific	**Falcons**
Saint Scholastica	**Saints**	Selma	**Bulldogs**
Saint Thomas Univ.	**Tommies**	Seneca	**Sting**
Saint Thomas, Univ. of	**Celts**	Seton Hall	**Pirates**
		Seton Hill	**Griffins**
Saint Thomas (NB)	**Tommies**	Sewanee	**Tigers**
Saint Thomas Florida	**Bobcats**	Shaw	**Bears**
Saint Thomas Aquinas	**Spartans**	Shawnee State	**Bears**
Saint Vincent	**Bearcats**	Shenandoah	**Hornets**
Saint Xavier	**Cougars**	Shepherd	**Rams**
Sainte-Anne	**Dragons**	Shepherd Technical	**Eagles**
Salem	**Tigers**	Sherbrooke	**Vert et Or**
Salem College	**Spirits**	Sheridan	**Bruins**
Salem State	**Vikings**	Shippensburg	**Raiders**
Salisbury	**Sea Gulls**	Shorter	**Hawks**
Salve Regina	**Seahawks**	Siena	**Saints**
Sam Houston State	**Bearkats**	Siena Heights	**Saints**
Samford	**Bulldogs**	Silver Lake	**Lakers**
San Diego	**Toreros**	Simmons	**Sharks**
San Diego Christian	**Hawks**	Simon Fraser	**Clan**
San Diego State	**Aztecs**	Simpson	**Red Hawks**
San Francisco	**Dons**	Simpson College	**Storm**
San Francisco State	**Gators**	Sioux Falls	**Cougars**
San Jose State	**Spartans**	Skidmore	**Thoroughbreds**
Santa Clara	**Broncos**	Slippery Rock	**The Rock**
Santa Cruz	**Banana Slugs**	Smith	**Pioneers**
Sarah Lawrence	**Gryphons**	Soka of America	**Lions**
Saskatchewan	**Huskies**	Sonoma State	**Seawolves**
Savannah Art & Design	**Bees**	South Alabama	**Jaguars**

South Carolina	Gamecocks	Southern Virginia	Knights
South Carolina Aiken	Pacers	Southern Wesleyan	Warriors
South Carolina Beaufort	Sand Sharks	Southern-New Orleans	Knights
South Carolina State	Bulldogs	Southwest	Mustangs
South Carolina Upstate	Spartans	Southwest Baptist	Bearcats
South Dakota	Coyotes	Southwest Minnesota	Mustangs
South Dakota Schl of Mines & Tech.	Hardrockers	Southwestern	Pirates
South Dakota State	Jackrabbits	Southwestern Assemblies of God	Lions
South Florida	Bulls	Southwestern Christian	Eagles
Southeast Missouri	Redhawks	Southwestern College	Eagles
Southeastern	Fire	Southwestern College	Moundbuilders
Southeastern Bible	Sabers	Southwestern Okla.	Bulldogs
Southeastern Louisiana	Lions	Spalding	Golden Eagles
Southeastern Okla.	Savage Storm	Spelman	Jaguars
Southern	Jaguars	Spring Arbor	Cougars
Southern Alberta	Trojans	Spring Hill	Badgers
Southern Arkansas	Muleriders	Springfield	Pride
Southern Calif.	Trojans/ Women of Troy	St. Clair	Saints
Southern Connecticut	Owls	St. Francis Xavier	X-Men/ X-Women
Southern Ill. Edwardsville	Cougars	St. Lawrence-Brockville	Schooners
Southern Illinois	Salukis	St. Lawrence-Cornwall	Sharks
Southern Indiana	Screaming Eagles	St. Lawrence-Kingston	Vikings
Southern Maine	Huskies	St. Louis Christian	Soldiers
Southern Methodist	Mustangs	St. Mary's Univ.	Huskies
Southern Mississippi	Golden Eagles	St. Mary's College	Lightning
Southern N.H.	Penmen	Stanford	Cardinal
Southern Nazarene	Crimson Storm	Staten Island	Dolphins
Southern Oregon	Raiders	Stephen F. Austin	Lumberjacks
Southern Polytechnic	Runnin' Hornets	Stephens	Stars
Southern Utah	Thunderbirds	Sterling	Warriors
Southern Vermont	Mountaineers	Stetson	Hatters

Stevens Institute	**Ducks**	Texas, El Paso	**Miners**
Stevenson	**Mustangs**	Texas, San Antonio	**Roadrunners**
Stillman	**Tigers**	Texas, Tyler	**Patriots**
Stonehill	**Skyhawks**	Texas Christian	**Horned Frogs**
Stony Brook	**Seawolves**	Texas Lutheran	**Bulldogs**
Suffolk	**Rams**	Texas of the Permian Basin	**Falcons**
Sul Ross State	**Lobos**	Texas Southern	**Tigers**
Susquehanna	**Crusaders**	Texas State-San Marcos	**Bobcats**
Swarthmore	**Garnet**		
Sweet Briar	**Vixens**	Texas Tech	**Red Raiders**
Syracuse	**Orange**	Texas Wesleyan	**Rams**
Tabor	**Bluejays**	Texas Woman's	**Pioneers**
Talladega	**Tornadoes**	Texas–Pan American	**Broncs**
Tampa	**Spartans**	The King's	**Eagles**
Tarleton State	**Texans**	Thiel	**Tomcats**
Taylor	**Trojans**	Thomas College	**Terriers**
Temple	**Owls**	Thomas Univ.	**Night Hawks**
Tennessee	**Volunteers**	Thomas More	**Saints**
Tennessee at Chattanooga	**Mocs**	Thompson Rivers	**Wolfpack**
		Tiffin	**Dragons**
Tennessee at Martin	**Skyhawks**	Toccoa Falls	**Eagles**
Tennessee State	**Tigers**	Toledo	**Rockets**
Tennessee Tech.	**Golden Eagles**	Toronto	**Varsity Blues**
Tennessee Temple	**Crusaders**	Tougaloo	**Bulldogs**
Tennessee Wesleyan	**Bulldogs**	Towson	**Tigers**
Texas	**Steers**	Transylvania	**Pioneers**
Texas A&M	**Aggies**	Trent	**Excalibur**
Texas A&M-C.C.	**Islanders**	Trevecca Nazarene	**Trojans**
Texas A&M-Commerce	**Lions**	Trine	**Thunder**
Texas A&M Int'l	**Dustdevils**	Trinity College	**Bantams**
Texas A&M-Kingsville	**Javelinas**	Trinity College (FL)	**Tigers**
Texas, Arlington	**Mavericks**	Trinity of Florida	**Tigers**
Texas, Austin	**Longhorns**	Trinity Bible	**Lions**
Texas, Brownsville	**Scorpions**	Trinity Christian	**Trolls**
Texas, Dallas	**Comets**	Trinity International	**Trojans**

Trinity Lutheran	**Eagles**	Vermont	**Catamounts**
Trinity Washington	**Tigers**	Vermont Technical	**Green Knights**
Trinity Western	**Spartans**	Victoria	**Vikes**
Troy	**Trojans**	Victory	**Eagles**
Truett-McConnell	**Bears**	Villanova	**Wildcats**
Truman State	**Bulldogs**	Virginia	**Cavaliers**
Tufts	**Jumbos**	Virginia Commonwealth	**Rams**
Tulane	**Green Wave**	Virginia Intermont	**Cobras**
Tulsa	**Golden Hurricane**	Virginia Military Inst.	**Keydets**
Tusculum	**Pioneers**	Virginia Polytechnic	**Hokies**
Tuskegee	**Golden Tigers**	Virginia State	**Trojans**
UCLA	**Bruins**	Virginia Union	**Panthers**
Union College	**Bulldogs**	Virginia Wesleyan	**Marlins**
Union College (NY)	**Dutchmen**	Virginia-Wise	**Cavaliers**
Union Univ.	**Bulldogs**	Viterbo	**V-Hawks**
Unity	**Rams**	Voorhees	**Tigers**
Univ. of the Rockies	**Avalanche**	Wabash	**Little Giants**
Upper Iowa	**Peacocks**	Wagner	**Seahawks**
Urbana	**Blue Knights**	Wake Forest	**Demon Deacons**
Ursinus	**Bears**	Waldorf	**Warriors**
Ursuline	**Arrows**	Walla Walla	**Wolves**
Utah	**Utes**	Walsh	**Cavaliers**
Utah State	**Aggies**	Warner	**Royals**
Utah Valley	**Wolverines**	Warner Pacific	**Knights**
Utica	**Pioneers**	Warren Wilson	**Owls**
Valdosta State	**Blazers**	Wartburg	**Knights**
Valley City State	**Vikings**	Washburn	**Ichabods/ Lady Blues**
Valley Forge Christian	**Patriots**	Washington College	**Shoremen**
Valor Christian	**Warriors**	Washington, Univ. of	**Huskies**
Valparaiso	**Crusaders**	Washington & Jefferson	**Presidents**
Vancouver Island	**Mariners**	Washington Adventist	**Shock**
Vanderbilt	**Commodores**	Washington and Lee	**Generals**
Vanguard	**Lions**	Washington -St. Louis	**Bears**
Vassar	**Brewers**	Washington State	**Cougars**
Vaughn	**Warriors**		

Waterloo	**Warriors**	Western Oregon	**Wolves**
Wayland Baptist	**Pioneers**	Western State-CO	**Mountaineers**
Wayne State College	**Wildcats**	Western Washington	**Vikings**
Wayne State Univ.	**Warriors**	Westfield State	**Owls**
Waynesburg	**Yellow Jackets**	Westminster Coll. (MO)	**Blue Jays**
Webb Institute	**Webbies**	Westminster Coll. (PA)	**Titans**
Webber International	**Warriors**		
Weber State	**Wildcats**	Westminster-Salt Lake	**Griffins**
Webster	**Gorloks**		
Wellesley	**Blue**	Westmont	**Warriors**
Wells	**Express**	Wheaton College (MA)	**Lyons**
Wentworth Inst.	**Leopards**	Wheaton College (IL)	**Thunder**
Wesley Dover	**Wolverines**	Wheeling Jesuit	**Cardinals**
Wesleyan College	**Pioneers**	Wheelock	**Wildcats**
Wesleyan Univ.	**Cardinals**	Whitman	**Missionaries**
West Alabama	**Tigers**	Whittier	**Poets**
West Chester	**Golden Rams**	Whitworth	**Pirates**
West Coast Baptist	**Eagles**	Wichita State	**Shockers**
West Florida	**Argonauts**	Widener	**Pride**
West Georgia	**Wolves**	Wilberforce	**Bulldogs**
West Liberty	**Hilltoppers**	Wiley	**Wildcats**
West Texas A&M	**Buffaloes**	Wilfrid Laurier	**Golden Hawks**
West Virginia	**Mountaineers**	Wilkes	**Colonels**
West Virginia State	**Yellow Jackets**	Willamette	**Bearcats**
West Virginia Tech	**Golden Bears**	William & Mary	**Tribe**
West Virginia Wesleyan	**Bobcats**	William Carey	**Crusaders**
		William Jessup	**Warriors**
Western Carolina	**Catamounts**	William Jewell	**Cardinals**
Western Connecticut	**Colonials**	William Paterson	**Pioneers**
Western Illinois	**Fighting Leathernecks**	William Penn	**Statesmen**
Western Kentucky	**Hilltoppers**	William Smith	**Herons**
Western Michigan	**Broncos**	William Woods	**Owls**
Western New England	**Golden Bears**	Williams	**Ephs**
		Williams Baptist	**Eagles**
Western New Mexico	**Mustangs**	Wilmington	**Quakers**
Western Ontario	**Mustangs**	Wilmington	**Wildcats**

Wilson	Phoenix	Wisconsin–Whitewater	Warhawks
Windsor	Lancers	Wittenberg	Tigers
Wingate	Bulldogs	Wofford	Terriers
Winnipeg	Wesmen	Wooster	Fighting Scots
Winona State	Warriors	Worcester Polytechnic	Engineers
Winston-Salem	Rams	Worcester State	Lancers
Winthrop	Eagles	Wright State	Raiders
Wisconsin Lutheran	Warriors	Wright State-Lake	Lakers
Wisconsin–Eau Claire	Blugolds	Wyoming	Cowboys
Wisconsin–Green Bay	Phoenix	Xavier	Musketeers
Wisconsin–La Crosse	Eagles	Xavier of Louisiana	Gold Rush/ Gold Nuggets
Wisconsin–Madison	Badgers	Yale	Bulldogs
Wisconsin–Milwaukee	Panthers	Yeshiva	Maccabees
Wisconsin–Oshkosh	Titans	York	Lions
Wisconsin–Parkside	Rangers	York of Pennsylvania	Spartans
Wisconsin–Platteville	Pioneers	York-Nebraska	Panthers
Wisconsin–River Falls	Falcons	Youngstown State	Penguins
Wisconsin–St. Point	Pointers		**TOTAL 1,592**
Wisconsin–Stout	Blue Devils		
Wisconsin–Superior	Yellow Jackets		

Chapter 3

The Definitive Lists

Animal Nicknames: **All Other Nicknames:**
51.2% **48.8%**

Every nickname (both men and women's for institutions that use separate names) has been categorized into one of the following lists.

THE CATS MEOW
All the felines with Lion and Tiger variations fleshed out accordingly.

Bobcats	15	Lynx	3
Catamounts	2	Mountain Cats	1
Cougars	35	Panthers	35
Golden Panthers	1	Pumas	1
Hill Cats	1	Tigers	47
Jaguars	6	Bengals	3
Leopards	3	Blue Tigers	1
Lions	36	Fightin(g) Tigers	2
Behrend Lions	1	Golden Tigers	2
Golden Lions	2	Tomcats	1
Mountain Lions	2	Wildcats	35
Nittany Lions	17		
Red Lions	1	Total	253

BEAR WITH ME
The Bear facts are listed with all the grizzly details.

Bears	21	Kermodes*	1
Battlin' Bears	1	Kodiaks	1
Black Bears	1	Nanooks**	1
Blue Bears	1	Pandas (w)	1
Bruins	6	Polar Bears	2
Golden Bears	7	Sugar Bears (w)	1
Golden Grizzlies	1		
Grizzlies	3	Total	47

*White furred black bear
**Inuit for "Polar Bear"

UNDER THE SEA
Muskies are the only exclusively freshwater mascot.

Dolphins	4	Sailfish	1
Fighting Muskies	1	Sand Sharks	1
Geoducks	1	Sea Lions	1
Marlins	1	Sharks	3
Muskies	1		
Otters	1	Total	17
Penguins	2		

GET THE FLOCK OUT OF HERE!

This list is for the birds except for fowl which are categorized separately.

Aigles Bleus	1		Night Hawks	2
Blackbirds	2		Red Hawks	5
Blue Jays	8		River Hawks	2
Cardinals	17		Scarlet Hawks	1
Condors	1		Seahawks	7
Eagles	66		Skyhawks	3
Bald Eagles	1		Thunder Hawks	1
Crimson Eagles	1		V-Hawks	1
Golden Eagles	13		War Hawks	3
Purple Eagles	1		Herons	1
Screaming Eagles	1		Mocs (Mockingbirds)	1
Soaring Eagles	1		Ooks	1
Falcons	21		Ospreys	2
Firebirds	1		Owls	12
Golden Falcons	1		Peregrines	1
Gulls	1		Petrels	1
Harriers	1		Raptors	1
Hawks	21		Ravens	5
Blue Hawks	3		Redbirds	1
Crimson Hawks	1		Roadrunners	4
Duhawks	1		Scarlet Raptors	1
Golden Hawks	1		Sea Gulls	1
Hawkeyes	1		Sunbirds	1
Jayhawks	1			
Kohawks	1		Total	226
Mountain Hawks	1			

DOG DAY AFTERNOON

The canine category, a breed apart from the others.

Bloodhounds	1		Ridgebacks	1
Boxers	1		Runnin' Bulldogs	1
Bulldogs	40		Salukis	1
Great Danes	1		Setters	1
Greyhounds	5		Terriers	5
Huskies	13			
Pointers	1		Total	72
Retrievers	1			

ANIMAL FARM
If folks breed, ride or eat 'em, they're listed here.

Bulls	2	Pacers	3
Colts	1	Razorbacks	1
Gee Gees*	1	Steers	1
Golden Bulls	1	Thoroughbreds	1
Jennies (w)	1	Thundering Herd	1
Longhorns	1	White Mules	1
Mavericks	6		
Mules	2	Total	38
Mustangs	15		

*1st horse out of the gate in a race

MAN, YOU BUG ME
Insects, bugs and other small, squashable creatures.

Banana Slugs	1	Spiders	1
Bees	1	Sting	1
Boll Weevils	1	Stingers	1
Fighting Bees	1	Wasps	1
Hornets	11	Yellow Jackets	17
Queen Bees (w)	1		
Runnin' Hornets	1	Total	39
Scorpions	1		

COLD BLOODED KILLERS
Reptiles only. Oddly enough, no team is named after an amphibian (TCU's horned frog is a lizard).

Cobras	2	Rattlers	2
Dinos	1	Terrapins	1
Gators	6		
Horned Frogs	1	Total	14
Moccasins	1		

FUR CRYIN' OUT LOUD!

The remaining mammals in these annals. We consider Bison, Buffaloes, Camels and Rams to be wild.

Anteaters	1		Mastodons	1
Antelopes	1		Moose	1
Badgers	4		Northern Timberwolves	1
Beavers	10		Prairie Wolves	1
Bison(s)	10		Pronghorns	1
Buffaloes	3		Rams	20
Camels	2		Red Foxes	1
Coyotes	5		Red Wolves	2
Fighting Koalas	1		Fighting Squirrels	1
Golden Gophers	1		Stags	2
Golden Rams	2		Timberwolves	1
Gophers	1		Vixens	1
Gorillas	1		Wolfpack	5
Jackrabbits	1		Wolverines	4
Javelinas	1		Wolves	9
Kangaroos	3			
Lopers*	1		Total	99

*Formerly Antelopes

CRY FOWL!

You won't find any turkeys here.

Bantams	1		Peacocks	2
Blue Hens	1		Peahens (w)	1
Chanticleers	1		Sagehens	1
Ducks	2			
Gamecocks	2		Total	11

CAPITAL IDEA!

Whether elected or appointed, they are all politicians. Don't like this list? Write your congressman.

Ambassadors	2		Senators	2
Diplomats	1		Statesmen	3
Governors	1			
Judges	1		Total	11
Presidents	1			

A ROYAL PAIN

Some folks need not work for a living because their blood is blue, so this list is for titled individuals only.

Barons	3	Queens (w)	1
Dukes	2	Regals (w)	1
Kings	1	Regents	1
Kingsmen	1	Royals	9
Ladies (w)	1	Student Princes	1
Lords	1		
Monarchs	3	Total	25

MEN OF THE CLOTH

Read this list religiously but don't choose the Blue Devils unless something possesses you to do so.

Battling Bishops	2	Monks	1
Crusaders	20	Parsons	1
Deacons	2	Quakers	3
Demon Deacons	1	Royal Crusaders	1
Friars	1	Saints	22
Hustlin' Quakers	1		
Maccabees	1	Total	57
Missionaries	1		

TAKE THIS JOB AND SHOVE IT!

Some of us work for a living but our advice is don't quit your day job.

Axemen	1	Mechanics	1
Boilermakers	1	Mounties	2
Brewers	1	Mystics	1
Builders	1	Oilers	1
Carabins*	1	Pipers	1
Hatters	1	Poets	1
Loggers	1	Railsplitters	1
Lumberjacks	4		
Magicians	1	Total	20

*a surgeon

HOME ON THE RANGE
Ranchers and farmhands doing what they do best.

Cobbers	1	Rustlers	1
Cornhuskers	1	Shockers	1
Cowboys	6	Threshers	1
Drovers	1		
Mule Riders	1	Total	18
Rangers	5		

COLOR ME BAD
Some teams have no imagination. They simply looked at the team jersey and decided color as a nickname was the way to go. These are the colorful teams without any other identifying characteristics.

Big Blue(s)	2	Orange	1
Big Green	1	Redmen	2
Big Red	2	Reddies	1
Blue(s)	2	Rouge et Or*	1
Blue Boys	1	Varsity Blues	1
Blugolds	1	Varsity Reds	1
Cardinal	1	Vert et Or**	1
Crimson	1		
Garnet	1	Total	22
Maroons	2		

*Red and Gold
**Green and Gold

SO, WHERE YA FROM?
The answer? Europe. Only two of these nicknames pertain to American-based peoples, the rest are Euro transplants.

Britons	1	Norse	2
Dutch	1	Ragin' Cajuns	1
Dutchmen	1	Scots	5
Fighting Irish	1	Terrible Swedes	1
Fighting Scots	5	Texans	1
Flying Dutch	1		
Flying Dutchmen	1	Total	21

OUR ANCESTORS
Here are all those ancient civilizations that failed to survive until the present day.

Aztecs	1	Trojans	12
Celtics	1	Vikes	1
Celts	1	Vikings	16
Clan	1	Women of Troy (w)	1
Gaels	3		
Saxons	1	Total	55
Spartans	17		

WATCH OUT FOR THAT TREE!
As you might guess, fauna wins out over flora when it is time to naming your team.

Buckeyes	1	Silverswords*	1
Cotton Blossoms (w)	1	Sycamores	1
Foresters	2	Violets	1
Maple Leafs	1		
Mighty Oaks	2	Total	11
Oaks	1		

*A Hawaiian plant

THE HILLS HAVE EYES
It appears that some founders simply looked around when they settled in and named the team after local topography. This is probably why there are no teams called the Volcanoes or Glaciermen.

Capers	1	Moundbuilders	1
Cascades	1	Mountaineers	9
Chaparrals	1	Seasiders	1
Fords	1	Shoremen	1
Highlanders	5	The Rock*	1
Hilltoppers	4		
Islanders	1	Total	36
Lakers	9		

* The Rock is the *only* nickname with an article preceding.

YOU'RE HISTORY!

These folks shaped our country (and French-speaking Canada) so we remember and celebrate their heroic souls by creating nicknames in their honor.

49ers	2	Pilgrims	1
Blazers	8	Pioneers	24
Citadins	1	Pionniers	1
Colonials	3	Rebels	2
Explorers	1	Sooners	1
Freemen	1	Trailblazers	2
Minutemen	1	Volunteers	1
Patriotes	1		
Patriots	9	Total	59

NONE BUT THE BRAVE

We know it's not politically correct but some schools still have Native American nicknames.

Braves	4	Indians	1
Chippewas	1	Seminoles	1
Choctaws	1	Tribe	1
Fighting Illini	1	Utes	1
Fighting Indians	1		
Fighting Sioux	1	Total	13

ANCHORS AWEIGH!

The lure of the sea drove us to this category, so shape up or ship out.

Anchormen	1	Privateers	2
Buccaneers	6	Schooners	1
Clippers	3	Sea Warriors	1
Corsairs	1	Seawolves	4
Flying Fleet	1	Tars	1
Keelhaulers	1	Voyageurs	2
Mariners	4	Yeomen	1
Midshipmen	1		
Pirates	7	Total	41

THAT'S AN ORDER!
Someone needs to command the troops. We salute these leaders of distinction.

Cadets*	1	Generals	2
Captains	1	Majors	1
Colonels	5		
Commodores	1	Total	11

* Training to become an officer.

BATTLE STATIONS!
War can be a sports metaphor and these are the weapons and well-trained soldiers needed for battle.

Archers	1	Green Knights	2
Arrows	1	Purple Knights	2
Battlers	2	Scarlet Knights	1
Blue Raiders	2	Lancers	7
Bullets	1	Marauders	4
Cannoneers	1	Musketeers	1
Cavaliers	7	Paladins	2
Chargers	9	Purple Raiders	1
Conquerors	2	Raiders	7
Defenders	2	Rainbow Warriors	1
Excalibur	1	Red Raiders	2
Fighting Leathernecks	1	Sabers	2
Grenadiers	1	Sabres	1
Gyrenes	1	Scarlet Raiders	1
Knights	25	Soldiers	1
Black Knights	1	Vandals	1
Blue Knights	2	Warriors	29
Fighting Knights	1		
Golden Knights	3	Total	130
Gothic Knights	1		

LOOK, UP IN THE SKY...

To be successful we need an air attack. We have just the flying aces for such a mission.

Blue Angels	2	Pilots	3
Bombers	1	Purple Aces	1
Flyers	2		
Golden Flyers	1	Total	11
Jets	1		

STORMY WEATHER

Pleasant weather does not a nickname make. Wind, rain and the power of the ocean are the theme here. Surprisingly, no tidal waves or tsunamis.

Avalanche	1	Lightning	3
Crimson Storm	1	Nor'easters	1
Crimson Tide	1	Red Storm	3
Crimson Wave	1	Savage Storm	1
Cyclones	3	Scarlet Wave	1
Dustdevils	1	Storm	5
Golden Hurricane	1	Thunder	4
Golden Tornadoes	1	Tornado(es)	4
Green Wave	1	Waves	1
Gusties	1	Westwinds (w)	1
Heat	1		
Hurricanes	2	Total	39

WHERE ARE ALL THE UNICORNS?

The most interesting group of nicknames might just be this mythical collection of man and beasts.

Argonauts	1	Red Dragons	2
Argos	2	Thunderbirds	3
Athenas (w)	1	Thunder Wolves	2
Avenging Angels	1	Titans	7
Dragons	5	Tritons	3
Giants	1	Trolls	1
Griffins	8	Valkyries	1
Little Giants	1	Vulcans	2
Martlets (w)	1		
Phoenix	3	Total	45

HEAVENLY BODIES

Space, the final frontier—especially for nicknames. Very few schools have upgraded past our atmosphere.

Astrelles (w)	1	Skylights (w)	1
Aurora	1	Stars	3
Comets	3	Suns	1
Golden Suns (w)	1		
Prairie Stars	1	Total	13
Rockets	1		

GOING IN STYLE

Some names are so upbeat and upscale that they distinguish themselves from all the other ho-hum monikers.

Belles	1	Spirits	1
Continentals	1	Valiants	1
Gaillards	1	Wonder Boys	1
Gents	1		
Pride	5	Total	12

SPEED KILLS

Everyone wants their sports teams to be fast and these squads all have a need for speed.

Blue Streaks	1	Ramblers	1
Express	1	Zips	1
Gold Rush	1		
Racers	2	Total	7

YOU GOTTA WEAR SHADES

These may be the brightest student-athletes around.

Beacons	2	Lights	1
Fire	1	Prairie Fire	1
Flames	6	Red Flash	1
Golden Flashes	1		
Inferno	1	Total	13

SPELL THAT AGAIN?

Either these schools didn't stress academics or they just decided to be a little "different." In any case, a list of names you'll see elsewhere but with a twist.

Bearkats	1	What is a *bearcat* let alone one with a "k"?
Bronchos	1	Sounds like a bronco with asthma.
Griffons	1	Not a bad alternate spelling...
Gryphons	2	...compared to this one!
Keydets	1	The southern pronunciation of "cadets"?
Thorobreds	1	Horses owned by the God of Thunder?
Total	7	

SPECIAL EDUCATION

Special names for specialty schools.

Aggies*	9		Orediggers	2
Engineers	3		Penmen	1
Eutectic	1		Profs	1
Fightin' Engineers	1			
Hardrockers	1		Total	21
Miners	2			

*Short for "agriculture"

WHAT IS IT?

Some things are, well, just made up. The following nicknames are not in the dictionary and only exist in the hearts and minds of the denizens of the school and the surrounding area. At least these institutions have some imagination.

Bearcats	11		Hoyas	1
Billikens	1		Tar Heels	1
Gorlocks	1			
Hokies	1		Total	17
Hoosiers	1			

QUE ES ESTO?
Spanish for "what is it?" We'll explain in English.

Broncos	8	Wild horse
Broncs	2	Abbreviated "Broncos"
Dons	1	Spanish gentleman
Gauchos	1	Cowboy
Lobos	2	Wolf
Matadors	1	Bullfighter
Toreros	1	part of a bullfighter's team
Toros	1	Bull
Total	17	

THE NAME GAME
Some of the nicknames were derivatives of the founder or a wealthy philanthropist who kept them afloat. Still more are take-offs of the school name. Saints alive!

NICKNAME		NAMED AFTER...
AMCats	1	*Mother Anne Marie*
Auggies	1	*Augustus Augsburg*
Bonnies	1	*Saint Bonaventure*
Ephs	1	*Colonel Ephraim Williams, founder*
Ichabods	1	*Ichabod Washburn, benefactor*
Jaspers	1	*Brother Jasper, first baseball coach*
Jimmies	1	*Jamestown, where school resides*
Johnnies	1	*Saint John*
Lord Jeffs	1	*Lord Jeffrey Amherst, benefactor*
Lyons	2	*Mary Lyons, administrator/teacher*
Mighty Macs	1	*Immaculate Mary*
Oles	1	*Saint Olaf*
Pomeroys	1	*Mary Pomeroy, alumnus/instructor/booster*
Scotties	1	*Agnes Scott, mother of benefactor*
Tommies	2	*Saint Thomas*
Total	17	

AH, THE HELL WITH IT!

Devils and demons are scary to other teams. Here is the list, satanized for your protection.

Demons	1		Red Devils	1
Blue Demons	1		Sun Devils	1
Devils	2			
Blue Devils	7		Total	14
Delta Devils	1			

I CATEGORICALLY DENY...

Some nicknames literally defy description. There is simply no substantial list to put the following under, so we lumped 'em together under "other."

Blue Hose	1	The only actual article of clothing nickname.
Gaiters	1	Bishop's boot covering. Smartly began using Gator mascot.
Gold Nuggets (w)	1	Would be part of a minor miner category.
Green Terror	1	Why does green evoke such emotion?
Janes (w)	1	Along with the Tarzan men's team, cute couple.
Jumbos	1	Named after one *specific* elephant.
Lasers	1	Maybe the most unique name of all.
Lutes	1	The only musical instrument mascot (short for "Lutheran").
Mean Green	1	Why is green so mean?
Shock	1	Shock and Terror in their own category.
Spires	1	One of only two architectural mascots, along with the Archers.
Steels	1	The only metal alloy nickname.
Tartans	1	Denotes a style of fabric.
Tarzans	1	Tarzan was popular in Puerto Rico, what can we say?
Toppers	1	I guess they got to the top of the mountain.
Tracers	1	Type of special bullet or a beginning artist?
Wesmen	1	Did a guy named Wes start things?
X-Men	1	Marvel Comics superhero team.
Zias (w)	1	An ancient symbol.
Total	19	

Chapter 4
Didja Know?

This book is all about nicknames and they cannot be stopped—we can only hope to contain them. Here is our effort to categorize them in fun and interesting ways along with a bunch of other related tidbits we found during our research. Enjoy!

THE POPULAR VOTE

The most popular nicknames exactly as they are used by the schools.

1.	Eagles	68		12.	Hawks	21
2.	Tigers	47		15.	Crusaders	20
3.	Bulldogs	40		16.	Rams	20
4.	Lions	36		17.	Cardinals	17
5.	Wildcats	35		17.	Yellow Jackets	17
5.	Panthers	35		17.	Nittany Lions	17
5.	Cougars	35		17.	Spartans	17
8.	Warriors	29		21.	Vikings	16
9.	Knights	25		22.	Bobcats	15
10.	Pioneers	24		22.	Mustangs	15
11.	Saints	22		24.	Golden Eagles	13
12.	Falcons	21		24.	Huskies	13
12.	Bears	21				

The most used ROOT nicknames as they appear within each school nickname.

1.	Eagles	85		6.	Knights	38
2.	Lions	59		7.	Panthers	36
3.	Hawks	56		8.	Wildcats	35
4.	Tigers	52		9.	Bears	34
5.	Bulldogs	40		10.	Warriors	30

EARNING YOUR COLLEGE LETTER

What are most popular monikers for each letter of the alphabet? If you can name them you get an "A" for effort.

A	Aggies	9		N	Nittany Lions	17
B	Bulldogs	40		O	Owls	12
C	Cougars	35		P	Panthers	35
D	Dragons	5		Q	Quakers	3
E	Eagles	68		R	Rams	20
F	Falcons	21		S	Saints	22
G	Golden Eagles	13		T	Tigers	47
H	Hawks	21		U	Utes	1
I	Ichabods, Indians, Inferno, Islanders	1		V	Vikings	16
				W	Wildcats	35
J	Jaguars	6		X	X-Men	1
K	Knights	25		Y	Yellow Jackets	17
L	Lions	36		Z	Zips	1
M	Mustangs	15				

CURRENT STATE OF AFFAIRS

Here is the list of all schools by state and the Canadian schools by province. The list is surprising considering the population ratios in certain areas.

United States

1.	Pennsylvania	118		27.	Connecticut	20
2.	New York	116		27.	Louisiana	20
3.	California	73		27.	Oregon	20
4.	Texas	66		30.	Washington	19
5.	Ohio	60		31.	Nebraska	18
6.	Massachusetts	58		31.	West Virginia	18
7.	Illinois	55		33.	Colorado	17
8.	North Carolina	50		34.	Maine	16
9.	Georgia	43		35.	Mississippi	14
10.	Missouri	43		36.	New Hampshire	11
11.	Indiana	42		36.	South Dakota	11
11.	Virginia	42		36.	Vermont	11
13.	Florida	41		39.	Montana	9
13.	Tennessee	41		39.	North Dakota	9
15.	Michigan	38		41.	Dist. of Columbia	8
16.	Wisconsin	34		41.	New Mexico	8
17.	Minnesota	33		41.	Rhode Island	8
18.	Iowa	31		41.	Utah	8
19.	Kentucky	29		45.	Arizona	7
20.	New Jersey	28		46.	Idaho	6
21.	Alabama	27		47.	Delaware	5
22.	Oklahoma	26		47.	Hawaii	5
22.	South Carolina	26		49.	Alaska	2
24.	Kansas	24		49.	Nevada	2
25.	Arkansas	21		51.	Wyoming	1
25.	Maryland	21				

Puerto Rico   2

Canada

Ontario	41		New Brunswick	7
Alberta	22		Saskatchewan	5
British Columbia	13		Manitoba	4
Quebec	12		Newfoundland	1
Nova Scotia	9		Prince Edward Island	1

NO "S" TO SPEAK OF

69 nicknames do not end in the letter S and we have subdivided them into seven "es"oteric categories.

Men Without Hats
Anchormen
Axemen
Dutchmen
Flying Dutchmen
Freemen
Midshipmen
Minutemen
Penmen
Redmen
Shoremen
Statesmen
Wesmen
X-Men
Yeomen

Coloring Book
Big Blue
Big Green
Big Red
Blue
Blue Hose
Cardinal
Crimson
Garnet
Gold Rush
Orange
Rouge et Or

Vert et Or

Animal Magnetism
Bison
Lynx
Moose
Sailfish
Thundering Herd
Wolfpack

Weather Report
Avalanche
Crimson Storm
Crimson Tide
Crimson Wave
Golden Hurricane
Green Wave
Heat
Lightning
Red Storm
Savage Storm
Scarlet Wave
Storm
Thunder
Tornado

Face the Nation
Clan

Dutch
Fighting Illini
Fighting Irish
Fighting Sioux
Flying Dutch
Norse
Tribe

Bright Future
Aurora
Fire
Inferno
Prairie Fire
Red Flash

Emotional Rescue
Green Terror
Mean Green
Pride
Shock

Table Scraps
Eutectic
Excalibur
Flying Fleet
Phoenix
Sting
The Rock

Didja Know? The Chicago Bears are often referred to as the *Monsters of the Midway* but the term was originally applied to the University of Chicago's football team (the Maroons) under the leadership of Amos Alonzo Stagg. "Midway" is a reference to the *Midway Plaisance*, a long, green swath of boulevard bordering the southern end of the campus between 59th and 60th Streets and running from Washington Park to Jackson Park on Chicago's South Side.

Didja Know? The official logo of The University of West Florida shows a Chambered Nautilus and because of this, students sometimes refer to themselves as the "Fighting Snails."

GET YOUR MOTOR RUNNING

Here is a category that many teams fit into auto-matically.

Alfa Romeo	Spiders		Falcons
AMC	Eagles		Fords
	Hornets		Mustangs
	Marlins		Rangers
	Matadors		Thunderbirds
	Pacers	**Geo**	Storm
	Ramblers	**GMC**	Jimmies
	Rebels	**Jaguar**	Jaguars
Buick	(Le)Sabres	**Lincoln**	Continentals
	Skyhawks	**Mercury**	Bobcats
	Wildcats		Comets
Chevy	Blazers		Cougars
	Cavaliers		Lynx
	Corsairs		Marauders
	Lasers		Monarchs
	Trailblazers		Mountaineers
Chrysler	(Le)Barons	**Plymouth**	Arrows
Dodge	Chaparrals		Roadrunners
	Chargers		Valiants
	Diplomats	**Pontiac**	Firebirds
	Lancers		Phoenix
	Mavericks		Sunbirds
	Rams	**Stutz**	Bearcats
	Spirits	**Subaru**	Foresters
Ford	Broncos	**Toyota**	Highlanders
	Explorers		

INANIMATE OBJECTS

Only 14 inanimate objects are used for nicknames.

Archers*	1	Jets	1
Arrows	1	Rockets	1
Bullets	1	Sabers	2
Clippers	3	Sabres	1
Comets	3	Schooners	1
Excalibur	1	Spires	1
Gaiters	1	The Rock	1

*Refers to an Arch on the Moody Bible Institute campus.

RHYME TIME

If you sense some melodious match-ups below, you are quite right. A list to peruse that's sure to amuse.

49ers	vs.	Miners	Ephs	vs.	Lord Jeffs
Arrows	vs.	Toreros	Flyers	vs.	Friars
Athenas	vs.	Javelinas	Fords	vs.	Lords
Battlers	vs.	Rattlers	Gamecocks	vs.	Gorlocks
Beacons	vs.	Deacons	Gents	vs.	Presidents
Bears	vs.	Corsairs	Grenadiers	vs.	Mountaineers
Beavers	vs.	Retrievers	Gyrenes	vs.	Wolverines
Belles	vs.	Chaparrals	Hardrockers	vs.	Shockers
Blazers	vs.	Lasers	Huskies	vs.	Muskies
Bluejays	vs.	Ospreys	Knights	vs.	Lights
Blues	vs.	Kangaroos	Lakers	vs.	Quakers
Bonnies	vs.	Johnnies	Lumberjacks	vs.	Razorbacks
Braves	vs.	Waves	Lutes	vs.	Utes
Buccaneers	vs.	Chanticleers	Matadors	vs.	Sycamores
Buffaloes	vs.	Blue Hose	Mocs	vs.	Peacocks
Bulldogs	vs.	Horned Frogs	Pacers	vs.	Racers
Cadets	vs.	Jets	Pilots	vs.	Violets
Cavaliers	vs.	Privateers	Pioneers	vs.	Steers
Crimson Tide	vs.	Pride	Pomeroys	vs.	Wonder Boys
Crusaders	vs.	Raiders	Shock	vs.	The Rock
Great Danes	vs.	Hurricanes	Spartans	vs.	Tartans
Diplomats	vs.	Mountain Cats	Stars	vs.	Tars
Eagles	vs.	Regals	Titans	vs.	Tritons
Engineers	vs.	Volunteers			

FAMOUS NAMES

Many schools are missing out on a brilliant marketing scheme, namely, bringing the most famous representative of the school nickname out to the ballgame.

Anchorman	Ron Burgundy (Will Ferrell)	Blues	BB King
		Bobcat	Bobcat Goldthwaite
Archer	William Tell		
Argonaut	Jason	Bonnie	Bonnie Parker (Bonnie & Clyde)
Auggie	Auggie Doggy		
Aztec	Montezuma	Boxer	Muhammad Ali
Baron	Baron von Richthofen	Brewer	Adolphus Busch
		Builder	Bob Vila
Bear	Yogi Bear	Bulldog	Bulldog Turner
Beaver	Theodore Cleaver	Camel	Joe Camel

Captain	James T. Kirk	Islander	Robinson Crusoe
Clipper	Joe DiMaggio, (Yankee Clipper)	Indian	Mahatma Ghandi
		Jimmie	Jimmie Johnson
Colonel	Colonel Sanders	Johnny	Johnny Depp
Commodore	Robert Peary	Judge	Judge Dredd
Conqueror	William the Conqueror	Kangaroo	Captain Kangaroo
		Knight	Bobby Knight
Coyote	Wile E. Coyote	Lion	Simba (Lion King)
Crusader	Batman (Caped Crusader)	Lobo	Rebecca Lobo
		Lumberjack	Paul Bunyan
Deacon	Deacon Jones	Magician	David Blaine
Defender	Johnny Cochran	Major	Old Major (Animal Farm)
Demon	Beelzebub		
Devil	Satan	Marlin	Marlin Perkins
Dino	Dino (the Flintstones)	Maverick	Tom Cruise (*Top Gun*)
Dolphin	Flipper	Missionary	Mother Teresa
Don	Don Corleone	Monarch	King Henry VIII
Dragon	Puff the Magic Dragon	Monk	Rasputin
		Moose	Bullwinkle
Duck	Daffy Duck	Mountaineer	Sir Edmund Hillary
Duke	Duke Ellington	Mountie	Dudley Do-Right
Dutchman	Vincent Van Gogh	Mule	Francis the Talking Mule
Eagle	Don Henley		
Engineer	Mighty Casey	Musketeer	Athos, Porthos, Aramis
Explorer	Columbus		
Express	Ernie "The Express" Davis	Mystic	Nostradamus
		Norseman	Leif Erickson
Fightin' Squirrel	Rocky Squirrel	Ole	Olaf Kolzig (Ole the Goalie)
Flyer	Amelia Earhart		
Ford	Harrison Ford	Owl	Woodsy Owl
Friar	Friar Tuck	Patriot	Nathan Hale
Gator	Wally Gator	Penguin	Burgess Meredith
General	Ulysses S. Grant	Pilot	Charles Lindbergh
Giant	Jolly Green Giant	Piper	Peter Piper
Golden Bear	Jack Nicklaus	Pirate	Captain Hook
Gorilla	Magilla Gorilla	Poet	Longfellow
Great Dane	Scooby Doo	Prairie Star	Michael Landon
Grizzly	Grizzly Adams	President	George Washington
Hatter	The Mad Hatter		
Hawkeye	"Hawkeye" Pierce (M*A*S*H)	Prof	Professor Plum
		Quaker	William Penn
Hawk	Tony Hawk	Racer	Dale Earnhart
Ichabod	Ichabod Crane	Ranger	The Lone Ranger

Rebel	James Dean		
Red Fox	Redd Foxx	Texan	JR Ewing
Reddie	Helen Reddy		(Larry Hagman)
Roadrunner	The Road Runner	The Rock	Dwayne "The
	(Looney Tunes)		Rock" Johnson
Rocket	Roger Clemens	Thoroughbred	Secretariat
Royal	Princess Diana	Thunder	Thor, the God of
Saint	Saint Patrick		Thunder
Scot	Sean Connery	Tiger	Tiger Woods
Scottie	Scotty (Star Trek)	Tommie	Tommy Lee Jones
Sea Gull	Jonathan	Topper	Topper Headon
	Livingston		(The Clash)
	Seagull	Trailblazer	Lewis & Clark
Shocker	Wes Craven	Trojan	Helen of Troy
Soldier	Beetle Bailey	Valiant	Prince Valiant
Spartan	Leonidas	Viking	Erik the Red
Spider	Itsy Bitsy Spider	Vulcan	Mister Spock
Spirit	Casper	Wolf	The Big Bad Wolf
	(Friendly Ghost)	X-Men	Wolverine
Tarzan	Johnny	Yeomen	Beefeaters
	Weissmuller		

THE BOOB TUBE

Here is your TV screen pass to view all the top programs.

30 **Rock**	**Duck** Factory	The Nanny & the
Angel	**Duck**man	**Professor**
Angels	The **Dukes** of Hazzard	NYPD **Blue**
Baby **Blues**	**Falcon** Crest	The **Rebel**
Bay City **Blues**	First **Wave**	School House **Rock**
Big Blue Marble	The **Golden** Girls	**Shark**
B.J. and the **Bear**	**Green** Acres	Sky **King**
Blue Thunder	The **Green Hornet**	**Star** of the Family
The **Blue Knight**	**Grizzly** Adams	**Star**man
Brave **Eagle**	**Highlander**	**Tarzan**: **King** of
Buffalo Bill	The High **Chaparral**	the Jungle
Captain(s) Kangaroo	Hill Street **Blues**	That's So **Raven**
Card **Sharks**	**Johnny** Quest	Touched by an **Angel**
Charlie's **Angels**	**Knight** Rider	**Topper**
City of **Angels**	**Knights** of Prosperity	Walker, Texas **Ranger**
Crusader	Land of the **Giants**	Wizards and **Warriors**
Dark **Angel**	Leave it to **Beaver**	**X**-Files
The **Defenders**	Man Called **X**	Xena, **Warrior** Princess

LIGHTS, CAMERAS, ACTION!

Of the 500 greatest movies of all time there are relatively few (only 45) that contain a college nickname in one form or another. Pass the popcorn!

Crouching **Tiger**, Hidden **Dragon** (2000)
Jailhouse **Rock** (1957)
Sweeney Todd: The **Demon** Barber of Fleet Street (2007)
The **Big Red** One (1980)
Rebel Without a Cause (1955)
Pirates of The Caribbean: Dead Man's Chest (2006)
Enter the **Dragon** (1973)
Spider-Man (2002)
Wonder Boys (2000)
Pirates of The Caribbean: The Curse of the **Black** Pearl (2003)
The **Gold** Rush (1925)
The **Green** Mile (1999)
Lone **Star** (1996)
The **Lion King** (1994)
Midnight **Cowboy** (1969)
Indiana Jones and the Last **Crusade** (2007)
The **Red** Balloon (1956)
A Place In The **Sun** (1951)
The Maltese **Falcon** (1941)
The **Black** Cat (1997)
The **Blues** Brothers (1980)
The **Leopard** (1963)
King Kong (1933)

Black Narcissus (1947)
Big (1988)
Betty **Blue** (1986)
School of **Rock** (2003)
Goldfinger (1964)
The **Red** Shoes (1948)
Dances With **Wolves** (1990)
Duck Soup (1933)
The Man Who Would Be **King** (1975)
The **King** Of Comedy (1983)
Blue Velvet (1986)
The Thin **Red** Line (1998)
Three Colours **Red** (1994)
The **Lord** of the Rings: The Two Towers (2002)
A Clockwork **Orange** (1971)
The **Lord** of the Rings: The Return of the **King** (2003)
The **Lord** of the Rings: The Fellowship of the Ring (2001)
Star Wars Episode IV: A New Hope (1977)
The Dark **Knight** (2007)
Raging **Bull** (1980)
Star Wars Episode V: The Empire Strikes Back (1980)
Raiders of the Lost Ark (1981)

Didja Know? The UC Santa Cruz Banana Slug was featured along with the school's logo on Vincent Vega's (John Travolta) t-shirt in the 1994 film, *Pulp Fiction*.

Didja Know? Much of the movie *Animal House* was filmed on the University of Oregon campus.

Didja Know? A portion of Adam Sandler's movie *Water Boy* (1998) was filmed on the Stetson University campus.

PLAY FOR PAY

No, not the college athletes! That would lead to sanctions and banishment from the amateur ranks. We're talking about teams that share their nicknames with the pros.

MLB
American League
Blue Jays
Indians
Mariners
Rangers

Royals
Tigers

National League
Braves

Brewers
Cardinals
Giants
Marlins
Pirates

NBA
Western Conference
Clippers
Grizzlies
Hornets
Lakers
Mavericks
Rockets
Suns

Thunder
Timberwolves
Trailblazers
Warriors

Eastern Conference
Bobcats
Bulls

Cavaliers
Celtics
Hawks
Heat
Pacers
Raptors

NFL
AFC
Bengals
Broncos
Chargers
Colts
Dolphins
Jaguars
Jets
Patriots
Raiders

Ravens
Texans
Titans

NFC
49ers
Bears
Buccaneers
Cardinals
Cowboys

Eagles
Falcons
Giants
Lions
Panthers
Rams
Saints
Seahawks
Vikings

NHL
Western Conference
Avalanche
Blues
Coyotes
Ducks
Flames
Kings
Oilers

Sharks
Stars

Eastern Conference
Bruins
Devils
Flyers
Hurricanes

Islanders
Lightning
Maple Leafs
Panthers
Penguins
Rangers
Sabres
Senators

WNBA

Lynx   Mystics   Shock   Storm

Defunct Pro Teams

Pilots	Seattle, MLB	Muskies	Minnesota, ABA
Bombers	St. Louis, NBA	Oaks	Oakland, ABA
Bullets	Baltimore, NBA	Pipers	Pittsburgh, ABA
Stags	Chicago, NBA	Spirits	St. Louis, ABA
Chaparrals	Dallas, ABA	Barons	Cleveland, NHL
Colonels	Kentucky, ABA	Fighting Saints	Minnesota, WHA
Comets	Houston, WNBA	Racers	Indianapolis, WHA
Cougars	Carolina, ABA	Roadrunners	Phoenix, WHA
Monarchs	Sacramento, WNBA	Toros	Toronto, WHA

COLOR MY WORLD

A veritable technicolor dreamcoat of a category. Guess the most popular and you win a gold medal.

Black (3)	Bears, Birds, Knights
Blue (16)	Angels, Bears, Big, Blue, Blues, Boys, Demons, Devils, Hawks, Hens, Hose, Jays, Knights, Raiders, Streaks, Tigers
Cardinal (1)	Cardinal
Crimson (6)	Crimson, Eagles, Hawks, Tide, Wave, Storm
Garnet (1)	Garnet
Golden (18)	Bears, Blu-, Bulls, Eagles, Falcons, Flashes, Flyers, Gophers, Grizzlies, Hawks, Hurricanes, Knights, Lions, Panthers, Rams, Rush, Tigers, Tornadoes
Gray/Grey (2)	Hounds, Wolves
Green (6)	Big, Knights, Mean, Terror, Vert et Or, Wave
Maroon (1)	Maroons
Orange (1)	Orange
Purple (4)	Aces, Eagles, Knights, Raiders
Red (13)	Big, Birds, -dies, Devils, Dragons, Flash, Hawks, Lions, Men, Raiders, Rouge et Or, Storm, Wolves
Scarlet (5)	Hawks, Knights, Raiders, Raptors, Wave
Silver (1)	Swords
White (1)	Mules
Violet (1)	Violets
Yellow (1)	Jackets

Didja Know? In 1973, Assistant Attorney General, Howard Koop suggested the University of Wisconsin do away with their Bucky Badger mascot to be replaced by Henrietta Holstein, arguing, "Kids love cows." Thankfully, Koop's effort failed.

BAND ON THE RUN

Bands with a nickname (or two) contained within and their best known song. Ah, music to my ears!

A Flock of **Seagulls**	*I Ran*
Arcade **Fire**	*Wake Up*
Barenaked **Ladies**	*One Week*
The Belle **Stars**	*The Clapping Song*
Bill Halley and the **Comets**	*Rock Around the Clock*
Brewer and Shipley	*One Toke Over the Line*
Buffalo Springfield	*For What It's Worth*
The **Captain** & Tennille	*Love Will Keep Us Together*
The **Commodores**	*Brick House*
The **Corsairs**	*Smoky Places*
Cowboy Junkies	*Anniversary Song*
The **Crusaders**	*Scratch*
Def **Leppard**	*Rock of Ages*
The **Eagles**	*Hotel California*
Gladys **Knight** and the Pips	*Midnight Train to Georgia*
Gorillaz	*Demon Days*
Green Day	*American Idiot*
The **Hawks**	*Patricia*
Hot Hot **Heat**	*Get In or Get Out*
Jet	*Are You Gonna Be My Girl?*
King **Crimson**	*Heartbeat*
Kings of Leon	*Use Somebody*
The **Kings**men	*Louie, Louie*
Los **Lobos**	*La Bamba*
The Moody **Blues**	*Nights in White Satin*
The **Nighthawks**	*Mighty Long Time*
Night **Ranger**	*Sister Christian*
Paul Revere and the **Raiders**	*Kicks*
The **Rebels**	*Wild Weekend*
Rory **Storm** and the **Hurricanes**	*Dr. Feelgood*
The **Scorpions**	*Rock You Like a Hurricane*
The **Spiders**	*Witchcraft*
Sting	*If You Love Somebody Set Them Free*
Stone Temple **Pilots**	*Big Bang Baby*
They Might Be **Giants**	*Birdhouse in Your Soul*
Vixen	*Edge of a Broken Heart*
Wu Tang **Clan**	*C.R.E.A.M.*

Didja Know? Singer-songwriter Jim Croce died in a plane crash hours after finishing a 1973 concert on the Northwestern State University campus.

ALITERAL INTERPRETATION

Some of our favorite college nicknames are alliterative and some names were chosen for just that reason, but how many schools can boast *triple* alliteration? Go to the list to find out.

Bluefield Big Blues
Cabrini College Cavaliers
Caldwell College Cougars
Centenary College Cyclones
Centre College Colonels
Coastal Carolina Chanticleers
College of Charleston Cougars
Clarke College Crusaders
Clermont College Cougars
Coker College Cobras
Colorado Christian Cougars
Columbia College Cougars

Concordia College Cobblers
Concordia College Clippers
Connecticut College Clippers
Maine Maritime Mariners
Minnesota-Mankato Mavericks
Mount Mercy Mustangs
Point Park Pioneers
Saint Scholastica Saints
Sonoma State Seawolves
University of Utah Utes
Walla Walla Wolves
Wisconsin-Whitewater Warhawks

Only two schools can brag that they have *quadruple* alliteration.

Cincinnati Christian College Crusaders
Clearwater Christian College Cougars

One would think that alliteration would play an important part in choosing a nickname but only 212 schools (13.3%) are alliterative.

Some letters lend themselves to alliteration better than others (the letter "B" is 38% alliterative while "A" is only 1%).

Letter/alliterative schools/total schools/percentage alliterative

A	1	74	1%	N	3	107	3%
B	32	84	38%	O	0	35	0%
C	35	167	21%	P	13	73	18%
D	3	44	7%	Q	0	4	0%
E	8	42	19%	R	9	46	20%
F	6	44	14%	S	24	168	24%
G	5	31	16%	T	16	63	25%
H	9	49	20%	U	1	17	6%
I	0	28	0%	V	3	25	12%
J	1	18	6%	W	18	109	17%
K	1	20	5%	X	0	2	0%
L	12	68	18%	Y	0	6	0%
M	24	146	16%	Z	0	1	0%

MIRROR, MIRROR ON THE WALL
Did the founders of these schools have long lost twins? The only way to tell these apart is by the state in which they reside. All this puts us in a state of confusion.

Augustana (IL) Vikings	vs.	Augustana (SD) Vikings
Berkeley (NJ) Knights	vs.	Berkeley (NY) Knights
Embry-Riddle Aero (AZ) Eagles	vs.	Embry-Riddle Aero (FL) Eagles
Johnson & Wales (CO) Wildcats	vs.	Johnson & Wales (RI) Wildcats

THE MIRROR CRACK'D
Thank god for nicknames or the cheerleaders wouldn't know who to root for.

Anderson (IN) Ravens	vs.	Anderson (SC) Trojans
Baptist Bible (PA) Defenders	vs.	Baptist Bible (MO) Patriots
Benedictine (IL) Eagles	vs.	Benedictine (IL) Ravens
Bethany (WV) Bison	vs.	Bethany (KS) Terrible Swedes
Bethel (IN) Pilots	vs.	Bethel (KS) Threshers
Bethel (TN) Wildcats	vs.	Bethel (MN) Royals
Carroll (MT) Saints	vs.	Carroll (WI) Pioneers
Centenary (NJ) Cyclones	vs.	Centenary (LA) Gents
Charleston (SC) Cougars	vs.	Charleston (WV) Golden Eagles
Cincinnati Christian (OH) Eagles	vs.	Cincinnati Christian (OH) Crusaders
Columbia (MO) Cougars	vs.	Columbia (PA) Fighting Koalas
Concordia (NY) Clippers	vs.	Concordia (MN) Cobbers
Crown (MN) Storm	vs.	The Crown (TN) Royal Crusaders
Dominican (IL) Stars	vs.	Dominican (CA) Penguins
Emmanuel (MA) Saints	vs.	Emmanuel (GA) Lions
Farleigh Dickinson (NJ) Devils	vs.	Farleigh Dickinson (NJ) Knights
Grace (IN) Lancers	vs.	Grace (NE) Royals
Holy Cross (IN) Saints	vs.	The Holy Cross (MA) Crusaders
Lincoln (MO) Blue Tigers	vs.	Lincoln (PA) Lions
Lindenwood (MO) Lions	vs.	Lindenwood (IL) Lynx
Long Island (NY) Blackbirds	vs.	Long Island (NY) Pioneers
Loyola (CA) Lions	vs.	Loyola (IL) Ramblers
Loyola (MD) Greyhounds	vs.	Loyola (LA) Wolfpack
Marian (IN) Knights	vs.	Marian (WI) Sabres
Maryville (TN) Scots	vs.	Maryville (MO) Saints
Miami (OH) Redhawks	vs.	Miami (FL) Hurricanes
Monmouth (IL) Fighting Scots	vs.	Monmouth (NJ) Hawks
Mount St. Mary (NY) Knights	vs.	Mount St. Mary's (MD) Mountaineers
New England (NH) Pilgrims	vs.	New England (MA) Nor'easters

North Central (IL) Cardinals	vs.	North Central (MN) Rams
Northwestern (MN) Eagles	vs.	Northwestern (IA) Red Raiders
Northwood (FL) Seahawks	vs.	Northwood (MI) Timberwolves
Notre Dame (CA) Argos	vs.	Notre Dame (IN) Fighting Irish
Notre Dame (OH) Falcons	vs.	Notre Dame (MD) Gators
Pacific (OR) Boxers	vs.	The Pacific (CA) Tigers
Providence (CANADA) Freemen	vs.	Providence (RI) Friars
Regis (MA) Pride	vs.	Regis (CO) Rangers
Robert Morris (PA) Colonials	vs.	Robert Morris (IL) Eagles
Rochester (MI) Warriors	vs.	Rochester (NY) Yellowjackets
Rutgers (NJ) Scarlet Knights	vs.	Rutgers (NJ) Scarlet Raptors
St. Catharine (KY) Patriots	vs.	St. Catherine (MN) Wildcats
St. Francis (NY) Terriers	vs.	St. Francis (PA) Red Flash
St. Francis (IN) Cougars	vs.	St. Francis (IL) Saints
St. John's (MN) Johnnies	vs.	St. John's (NY) Red Storm
St. Joseph (CT) Blue Jays	vs.	St. Joseph (VT) Fighting Saints
St. Joseph's (NY) Bears	vs.	St. Joseph's (NY) Golden Eagles
St. Joseph's (IN) Pumas	vs.	St. Joseph's (PA) Hawks
St. Mary (NE) Flames	vs.	St. Mary (KS) Spires
St. Mary's (CA) Gaels	vs.	St. Mary's (ID) Belles
St. Mary's (MD) Seahawks	vs.	St. Mary's (TX) Rattlers
St. Thomas (TX) Celts	vs.	St. Thomas (MN) Tommies
Salem (MC) Spirits	vs.	Salem (WV) Tigers
Simpson (IA) Storm	vs.	Simpson (CA) Red Hawks
Southern (LA) Jaguars	vs.	Southern (LA) Knights
Southwestern (AZ) Eagles	vs.	Southwestern (KS) Moundbuilders
Thomas (ME) Terriers	vs.	Thomas (GA) Night Hawks
Trinity (CT) Bantams	vs.	Trinity (FL) Tigers
Union (KY) Bulldogs	vs.	Union (NY) Dutchmen
Wayne State (NE) Wildcats	vs.	Wayne State (MI) Warriors
Wesleyan (GA) Pioneers	vs.	Wesleyan (CT) Cardinals
Westminster (MO) Blue Jays	vs.	Westminster (PA) Titans
Wheaton (MA) Lyons	vs.	Wheaton (IL) Thunder
Wilmington (OH) Quakers	vs.	Wilmington (DE) Wildcats
Xavier (OH) Musketeers	vs.	Xavier (LA) Gold Rush
York (NE) Panthers	vs.	York (PA) Spartans

Didja Know? Since 1956 the student mascot inside the St. Joseph's Hawk costume famously flaps his wings continually during basketball games. ESPN once used a "flap-o-meter" on the national telecast to estimate that the Hawk flaps its wings 3,500 times during a regulation game.

THE FAIRER SEX

When women's schools started competing it was obvious their nicknames would not, for the most part, follow traditional standards. Women's schools have a higher percentage of top-10 nicknames (26% vs. 23% of co-ed schools) and of the 42 schools listed, 15 have one-of-a-kind nicknames (36% vs. 22% overall). One-of-a-kind are in **bold**.

Agnes Scott Scotties	Regis Rangers
Alverno Inferno	Russell Sage Gators
Bay Path Wildcats	Saint Benedict Blazers
Breneau Golden Tigers	Saint Catherine Wildcats
Bryn Mawr Owls	Saint Elizabeth Eagles
Carlow Celtics	Saint Joseph's Blue Jays
Cedar Crest Falcons	Saint Mary Flames
Chatham Cougars	**Saint Mary-of-the-Woods Pomeroys**
Columbia Fighting Koalas	**Saint Mary's Belles**
Converse Valkyries	**Salem Spirits**
Georgian Court Lions	Simmons Sharks
Hollins--No Nickname	Smith Pioneers
Lesley Lynx	Spelman Jaguars
Mary Baldwin Fighting Squirrels	Stephens Stars
Meredith Avenging Angels	**Sweet Briar Vixens**
Midway Eagles	Texas Women's Pioneers
Mills Cyclones	Trinity Washington Tigers
Mount Holyoke Lyons	**Ursuline Arrows**
Mount Mary Blue Angels	**Wellesley Blue**
New Rochelle Blue Angels	**Wells Express**
Notre Dame Gators	Wesleyan Pioneers
Peace Pacers	Wilson Phoenix

For some reason, four schools changed·from unique nicknames to something more traditional, a trend we hope does not continue. Former names: Cedar Crest Classics, Converse All-Stars, Chatham Seals, Simmons Thunderbolts.

FOR MEN ONLY

Only three all-men's colleges remain. Two of the three schools (Morehouse and Wabash) use one-of-a-kind nicknames.

Hampden-Sydney Tigers
Morehouse Maroon Tigers
Wabash Little Giants

NATURAL RIVALRIES

49ers vs. Gold Rush	Gold Rush doesn't pan out and the 49ers have to dig deep to win.
Bees vs. Ephs	Bees grade higher and Ephs fail.
Billikens vs. Trolls	Charming match between two tiny foes. Good luck!
Angels vs. Blue Devils	With Armageddon on the line, overtime!
Britons vs. Colonials	Colonials prevail in democratic fashion.
Bulls vs. Bears	Bears' stock on Wall Street rises.
Golden Bulls vs. Matadors	Bulls gore Matadors.
Cobbers vs. Cornhuskers	Cobbers grab Huskers by the ear (oh dear!).
Cowboys vs. Indians	Cowboys circle wagons - Indians settle for a truce.
Coyotes vs. Roadrunners	Beep beep! Roadrunner wins cliff hanger.
Cyclones vs. Shoremen	Cyclones tear roof off the place but peter out.
Ducks vs. Webbies	Ducks give opposition a good paddling.
Fighting Irish vs. Britons	Opposing sides toss spuds from stands.
Foresters vs. Inferno	Inferno coach fired after hot start is extinguished.
Gamecocks vs. Beavers	Both teams enjoy tussle and come away satisfied.
Islanders vs. Hurricanes	Islanders get leveled by Cane air attack.
Judges vs. Vandals	Good defense frees Vandals to run wild, but offense hurts record.
Knights vs. Dragons	Dragons win when Knight throws chair, gets tossed.
Lightning vs. Thunder	Lightning strikes first but Thunder rolls.
Little Giants vs. Big Red	Big Red chews up the competition.
Loggers vs. Sycamores	Sycamore defense foils every attempt to cut them down. Tree-mendous!
Lumberjacks vs. Oaks	Oaks run rings around the Jacks to claim The Axe.
Magicians vs. Jackrabbits	Magicians pull this one out of their hat at the buzzer.
Mariners vs. Waves	Waves makes a big splash but Mariners navigate to victory.
Mechanics vs. Fords	Fords have Tempo problems and lose Focus.
Musketeers vs. Cardinal	Athos to Porthos beats Richelieu as Musketeers play as a unit.
Mustangs vs. Pacers	Vroom, vroom. Mustangs race to victory.
Nor'easters vs. Seasiders	Nor'easters blow Seasiders off the map.
Orediggers vs. The Rock	The Rock is solid; Orediggers blow lode and don't show their metal.
Pacers vs. Thoroughbreds	Photo finish!
Penmen vs. Sabers	The pen is mightier than the sword.

Pilgrims vs. Braves	Both teams feast during this Thanksgiving Day classic.
Pirates vs. Clippers	Pirates sink Clippers.
Pointers vs. Retrievers	Pointers show the way but Retrievers want it more.
Profs vs. Student Princes	Profs teach a lesson but Princes still go for the crown.
Rustlers vs. Cowboys	Cowboys hang Rustlers out to dry.
Salukis vs. Greyhounds	Two lightning fast teams eventually get dog-tired.
Sharks vs. Jets	Gang tackling leave both teams battered and beaten.
Terrapins vs. Jackrabbits	Slow and steady wins the race.
Tomcats vs. Bulldogs	Cats really meow mix it up but Bulldogs triumph.
Toros vs. Toreros	Toreros prevail as Toros fall for the fake.
Trojans vs. Spartans	Trojans lose due to a breakdown in protection.

BY THE NUMBERS

1,592	Total schools listed
824	Schools using an animal nickname (51.8%)
538	Different nicknames used
522	Mammal nicknames
374	Schools that use top ten nicknames (23%)
354	Nicknames unique to only one school (22%)
252	Eagle, Lion, Hawk and Tiger name derivatives (16%)
243	Bird nicknames
69	Nicknames not ending in the letter "s"
37	Insect nicknames
14	Reptile nicknames
14	Inanimate nicknames
11	Plant nicknames
8	Fish/sea creature nicknames
5	Letters of the alphabet (I, Q, U, X, Z) that account for only 11 nicknames (.007%)
5	Letters of the alphabet (B, C, P, S, T) that account for 741 nicknames (46.54%)
1	Nickname that starts with a number (49ers)
1	School with no nickname (Hollins University)
0	Amphibian nicknames

Didja Know? Spring Hill College's baseball field, Stan Galle Field ("The Pit"), is the oldest continually used college baseball field in the country. Many former major league players have used the field including Babe Ruth and Hank Aaron.

In the summer of 1963, Lee Harvey Oswald gave a speech at Spring Hill, just months before assassinating President John F. Kennedy.

WE'RE NUMBER ONE!

Since the start of the rock n' roll era in 1955, 38 songs containing some form of a college nickname in the title have gone to the top of the Billboard Pop Chart. Elvis Presley, Elton John and Michael Jackson lead the way with two apiece.

SONG	YEAR	WKS #1	ARTIST
Rock Around the Clock	1955	8	Bill Haley and the Comets
Rock and Roll Waltz	1956	1	Kay Starr
Singing the **Blues**	1956	9	Guy Mitchell
Let Me Be Your Teddy **Bear**	1957	7	Elvis Presley
Jailhouse **Rock**	1957	7	Elvis Presley
Mr. **Blue**	1959	1	The Fleetwoods
Running **Bear**	1960	1	Johnny Preston
Teen **Angel**	1960	1	Mark Dinning
Blue Moon	1961	2	The Marcells
The **Lion** Sleeps Tonight	1961	3	The Tokens
Duke of Earl	1962	3	Gene Chandler
He's a **Rebel**	1962	2	The Crystals
Johnny **Angel**	1962	2	Shelley Fabares
Blue Velvet	1963	3	Bobby Vinton
Heart of **Gold**	1972	1	Neil Young
Song Sung **Blue**	1972	1	Neil Diamond
Crocodile **Rock**	1973	3	Elton John
Delta Dawn	1973	1	Helen Reddy
Bennie and the **Jets**	1974	1	Elton John
Rock the Boat	1974	1	Hues Corporation
Rock Me Gently	1974	1	Andy Kim
Rhinestone **Cowboy**	1975	2	Glen Campbell
Rock With You	1980	4	Michael Jackson
It's Still **Rock** n' Roll To Me	1980	2	Billy Joel
I Love **Rock** n' Roll	1982	7	Joan Jett
Eye of the **Tiger**	1982	6	Survivor
Rock Me Amadeus	1986	3	Falco
Eternal **Flame**	1989	1	The Bangles
Rock On	1989	1	Michael Damian
Black Velvet	1990	2	Alannah Myles
Black Cat	1990	1	Janet Jackson
Black and White	1991	7	Michael Jackson
How Do You Talk To An **Angel**	1992	2	The Heights
I'm Your **Angel**	1998	6	R. Kelly and Celine Dion
Angel of Mine	1999	4	Monica
Angel	2001	1	Shaggy
Gold Digger	2005	10	Kanye West
Party **Rock** Anthem	2005	6	LMFAO

WE CAN DO BETTER!!!

Given the opportunity we could improve many school's nicknames—not that we'll be given the chance, but if we were...

NAMES THAT MAKE SENSE

Baptist Bible Thumpers
Chattanooga Choo Choos
Connecticut Yankees
Crown Jewels
Daniel Webster Devils
Delta Force
Fisher Kings
Florida Atlantic Salmon
Gordon Flash
Hendrix Purple Haze
Humboldt Lightning
Kalamazoo Animals
Kentucky Fried Chickens
King's English
Louisiana Lightning
Lynchburg Hangmen
Midway Monsters
Nevada-Las Vegas Gamblers
North Park Rangers
Notre Dame Hunchbacks
Patten Tanks
Peace Knicks
Rhodes Scholars
Salem Witches
Sterling Silver
Vanguard Dogs
Wabash Cannonballs
West Liberty Belles
Wiley Coyotes

Names That Sound Like People

Alaska-Fairbanks Douglases
Albright Madelines
Alfred Enu Men
Alice Lloyd Bridges
Allen Iversons
Austin Cars

Barton Finks
Benedict Arnolds
Bradley Miltons
Briarcliff Clavins
Bryant Gumbels
Calvin Kleins
Carleton Fisks
Carroll Brunettes
Chico Marks
Clarke Kents
Cleveland Grovers
Dakota Fannings
Dallas Green
Davenport Lindseys
Dickinson Angies
Drew Barrymores
Duke Kahanamokos
Elmira Sorvinos
Elon Chaneys
Emerson Boozers
Evangel Holyfield
Ferris Buellers
Fisk Carltons
Francis Marion Motleys
George Fox Mulders
George Washington Carvers
Grace Kellys
Hannibal-LaGrange Red Lectors
Henderson Rickeys
Hobart Simpsons
Houston-Victoria Principals
Howard Johnsons
Indiana Jones'
Jackson Pollacks
Kennesaw Mountain Landises
La Salle Mini-O's
Lane Night Train
Laverne Jewels

Lawrence Oliviers
Lee Marvins
Lenoir-Rhyne Sandbergs
Lesley Neilsons
Lewis Jerries
Lindsey Wilson Picketts
Lipscomb Big Daddies
Livingstone Bramble
Luther Vandross
Lyndon Johnsons
Lynn Red Graves
MacMurray Freds
Madonna Material Girls
Manchester Melissas
Marist Rogers
Martin Luther Kings
McDaniel Boons
McPherson Elles
Meredith Burgesses
Miles Standishes
Mills Lane
Millsaps Rodneys
Montana Q-Bees
Murray Fred Macs
New Jersey Joe Walcotts
Norwich Hazel
Pfeiffer Michelles
Quincy Joans
Randolph Scots
Regis Philbins
Rochester Andersons
Rollins Tree
Roosevelt Browns
Saint Benedict Arnolds
Saint Elizabeth Tailors
Saint Martin Landaus
San Diego Riveras
Seattle Slew
Selma Diamonds
Shorter Francs
Simmons Bills
Simon Fraser Cranes

Simpson Homers
Spalding Gray
Stephens Kings
Stony Brook Shields
Tennessee-Martin Shorts
Texas-Austin Powers
Texas-San Antonio Banderas
Troy Ache Men
Truman Capotes
Vaughn Vinces
Virginia Dares
Webster Slaughter
Wellesley Snipes
Wilkes Booths
William Carey Nation
William Jewell Thieves
Wilson Phillips
Winona Riders
Xavier Cugats

Names That are Products or Foods
Agnes Scott Towels
Caldwell Bankers
Campbell Soups
Cedar Crest Toothpaste
Charleston Chews
Clark Bars
Coker Pepsi
Colby Cheese
Denver Omelets
Liberty Mutuals
Long Island Ice T's
New England Chowder
Philadelphia Cream Cheese
Pittsburgh Paints
Plymouth Dusters
Post Grape Nuts
Shepherd Pies
Southern Comfort
Stetson Cologne
Texas Toast
Thomas English Muffins

Union Labels
Wagner Power Painters
Webber Barbecues
Wells Fargo
Whitman Samplers
York Peppermint Patties

Names That are Familiar Phrases
Adams Family
American Bandstand
Boston Stranglers
Brown Bag Lunches
Capital Gains
Capitol Ideas
Centenary Plots
Centre Peace
Coe Operation
Columbia Cartel
Cumberland Gap
Davis Cups
Emory Boards
Hope Chests
Idaho Spuds
Keystone Combination
King Kongs
Lyon Tamers
Maine Squeeze
Mobile Homes
Niagara Falls
Pace Makers
Paine Relievers
Park Benches
Pratt Falls
Suffolk Tails
Taylor Maids
Temple Worshippers
Tulane Highway
Victory Dance
Washington Monuments
Webb Sites
Westminster Abbeys

Rhyming Names
Defiance Alliance
Felican Pelicans
Furman Vermin
Hilbert Dilberts
Knox Jocks
Kutztown Klutzes
Kyper Vipers
LaGrange Mange
Lander Ganders
Maine-Presque Isle Crocodiles
Milligan Gilligans
Minnesota-Duluth Truth
Missouri Fury
Nevada-Reno Keno
New York-Oswego Amigos
Newberry Blueberries
Quinnipiac Quack Attack
Saint Scholastica Spasticas
Salve Regina Hyenas
Shenandoah Boas
Sonoma Melanomas
Sweet Briar Choir
Syracuse Caboose
Tougaloo Boogaloos
Ursuline Machine

Sounds Good but Whacked
Akron Nimhs
Albion Time
Amherst Castle
Augusta Wind
Aurora Borealis
Austin Peay Brains
Bacone Cheeseburgers
Barber-Scotia Novas
Bard The Door
Barry The Hatchet
Bates The Hook
Bellevue Ravin' Lunatics
Berry Interesting
Brigham Young Guns

Butler Didit
Cardinal Stritch Armstrongs
Carnegie-Mellon Heads
Carthage Carnage
Cazenovia Lovers
Chowan Down
Clarion My Wayward Son
Colgate Flouridians
Concord Everest
Converse Satians
Coppin Attitude
Creighton Cretins
Dayton Kardashians
Delhi Sandwiches
Dordt Dorks
Duquesne Mutiny
Emmanuel Labor
Eureka Manure
Flagler Marvelous Marvin Haglers
Florida International Men of Mystery
Franklin Pierce Arrows
Gannon Balls
George Mason Jars
Georgian Court Jesters
Goshen G-Whiz
Graceland Elves
Grand View Masters
Great Falls of Fire
Harris Stowe Aways
Hawaii-Hilo Copters
High Point Acmes
Holy Family Trees
Hood Ornaments
Hunter Self-Inflicted Wounds
Husson First
Iona Pack of Trojans
Iowa Bundle
James Madison Avenue
Johnson & Wales Sperm Whales
Keene Peachies
Lake Erie Silence
Lake Forest Gumps

Lake Superior Intellect
LaRoche Clips
Lehigh Voltage
Limestone Cowboys
Lincoln Logs
Long Beach Combers
Longwood Braggarts
Louisville Sluggers
Malone Gunmen
Manhattan Transfer
Mansfield Bust Lines
Marian Brides
Marietta Little Lambs
Mary Old Souls
Medgar Evers to Chance
Messiah Relief
Miami Vice
Millikin Cookies
Minot Doctrine
Misericordia Luvs Company
Montana-Bozeman Bozos
Morehouse Dressing
Morningside Swipers
Mount Ida Ho's
Mount Mary Pro Creators
Mount Olive Oyls
Multnomah Mr. Nice Guy
Neumann Disgruntled Postmen
New York-Binghamton Captains
North Carolina-Charlotte Webs
Nyack Yaks
Occidental Death
Oglethorpe Leering Jims
Oklahoma-Panhandle Hustlin' Beggars
Old Dominion Dominatrix
Otterbein Burritos
Ouachita Cheetahs
Ozarks Mountain Daredevils
Paul Quinn Tuplets
Penn State-Altoona Piano
Penn State-Beaver Cleavers
Pittsburgh-Johnstown Floods

Puget Sound Barriers
Queens Reich
Randolph Macon Friends
Rio Grande Mothers
Ripon The Establishment
Roanoke Lost Colony
Rockford Philes
Rocky Mountain High
Rowan Boats
Russell Sage Rosemary & Thyme
Sacred Heart Attack
Saint Bonaventure Capitalists
Saint Cloud State Cumulonimbi
Salisbury Steaks
Samford and Son
San Jose Cardenals
Santa Clara Bartons
Santa Cruz Ships
Savannah Whites
Seton Hall Monitors
Shaw Shanks
Siena Crayons
Sioux Falls Honor Ass
Skidmore Skidmarks
Slippery Rock Candy
South Carolina-Aiken Backs
Susquehanna and Her Sisters

Tabor Cloths
The Master's Baiters
Thiel Thecond Bathe
Tiffin E-Lamps
Transylvania Bloodsuckers
Trine In Vain
Tufts O-Hare
Ursinus Infection
Utah Puddytats
Vassar Lean
Virginia-Wise Crackers
Viterbo Jangles
Vorhees a Jolly Good Fellow
Waldorf Salads
Warner Brothers
Wartburg Warthogs
Wayne Batmen
Wheaton Barley
Whittier Than Thou
Wilberforce Field
William Penn Pals
Winston-Salem Smokers
Wisconsin-Superior Beings
Wisconsin-Whitewater Rafts
Worcester Sure Sauce
Wright Place Wrong Time

FOR SERIOUS CONSIDERATION

There are still plenty of good nicknames that have never been used and instead of schools going with the standard Eagles, Hawks or Pioneers we offer a few valid nicknames for schools to consider.

Admirals	Cheetahs	Rattlesnakes
Anacondas	Commanders	Rhinos
Bandits	Crocs	Sting Rays
Black Widows	Dragonflies	Superiors
Blitz	Gila Monsters	Tarantulas
Blizzard	Hyenas	T-Rex
Bullfrogs	Polecats	
Buzzards	Praying Mantises	

Chapter 5

How They Got Their Nickname

Typically, nicknames and mascots have been chosen to engender school spirit and to inspire students, alumni, faculty, the administration and fans.

As far back as the late 1800s administrators allowed the student body to choose (usually via an election) what a school nickname would be and this method is by far the most common determination. For the most part, school officials have stayed clear of cognomens except for nudges in an appropriate direction.

Although newspapers played an important role in many nicknames, this was generally true only of those schools that adopted nicknames in the 19th Century and early decades of the 20th. Many schools had never competed in athletics so there was no need for a nickname. It was only when intercollegiate athletics began in earnest that newspapers were forced to make up nicknames where none had existed before simply so they'd have something that easily fit into their headline to determine one school from another.

In the early years people cheered for (or against) a school, and not a "name" because nicknames often changed for no other reason than new colored uniforms or some animal was found roaming around on campus. Some teams stuck with a name for only a year or two before moving onto something else.

In the "modern" era, when new schools have been opened one of the first items on the agenda is to get a nickname because it gives the student body something to rally behind. They *become* "Bulldogs" or "Golden Eagles."

Collegiately, in 1889 Yale was the first to adopt a mascot (a bulldog) but by no means was this anything new. As far back in American history as the Revolutionary War a military division in Delaware took to calling itself the "Blue Hens," a name that later transferred to Delaware University's "Fightin' Blue Hens." During the Civil War many divisions and brigades on both sides adopted nicknames (New York's Irish Brigade, the Louisiana Tigers are just two examples). But it was athletics, particularly football, which brought rise to nicknames if for no other reason than to differentiate one team from another, particularly in newspapers.

It's interesting to note that there are very few "modern" nicknames used (Rockets, Lasers) and there is a nostalgic overtone to the vast majority of nicknames. There are a few Jets and all of the Sharks names have only come about in the past ten years, but little else that captures the second half of the 20th Century and into the 21st. Even when schools have adopted new nicknames in the recent past (for whatever reason, but most often to do away with Native American references), traditional names are still chosen (Eagles and its derivatives, Pioneers, Hawks) perhaps for nostalgic purposes and perhaps because they're "safe," non-controversial and politically correct. However, new names keep arising (Clan, Tracers, Archers) but they are few in number.

Although it is beyond the scope of this book, it's also worth noting that the logos representing nicknames have changed drastically in the past decade or so. This could be called the "Sharks Effect" for it was the San Jose Sharks of the NHL that brought branding and marketing of a team's nickname to a new level. The emphasis on marketing and branding in college sports is now pervasive and whole companies exist for just that purpose. Hundreds of colleges have updated their representation of nicknames and mascots to contemporary levels because it helps "sell" the school and offers additional money for athletic coffers.

North Carolina-Charlotte 49ers

Originally UNCC was a night school serving World War II veterans on the GI Bill, and the athletic teams were called the Owls. The 49ers nickname derives from the fact that the school was saved from closure in 1949 and that the fledgling institution exuded a "49er spirit," in reference to the hardships faced by those who traveled west seeking fortunes during the California Gold Rush.

Long Beach State 49ers

The 49ers nickname honors the school's founding in 1949 and the fact that like all of California, the city of Long Beach prospered due to the 1849 Gold Rush. An unofficial name for the school is "The Beach" due to the fact LBSU is the only NCAA Division I school with the word "Beach" in their name.

The official name of the university's baseball team is the "Dirtbags" (see *Long Beach State Dirtbags*).

California-Davis Aggies

The Aggies nickname is in honor of Davis' agricultural heritage and animal husbandry curriculum. The official school mascot is a mustang, named Gunrock, a name that dates to 1921 when the US Army brought a horse named Gunrock to the campus to supply high-quality stock for cavalry horses. During his 1921–31 stay at UC Davis, Gunrock was bred with 476 mares. In 1924, he was adopted as the official mascot and accompanied teams to games and rallies.

There was once a movement afoot to change the school's mascot from the mustang to the cow, but despite student support this was turned down after opposition from alumni.

New Mexico State Aggies

Opened in 1888 as the land-granted New Mexico College of Agriculture and Mechanic Arts, when athletics began teams were called the Aggies.

When legendary cowboy Frank "Pistol Pete" Eaton appeared in a homecoming parade in the 1950s he was chosen as the school's mascot.

As a child, Eaton's father was killed six members of the Regulators. In 1868, Mose Beaman, his father's friend, said to Frank, "My boy, may an old man's curse rest upon you, if you do not try to avenge your father."

By the age of 15 Eaton had become a quick draw and a marksman and gained the nickname, "Pistol Pete" at Fort Gibson in Indian Territory and was a U.S. Marshal at the age of seventeen. From the start of his career as a lawman he tracked down his father's killers, claiming that by 1887 he had killed five, and the sixth only escaped his six-shooter by being shot by someone else.

Anna Maria AMCats

Surely one of the most unusual nicknames in college sports, Anna Maria's nickname is an acronym of **A**nna **M**aria **C**ollege **A**thletic **T**eams.

Meredith College Avenging Angels

For decades the Meredith teams were known simply as the "Angels" and two stories relate the name's origin. Meredith's brother school, Wake Forest, had the nickname "Demon Deacons,' therefore, "Angels" was chosen for Meredith. The other explanation states that the land Meredith was built upon was known as "The Angel Farm." During the summer of 2007 the name of the sports teams was changed to Avenging Angels to emphasize the prowess of Meredith athletes.

California-Irvine Anteaters

In 1965 students were allowed to submit mascot candidates to be voted on in a campus-wide election. Disappointed with the choices, undergrad Schuyler Hadley Basset III is credited with choosing the Anteater and for designing its cartoon representation. The Anteater was inspired by "Peter the Anteater" from the Johnny Hart comic strip, "B.C."

Before the voting took place on campus the men's water polo team highly encouraged the students to vote for the anteater since it was "original and slightly irrelevant." The Anteater won with 56% of the vote, beating "None of the Above" by a wide margin.

Moody Bible College Archers

The famous Moody Arch is the unofficial main entrance to the campus and from which the nickname is derived.

St. Ursuline Arrows

According to Kevin Alcox, Sports Information Director at St. Ursuline, the name Arrows was first used when athletics began at Ursuline College in 2000. The school chose the name based on the story of St. Ursula (for whom the college was named).

Legend states Ursula was a Romano-British princess who, at the request of her father, King Donaut of Dumnonia, set sail in 383 to join her future husband, the pagan Governor Conan Meriadoc of Armorica, along with 11,000 virginal handmaidens. Before her marriage Ursula undertook a pilgrimage to Rome with her followers and after setting out for Cologne, which was being besieged by Huns, all the virgins were beheaded in a horrific massacre. The Huns' leader personally shot Ursula dead with an arrow.

An arrow is most commonly associated with St. Ursula and the shield of the Ursuline Sisters (founded by Saint Angela de Merici in 1535, primarily for the education of girls) displays an arrow pointing to the heavens and to God.

Augsburg Auggies

The Auggies nickname first appeared in the mid-1920s and is merely an extension of the school name. The eagle has often been associated with Auggie athletic teams for decades because a baby eagle is often referred to as an "auggie."

Sir Sanford Fleming College Auks

The Auks nickname is in reference to the Great Auk, a large, flightless bird that became extinct in the mid-19th century. 30 inches tall and weighing 11 pounds the auks ranged as far south as the New England region and northern Spain through Canada, Greenland, Iceland, Norway, Ireland, and Great Britain.

The last colony lived on Geirfuglasker (the "Great Auk Rock") off Iceland. The last pair, found incubating an egg, was killed there on 3 July 1844, with Jón Brandsson and Sigurður Ísleifsson strangling the adults and Ketill Ketilsson smashing the egg with his boot.

San Diego State Aztecs

In the fall of 1924, Athletic Director C.E. Peterson urged students to select a nickname to replace Staters and Professors and the school newspaper invited suggestions. Student leaders chose the nickname Aztecs over Balboans.

Wisconsin Badgers

The Badger started as the official UW mascot with the inception of football in 1889 and was borrowed from the state of Wisconsin which was dubbed the "Badger State." The name didn't come from the animals in the region, but rather from an association with lead miners in the 1820s. Without shelter in the winter, the miners had to "live like badgers" in tunnels burrowed into hillsides.

Wisconsin's mascot, Bucky Badger, was first drawn in 1940 and a cheerleader first wore a badger outfit with a papier-mâché head in 1949.

California-Santa Cruz Banana Slugs

In 1981 the school's chancellor declared the team's nickname to be the Sea Lions.

Most students disliked the offering and suggested an alternative mascot; the Banana Slug. In 1986, students voted to declare the Banana Slug the official mascot — a vote the chancellor refused to honor, arguing that only athletes should choose the mascot. When a poll of athletes showed that they, too, wanted to be "Slugs" the chancellor relented.

Lock Haven Bald Eagles
Tradition states that during a 1890s baseball game in which Lock Haven was losing, a bald eagle perched itself outside the left field fence. Lock Haven rallied to win the game and credited the eagle with bringing the team good luck.

Trinity Bantams
At an 1899 dinner in of the Princeton Alumni Association of Western Pennsylvania, Hon. Judge Joseph Buffington, '75, referred to his alma mater's competitiveness and spirit by saying in part; "They tell me that Trinity is in great company tonight. In the presence of these mighty chanticleers of the collegiate barnyard, I presume the Trinity bantam should feel outclassed, possibly, if he took your estimate of your-selves and yours of him he would." Within a short time, newspapers were referring to Trinity athletic teams as the "Bantams."

Franciscan University of Steubenville Barons
The town of Steubenville was laid out in 1797 and was built on the site of Fort Steuben which was named in honor of 'Baron' Friedrich Wilhelm von Steuben. Von Steuben was a Prussian-born military officer who served as inspector general and Major General of the Army during the Revolutionary War.

Alderson–Broaddus College Battlers
Alderson–Broaddus, in Philippi, West Virginia, uses the "Battlers" in reference to the Battle of Philippi that was fought nearby on June 3, 1861 in the first organized land action of the Civil War.

Ohio Wesleyan Battling Bishops
Before 1925 teams were simply known as the Red and Black or the Methodists. In 1925, the alumni magazine lamented at the lack of an inspiring nickname by stating, "There are countless colleges throughout the country claiming red and black as their colors, and fourteen Methodist colleges in Ohio alone." The Pi Delta Epsilon fraternity sponsored a contest to find a name and the winning entry, "The Battling Bishops," came from senior Harold Thomas.

Cincinnati Bearcats

During the second half of a hard-fought game against Kansas in 1914, a UC cheerleader created the chant "They may be Wildcats, but we have a Baehr-cat on our side" in reference to fullback, Leonard K. "Teddy" Baehr. The crowd took up the cry "Come on, Baehr-cat!" and when Cincinnati prevailed, 14-7, the victory was memorialized in a cartoon published on the front page of the student newspaper depicting a bedraggled Kentucky Wildcat being chased by a creature labeled "Cincinnati Bear Cat."

Following Baehr's graduation in 1916 the name dropped out of use, but when Cincinnati played at Tennessee in November, 1919, *Cincinnati Enquirer* writer Jack Ryder's dispatch on the game used "Bearcats" and the university's teams were regularly called Bearcats ever since.

Brown Bears

Introduced in 1902, Brown's first mascot was a burro that appeared at a game against Harvard. Skittish by the game's noise it was not retained. The university eventually settled on Bears after the head of a brown bear was carved on an archway above the student union in 1904.

Maine Black Bears

The black bear has been the mascot since 1914 when Jeff, a black bear cub who was found on the slopes of Mt. Katahdin was loaned to the university by Old Town police chief, O.B. Fernandez. Jeff made his debut at a pep rally before the Colby game, and, as he entered the auditorium the surprised crowd went "bananas!" The mascot's name has been "Bananas" ever since.

Northern Colorado Bears

UNC used the nickname Teachers before adopting Bears in 1923. Inspiration for the name had come in 1914 from a bear on top of an Alaskan totem pole donated to the school by an 1897 alum.

Washington University Bears

Early WU teams were called the Pikers, a name whose roots lie in the 1904 St. Louis World's Fair. The "Pike" was the fair's amusement section. By 1920 the term "Pikers" had taken on a different, less complimentary meaning but an effort to rename the team in was soundly quashed by a 504-106 vote.

In 1925, a meeting of the student body was held to discuss the nickname issue and several were considered, including Eagles, Bearcats and Bears. When a vote was held the students chose Bears, 320-106.

Sam Houston Bearkats
When the school was called the Sam Houston Normal Institute the athletic teams were known as the Normals. When the name changed to Sam Houston State Teachers College the nickname Bearkats was chosen with inspiration coming from a local saying; "Tough as a Bearkat." In the 1940s there was a movement afoot to dump the Bearkat in favor of the Raven, but a vote taken by the student body relegated the Raven to nevermore.

Buena Vista Beavers
In the early 1900s, the football team was called the BVers. By the spring of 1921 the name had morphed to Beavers.

Caltech Beavers
The beaver was chosen as Caltech's mascot and nickname because they are known for making dams and people think they are the animal most like engineers.

With 31 Nobel laureates to its name, Caltech has never been known for its athletics. On January 6, 2007, the men's basketball team snapped a 207-game losing streak to Division III schools, beating Bard College, 81-52. On February 22, 2011, the Beavers recorded their first conference victory since 1985 (310 consecutive losses) and on January 13, 2007, the Caltech women's basketball team snapped a 50-game losing streak. On the bench as honorary coach for the evening was Dr. Robert Grubbs, 2005 Nobel Laureate in Chemistry. On March 5, 2009, the men's soccer team snapped a 201-game losing streak.

Oregon State Beavers
In the early days teams were known variously as the Aggies, Coyotes and Bulldogs. When orange uniforms were bought the teams were referred to as the Orangemen. In 1916 the school yearbook was renamed *The Beaver* and, as the state's official animal, the name Beaver became associated with the school. The name gained instant popularity among alumni and students.

Saint Mary's College Belles
St. Mary's was founded in 1844 but didn't to compete athletically until 1975. At their first basketball game the St. Mary's women unveiled new t-shirts with "Belles" spelled out across the chest. The nickname is in reference to the 1945

movie, *The Bells of St. Mary's*, starring Bing Crosby and Ingrid Bergman. The movie tells the story of a priest (Crosby) and a nun (Bergman) who set out to save their fictitious New York school (St. Mary's) from being shut down.

Buffalo State Bengals

Early teams were variously called the Teachers, Normals, Frontiersmen, Orangemen and in the 1950s, Billies.

In 1969, a campus-wide contest was held to find a new nickname and mascot. On December 1, 1969, the men's basketball team opened its season against Toronto University. At halftime, the winning nickname was announced, and Buffalo State returned from the locker room for the second half as the "Bengals."

Idaho State Bengals

When ISU was known as the Idaho Technical Institute, teams were dubbed the "Bantams," but as it conjured up all things "little" the name was never very popular. In 1921, Ralph H. Hutchinson became Director of Physical Education and Athletics and as a graduate of Princeton he immediately organized an "I" Club, and the group's members adopted Princeton's Bengal Tiger as its mascot. Merrill Beal's 1952 *History of Idaho State College* noted of the Bengal Tiger: ". . . a creature that has never been found hereabouts, living or dead."

Cornell Big Red

Cornell's colors, carnelian red and white, date back to 1868, but the school's teams had no official nickname until 1905. That year, graduate Romeyn Berry, wrote lyrics for a new fight song that included the words "the big, red team." The nickname stuck. Cornell has no official mascot but the bear has been used as a symbol for more than a hundred years.

St. Louis Billikens

In the early 1900s, a Kansas City artist, Florence Pretz, created her version of an ancient Asian figure with chubby cheeks, pixie ears and a big grin. The Billiken Company of Chicago adopted the likeness, giving it its eventual name.

For a few years in the early 1900s the Billiken was everywhere and turned up on dozens of items including dolls, candies, metal banks, hatpins, pickle forks, belt buckles, auto hood ornaments, watch fobs, salt and pepper shakers and glass bottles. It also became a universal symbol of good fortune. To buy a Billiken gave the purchaser luck; to have one given to you is better luck; to have one stolen from you was the best luck of all. At least two Billiken-themed songs were recorded but after a few years the fad died down.

The name came to be associated with St. Louis University in 1911 when two St. Louis sportswriters decided that the SLU football coach, John Bender, looked just like the impish creature. One of them drew a cartoon of Bender as a Billiken and named the football team "Bender's Billikens." The public enthusiastically took up the name and it soon became official for all SLU teams.

Gallaudet Bison

Gallaudet University is a federally-chartered university for the education of the deaf and hard of hearing. Early teams were known as the Kendalls (after its founder, United States Postmaster General Amos Kendall) and Blues because of the school colors.

During the early 1940s, there was a general feeling that the Blues nickname wasn't "tough enough." A sportswriter for the student newspaper proposed changing the team name from the Blues to the Blue Bisons. No one complained and in a November 7, 1941 column the new nickname was announced.

Howard Bison

Howard, a traditionally Black university in Washington DC uses the Bison nickname in homage to the Buffalo Soldiers (a name given to the Negro Cavalry by Native American tribes they fought against) who were originally members of the 10th Cavalry Regiment of the United States Army.

North Dakota State Bison

North Dakota's athletic teams have evolved from the Farmers to the Aggies and finally the Bison in 1919. Head football coach Stan Borleske changed the name because he wanted a strong and fierce mascot and Bison was a logical choice since great herds of that animal once roamed the North Dakota prairie.

United States Military Academy Black Knights

The original nickname for the Academy's football team was the "Black Knights of the Hudson" due to the color of its uniforms. The name was later shortened to Black Knights.

The mule has served as the Academy and its Corps of Cadets mascot since the 1899 Army-Navy game when Academy officials selected the animal in an effort to counter the Naval Academy's goat.

Army's combination of black, gold and gray represent the colors of three ingredients that form gunpowder; charcoal, saltpeter and sulfur.

Hood Blazers
The Blazer nickname dates back to the 1920s when the college was an all-women's institution and the campus elected a rising senior as the "White Sweater" girl as someone who possessed the most sportsmanship and school spirit. In 1928, the sweater was changed to a 'blazer.'

Valdosta Blazers
Shortly after the all-women's Georgia State Women's College transformed into the coed Valdosta State College, the institution adopted the nickname Rebels, a name that lasted for nearly 50 years. In 1973, the university sought a more socially acceptable image and settled on Blazers, a reference to the school's "trailblazing" spirit.

DePaul Blue Demons
When DePaul's first athletics teams were formed in the early 1900s, the monogram "D" was selected for the uniforms. From this originated the nickname "D-men" which evolved into "Demons." The color blue, which signifies loyalty, was chosen in 1901 by a vote of the student body and was added to the name to create Blue Demons.

Duke Blue Devils
During World War I the *Chasseurs Alpins*, nicknamed *"les Diables Bleus,"* were well known French soldiers. Their distinctive blue uniform and jaunty beret captured public imagination. When the United States entered the World War I, units of the French Blue Devils toured the country helping raise money in the war effort.

As the war was ending in Europe, the Trinity College's Board of Trustees (Duke was then known as Trinity College) lifted its ban of football on campus and began intercollegiate competition in 1920. That first year the team had several nicknames including the Trinity Eleven, the Blue and White or the Methodists.

As campus leaders from the Class of 1923 made plans for their senior year, they decided to select a permanent nickname and the editors of two student publications, agreed. William H. Lander, editor-in-chief, and Mike Bradshaw, managing editor, of the *Trinity Chronicle* began the academic year 1922-23 referring to the athletic teams as the "Blue Devils." Their class had been the first post-war freshmen and the student body was full of returning veterans so the name needed no explanation. No opposition materialized, not even from the college administration. The newspaper staff continued its use and through repetition, Blue Devils eventually caught on.

Delaware Fightin' Blue Hens

The blue hen is the state bird of Delaware and came from a Revolutionary War regiment that took its name from a favourite breed of gamecock.

On December 9, 1775, the Continental Congress resolved that a military battalion was to be raised from Delaware. The second company enrolled was under the command of Capt. John Caldwell, an avid fan and owner of gamecocks. His troops often amused themselves by staging cock fights with a breed known as the Kent County Blue Hen, recognizable for its blue plumage. The renown of these chickens spread rapidly during the time when cock fighting was a popular form of amusement, and the "Blue Hens Chickens" developed quite a reputation for ferocity and fighting success. Capt. Caldwell's company likewise acquired a considerable reputation for its own fighting prowess, in engagements with the British at Long Island, White Plains, Trenton and Princeton, and soon it was nicknamed "Caldwell's Gamecocks."

Urbana Blue Knights

The earliest nickname for Urbana's athletic teams was the "Blue Streaks" in 1926-27. In 1965, the school newspaper held a contest to find a new nickname and in the January 25, 1966 edition, announced that the Blue Knights had won the day.

John Jay College of Criminal Justice Bloodhounds

The school's namesake, John Jay, was the first Chief Justice of the United States Supreme Court and one of the Founding Fathers of the United States. JJC is the only liberal arts college with a criminal justice focus in the United States and their Bloodhounds nickname is a perfect fit for such an institution.

Mount Mary Blue Angels

In 1950 the school first competed at the intercollegiate level as a member of the Athletic Federation of College Women. In 1994 the school joined the NCAA as the Crusaders. In response to the September 11, 2002 terrorist attacks discussions were begun on changing the nickname to something less violent in nature. By a vote of the student body, the name Blue Angels was adopted.

Elizabethtown Blue Jays

In the late 1930s, the student body selected Blue Jays as the name for its athletic teams because of its blue and gray coat that matched the school colors and, most importantly, because of its nature as a fighting, scrappy bird.

Presbyterian College Blue Hose

A story suggests that the Blue Hose name comes from a fierce band of Scotch-Irish, named "The Hose" who painted their entire bodies blue before going into battle (as in the movie *Braveheart*). In truth, Presbyterian's teams started using the name around 1915 when the football team's uniform was changed to include blue socks and a sports writer started calling the team "Blue Stockings." In 1954 the name was shortened to Blue Hose and was officially adopted by the school.

Johns Hopkins Blue Jays

Originally, teams were called the Black and Blue, a nickname derived from their uniform colors. It is theorized that the Blue Jay name stems from Hopkins' student humor magazine, *The Black and Blue Jay,* with the "Black and Blue" coming from the athletic colors and the "Jay" most likely stood for first initial in Johns Hopkins ("J").

Illinois College Blueboys

Many Illinois College students volunteered for the Union Army during the Civil War and because of the college's link to the Union cause, the students were dubbed "Blueboys" for their blue U.S. Army uniforms used at the time. The name eventually carried over to the school's athletic teams.

Creighton Bluejays

Into the mid-1920s Creighton's teams were referred to as the Hilltoppers. The *Omaha Bee* assisted the university's Athletic Board and Alumni Association in finding a new nickname by asking readers to submit possibilities. After reviewing over 200 entries, the Athletic Board decided upon "Bluejays" because of the school's colors, blue and white. Just outside the Creighton's Morrison Stadium stands a tall statue of the school's mascot, "Billy Bluejay."

Eau Claire Blugolds

Prior to 1940 the school went by a wide assortment of names including Normals, Blue and Gold Warriors, Zornmen (in honor of Bill Zorn, basketball and football coach from 1928–1968), Golden Tornadoes, Zornadoes, Golden Zornadoes, Blue and Gold Squad and the Blugold Squad before Blugolds became official.

Bates Bobcats

Because Bates was without a mascot, at an open forum before the Varsity Club in November, 1924, Clarence Archibald, '24, proposed the bobcat because of their fighting spirit despite its small size. A ballot in December gave the Bobcat an overwhelming victory with 490 votes in its favor while the panther, moose and stork each received little support (the stork received just three votes).

Ohio University Bobcats

Until 1925 the OU athletic teams were simply called the Green and White. That year a campus-wide contest was initiated and after great debate, the Bobcat won for its reputation as a sly, wily, scrappy animal.

Purdue Boilermakers

Prior to 1891 the Purdue teams were derisively known by such names as Grangers, Pumpkin-Shuckers, Railsplitters, Cornfield Sailors and Blacksmiths due to their status as a land-grant institution that schooled the sons and daughters of the working class for work that was considered "beneath" the high-born who attended liberal arts colleges such as nearby Wabash.

In 1891 Purdue hired two coaches from eastern power Princeton and in the season opener they traveled to Wabash College in Crawfordsville. After being drubbed 44-0, one Crawfordsville newspapers lashed out at Purdue's "Herculean wearers of the black and old gold." Beneath the headline "Slaughter of Innocents," the paper told of the injustice visited upon the "light though plucky" Wabash squad and stated in the headline, "Wabash snowed completely under by the boiler makers from Purdue."

Monticello Boll Weevils

As the story goes, a former university president is responsible for the Boll Weevils name as he once claimed the boll weevil was the only thing that had ever licked the South, and the name stuck. The women's teams are called Cotton Blossoms.

Ithaca Bombers

Ithaca teams had been known as the Blue Team, Blues, Blue and Gold, Collegians and Seneca Streeters before changing to the Cayugas by a student vote in 1937. The origin of the nickname Bombers is unclear, but the first known reference was in a December 17, 1938 issue of the *Rochester Times-Union* article on the basketball team that referred to the Ithaca's "bomb-like shots."

Pacific Boxers

The school's nickname became Boxers in 1968 after a student vote. Prior to that, Pacific's athletic teams had been known as the Badgers. The original Boxer was a 60-pound bronze statue; part-dog, part-dragon that was brought back from China by Rev. Joseph Elkanah Walker in 1898 and gifted to the university by his mother. The statue quickly became a coveted prize, stolen between clubs, fraternities and classes. *The Index*, Pacific's campus newspaper, coined the name "Boxer" in 1908 as a nod to the Boxer Rebellion.

Pembroke Braves

Pembroke was created in 1887 in response to a local petition, sponsored by North Carolina Representative Hamilton McMillian of Robeson County, with the goal of educating Native American teachers. Enrollment was originally limited to the Native American Indians of Robeson County.

Due to its heritage and support from the Lumbee Tribe of North Carolina, the school's use of the Braves nickname has largely been immune to the ongoing controversies related to Native American-themed nicknames and mascots.

Bradley Braves

The Braves nickname originally was in reference to the Peoria Tribe indigenous to the region. In August 2005, the NCAA instituted a ban on schools that use "hostile and abusive" Native American nicknames from hosting postseason games, beginning February 2006. Bradley was initially placed on a list of schools with such names but in April 2006, after a lengthy and contentious appeals process by Bradley officials, the NCAA agreed to remove Bradley from the list but placed it on a 5-year watch list.

Vassar Brewers

Brewing magnate, Matthew Vassar, founded Vassar College in 1861 when he gave half of his fortune, $408,000, and a deed of conveyance for 200 acres of land for the college site and farm.

A verse from a once popular Vassar song reads:

> *And so you see, to old V.C.*
> *Our love shall never fail.*
> *Full well we know that all we owe*
> *To Matthew Vassar's ale.*

Boise State Broncos

The Bronco nickname originated in 1932 when several students gathered after a basketball practice and chose the name because the area was still cattle country and most of the players still rode horses. When the coaches, administration and students approved the choice, it became official.

Santa Clara Broncos

A 1923 student report in the school's newspaper stated, "Wanted—a name for the varsity. Stanford has her Cardinals, Cal her Golden Bears, and Santa Clara may profit by their example. We have been dubbed the 'Missionites' by some, others have seen fit to label us the 'Prunepickers,' and still others have stretched the imagination to call us 'Friars,' 'Missions,' 'Padres...'"

The Rev. Hubert Flynn, S.J. is credited with creating the Broncos name 1923 when, after attending a rodeo he wrote: "The Bronco is a native westerner, a chunk of living dynamite, not very big but game to the core. If you turn him loose in an open field his speed outstrips the wind."

Western Michigan Broncos

First called Hilltoppers, reflecting the school's original Prospect Hill campus, the Broncos nickname dates to 1939 when the athletic board adopted it at the suggestions of WMU alumnus, John Gill, who was awarded a check for $10.00.

Belmont Bruins

In the mid-90s Belmont's Rebels nickname was replaced by Bruins due to the former's association with the Confederacy.

Belmont and its archrival, Lipscomb, are located only two miles apart on Belmont Boulevard in Nashville. Their propinquity allows the two schools to share a special basketball bond having played each other more than 126 times since Dec. 11, 1953 and the "Battle of the Boulevard" is touted as one of the greatest rivalries in college sports. On Feb. 17, 1990 over 16,000 fans packed Vanderbilt's Memorial Gym to watch Lipscomb defeat Belmont 124-107 in the largest-attended basketball game in NAIA history.

Top College Rivalries by distance (from middle of football/soccer fields):

Macalester/St. Catherine	.85 miles
St. Olaf/Carleton	1 mile
St. Catherine/St. Thomas	1.57 miles
Macalester/St. Thomas	2.14 miles
Belmont/Lipscomb	2 miles

Hamline/St. Thomas	2.14 miles
Hamline/Macalester	2.27 miles
Cincinnati/Xavier	2.34 miles
Hamline/St. Catherine	3.09 miles
Rice/Houston	3.64 miles

UCLA Bruins

In 1919 UCLA's first football team was known as the Cubs owing to their young relationship to the California Bears in Berkeley. In 1923, new coach Jimmie Cline adopted Grizzlies and when UCLA joined the Pacific Coast Conference there was a problem as the University of Montana, already a member of the PCC had prior rights to the Grizzlies nickname. In 1928 the school's teams became Bruins.

Beloit Buccaneers

Early Beloit teams were called The Gold or the Blue Devils. In 1949, an undergraduate announcer of the basketball games on the college radio station became incensed by the non-alliterativeness of the word "Devils." Singlehandedly, he convinced the faculty and the student body to cast out the "Devils" and replace them with the Buccaneers.

East Tennessee Buccaneers

The Buccaneers nickname comes from a local legend that pirates once used a subterranean river that stretched from the mountains of Eastern Tennessee all the way to the Atlantic as a hideout.

Ohio State Buckeyes

Ohio is commonly referred to as the Buckeye State due to the prevalence of Ohio Buckeye trees within its borders. Ohioans have referred to themselves as Buckeyes since at least the presidential election of 1840, when Ohio resident William Henry Harrison won the presidency. Harrison's supporters carved campaign souvenirs out of buckeye wood to illustrate their support for their fellow Ohioan.

Colorado Buffaloes

In 1934, The CU student newspaper decided to sponsor a national contest to find a permanent nickname with a $5 prize to go to the author of the winning selection. Previous nicknames included Silver Helmets, Yellow Jackets, Hornets, Arapahos, Big Horns, Grizzlies and Frontiersmen. Over 1,000 nominations arrived from almost every state in the union and the final tally chose Buffaloes.

Brooklyn Bulldogs
In 2009, new Brooklyn College president, Dr. Karen L. Gould, announced that the school would look for a nickname to replace Bridges, a name in use since 1994. After conferring with several committees, President Gould, a self-proclaimed lover of sports, chose Bulldogs.

Butler Bulldogs
Prior to 1919 Butler's athletic teams were known as the Christians but numerous losses that football season caused supporters to grow weary of the nickname.

   During the week leading up to the game with the Franklin Baptists, members of the school newspaper decided something "hot" must be conceived for the weekly pep rally. When the mascot of a Butler fraternity (a bulldog named Shimmy, because you couldn't shake him), wandered into the paper's office an idea was born. The next edition to come out with a cartoon showing Shimmy, labeled "Butler," taking a bite out of the pants seat of a figure labeled "John the Baptist." Butler lost the game to Franklin, 14-0, but the name "Bulldogs" stuck.

Georgia Bulldogs
Many old-timers say Georgia acquired the Bulldog nickname because of the strong ties with Yale (whose nickname is Bulldogs). However, on Nov. 3, 1920, the *Atlanta Journal* wrote about school nicknames and stated, "The Georgia *Bulldogs* would sound good because there is a certain dignity about a bulldog, as well as ferocity." After a 0-0 tie with Virginia in Charlottesville on Nov. 6, 1920, *Atlanta Constitution* writer Cliff Wheatley used the name "Bulldogs" in his story five times. The name has been used ever since.

   The name of one of the best known mascots in the country, Uga, is derived from an abbreviation of the **U**niversity of **G**eorgi**a**. Deceased Ugas are interred in a mausoleum near the main entrance to Sanford Stadium.

Gonzaga Bulldogs
Gonzaga teams went by the Fighting Irish but the name was dropped in 1921 in favor of the current Bulldogs. Although the school's official nickname and mascot is the Bulldog, marketing materials, fans and television announcers often use the term "Zags" to describe Gonzaga's teams and students.

Samford Bulldogs

In 1916, when the school was known as Howard College, students chose the Bulldog in a campus-wide contest replacing Tigers.

Truman State Bulldogs

Bulldogs became the official nickname for the college's teams in 1915.

At least three ghosts haunt Truman State's residence halls. "Joan," the "Ghost of Centennial Hall" is said to be a student killed in an auto accident in the 1970s. "Charlotte" and an unnamed little boy have haunted Grim Hall for more than 70 years, and "Gina" watches over the women of Ryle.

Yale Bulldogs

The Yale Bulldog is generally considered to be the first collegiate mascot, a tradition established by a young gentleman from Victorian England. When Princeton used to have a real tiger cub and Harvard always brought along the "Orange Man" as a stand-in for Puritan John Harvard, Yale undergraduates thought they were due for a mascot and one came in 1889. Undergraduate Andrew B. Graves had seen the dog sitting in front of a shop and purchased him from a New Haven blacksmith for $5. The students dubbed him the "Yale mascot," or, "Handsome Dan." "In personal appearance, he seemed like a cross between an alligator and a horned frog, and he was called handsome by the metaphysicians under the law of compensation," eulogized the *Hartford Courant*. "He was always taken to games on a leash, and the Harvard football team for years owed its continued existence to the fact that the rope held." *The Philadelphia Press* recalled that "a favorite trick was to tell him to "Speak to Harvard." He would then bark ferociously and work himself into physical contortions of rage never before dreamed of by a dog.

In 1897, Graves and Handsome Dan set out for a trip around the world but Dan died the following year. His stuffed body long stood in the old Yale gymnasium. When the gym was torn down, he was sent to the Peabody Museum for reconstruction. He now is in a sealed glass case in one of the trophy rooms of Yale's Payne Whitney Gymnasium, where "he is the perpetual guardian of the treasures which attest to generations of Yale athletic glory."

Along with being called Bulldogs, Yale's teams are also known as "Elis" in honor of school namesake Elihu Yale, who gave nine bales of goods, 417 books, and a portrait and arms of King George I to the Collegiate School, as the university was originally titled.

Gettysburg College Bullets
Teams at Gettysburg College were simply known as the Orange and Blue before being designated "Bullets" in 1924 by Paul L. Roy, city editor of the *Gettysburg Times*, a take-off on the Civil War Battlefield on which the school resides.

South Florida Bulls
In a 1962 election, five finalists were on the ballot: Buccaneers, Golden Brahman, Olympians, Cougars and Golden Eagles. Buccaneer received the most votes but wasn't adopted because it was believed that a junior college in Pensacola was using the name. The Golden Brahman, which had lost to the Buccaneer by only three votes, was chosen instead.

After it was learned that the junior college used Pirates, a 12-member committee decided that Buccaneer would serve USF. With the decision came controversy and a petition was formulated and collected more signatures than the actual number of votes cast in the original election. In the runoff, The Golden Brahman won the day and was officially unveiled Nov. 17, 1962.

Norwich Cadets
Founded in 1819 Norwich is the oldest of six Senior Military Colleges, and is recognized by the United States Department of Defense . The university's population is largely a Corps of Cadets but also includes traditional students.

Campbell Camels
Before 1934 Campbell's athletics teams were known as the Hornets, Campbells or Campbellites. The "Camels" origin is derived from a statement by early school patron, Zachary Taylor Kivett, who approached school founder James Archibald Campbell after a fire had destroyed the school's three buildings in 1900 and said, "Your name's Campbell; get a hump on you! We've got work to do."

Connecticut College Camels
After going co-ed in 1969, some of the men on campus asked for help in organizing a basketball team. Ex-Navy man, Mike Shinault, was head of the mail room and volunteered. Shinault had coached several service basketball teams and quickly went in search of a mascot. He remembered seeing a Pakistani team while in the Navy and chose their mascot as CC's own—the camel.

Pratt Cannoneers
In October, 1963 Cannoneers was chosen due to the fact that at one time the

college looked at the Sackets Harbor military site to be their permanent home.

When the college moved to its permanent home Rep. Robert C. McEwen presented a Civil War-era 300-pound Rodman cannonball, made of cast iron, to the college in 1966. He said at the time that he was "sworn to secrecy" about where he got it. Around 1967 a friend of the college recovered a War of 1812 cannon from the bottom of the St. Lawrence River and agreed to donate it to the school if transportation was provided. The cannon was delivered to the campus and the maintenance department built the carriage for it.

Christopher Newport Captains

Captain Christopher Newport (1561–1618) was an English seaman and privateer and is best known as the captain of the *Susan Constant*, the largest of three ships which carried settlers for the Virginia Company in 1607 on the way to find the settlement at Jamestown in the Virginia Colony (the first permanent English settlement in North America). The school and its nickname were named in Newport's honor.

Université de Montréal Carabins

It was from the university's school of medicine that the "Carabins" nickname is derived for a "carabin" is also known as a "sawhorse," or, a doctor or surgeon.

Stanford Cardinal

Indians was used as Stanford's nickname from 1930 until the 1970s. Deemed offensive, suggestions for a new nickname were sought. These included Robber Barons, Sequoias, Trees, Cardinals, Railroaders, Spikes and Huns but none of the suggestions were accepted. From 1972 until November 17, 1981, Stanford's official nickname was Cardinals, in reference to one of the school colors, not the bird.

In 1981 President Donald Kennedy declared that all Stanford athletic teams will be represented and symbolized exclusively by the color cardinal and stated, "While various other mascots have been suggested and then allowed to wither, the color has continued to serve us well, as it has for 90 years."

Ball State Cardinals

Changed from the "Hoosieroons" in 1929.

Lamar Cardinals

Lamar started out as South Park Junior College and its teams were called

Brahmas. When the school was set to change its name in 1932, a contest was held for a new *school* name with students voting and Lamar won out (Mirabeau Lamar, 1798–1859, was a Texas politician and second President of the Republic of Texas, soldier and a leading Texas political figure during the Texas Republic era).

With the new Lamar name, John Gray, head coach and athletic director at the time, dropped Brahmas and chose Cardinals in its place.

Louisville Cardinals
The name was chosen because the cardinal is the state bird of Kentucky.

Vermont Catamounts
In 1926 the student newspaper asked students to vote for a mascot, with lynx and wildcat among the choices. The response was unenthusiastic, so the paper offered another set of names that included tomcat, camel, cow and catamount. Only male students were allowed to vote, and they chose Catamounts.

Western Carolina Catamounts
A 1931 contest to replace the Teachers nickname resulted in such potential names as Bears, Indians and Panthers but something unique was desired. Eventually, the contest came down to a choice between Catamounts and Mountain Boomers, which are ground squirrels that are difficult to catch. Students overwhelmingly voted for Catamounts.

Virginia Cavaliers
Known variously as the V-men, Virginians and Old Dominion before taking Cavaliers more-or-less officially in 1923 when the college newspaper held a contest to choose an official fight song. *The Cavalier Song*, written by Lawrence Haywood Lee, Jr., '24, with music by Fulton Lewis, Jr., '25, was chosen the best and inspired the nickname "Cavaliers."

The unofficial nickname is Wahoos. Legend states that Washington & Lee baseball fans dubbed the Virginia players "Wahoos" during the fiercely contested rivalry that existed between the two in-state schools in the 1890s.

Carlow Celtics
Carlow University was founded in 1929, by the Sisters of Mercy from Carlow, Ireland and the Celtics nickname reflects those Irish origins.

St. Thomas Celts

When St. Thomas started intercollegiate competition in 1947 it was under the "Saints" banner but by the mid-50s Warriors had supplanted Saints. In 1983 the school held a Name That Team Contest and Fighting Celts won easily. In 2005 students again voted to shorten the name to Celts.

Coastal Carolina Chanticleers

In the mid-1960's Coastal's teams were known as the Trojans and as a two-year branch of the University of South Carolina, many people began to push for a nickname that was more closely related to USC's Gamecock and chose "Chanticleers."

The Chanticleer comes from Chaucer's *Canterbury Tales*. The Chanticleer is a proud and fierce rooster who dominates the barnyard. "For crowing there was not his equal in all the land. His voice was merrier than the merry organ that plays in church, and his crowing from his resting place was more trustworthy than a clock. His comb was redder than fine coral and turreted like a castle wall, his bill was black and shone like a jet."

Midland Chaparrals

A "chaparral" is better known as the "Great Roadrunner" (*Geococcyx californianus,* meaning "Californian Earth-cuckoo"). The bird is native to the American southwest and is known for its long tail feathers and impressive speed when running. At Midland the name is often shortened to "Chaps."

Hillsdale Chargers

In the fall of 1968 a vote was held to replace the Dales nickname because many students didn't know what a Dale *was*. Three names were on the ballot; Volunteers, Chiefs and Chargers. Volunteers honored the more than 400 students who volunteered to fight for the Union army in the Civil War, while Chiefs was in reference to Chief Baw Beese (a Potawatomi Indian chief in the area of Hillsdale in the 1830s). Chargers was added to the list because of its catchy sound and won the election by a wide margin.

Central Michigan Chippewas

Formerly the Normalites, Dragons and Bearcats before Chippewas was chosen in a school-wide vote in 1942. The Saginaw Chippewa Tribe has a positive relationship with the university and allows its use of the Chippewas nickname.

Université du Québec à Montréal Citadins
Citadins is French for "City Dwellers," as UQAM's campus is located in downtown Montreal.

Simon Fraser Clan
Simon Thompson Fraser (1776– 1862) was the son of Scottish Highlanders. He was a famous fur trader and explorer who charted much of what is now the province of British Columbia. The Clan nickname stems from Fraser's Scottish roots and the mascot is a costumed Scottish Terrier named McFogg the Dog.

Concordia College Cobbers
In the early 1900s the Concordia campus was not quite in the city of Moorhead. Moorhead State University students, in obvious reference to the many fields of corn then surrounding the campus, used to taunt Concordia students as country hicks by calling them "Cobbers." In time, what originated as a slur was embraced by the students who wear it proudly.

Curry Colonels
Curry was named for Samuel Silas Curry (1847-1921), an American professor of elocution and vocal expression and shared kinship with both Daniel Boone (a Lieutenant Colonel in the Fayette County militia) and Davy Crockett (a Lieutenant Colonel of the Fifty-seventh Regiment of Tennessee Militia) from whence the Colonels nickname is taken.

Nicholls State Colonels
Francis T. Nicholls (1834-1912), for whom the school is named, was a two term Louisiana Governor, a judge and rose to the rank of brigadier general in the Confederate Army during the Civil War. In the Shenandoah Valley Campaign he lost his left arm. On October 14, 1862, he was promoted from lieutenant colonel (from whence Nicholls State takes its Colonels nickname) to the rank of brigadier general and given command of a brigade of Louisiana infantry. During the Battle of Chancellorsville, Virginia, in 1863, a Union shell ripped off his left foot.

George Washington Colonials
When Columbian University changed its name to The George Washington University in 1904 its colors were also altered to buff and blue to match the uniform Washington wore as he resigned his position as Commander-in-Chief of the Continental Army on December 23, 1783.

The school's teams were referred to as the Buff and Blue, the Crummen (after coach Henry Watson Crum) and the Hatchetites (after the student newspaper) before Colonials came into use in 1926. An editorial in the *Hatchet* that year explained: "Dissatisfaction has been expressed for the past several years with the nicknames usually associated with our athletic teams. In the place of the names the *Hatchet* suggests the use of the connotation 'Colonials.' What name could be more fitting? This, the school named after George Washington should be entitled to bear the name of "Colonials" if any school is so entitled."

Western Connecticut Colonials

During the American Revolution, Danbury (where WCU is located) was an important military supply depot for the Continental Army. On April 26–27, 1777, the British under Major General William Tryon burned and looted the city. The central motto on the seal of the City of Danbury is *Restituimus* ("We have restored"), a reference to the destruction caused by the Loyalist army troops. The Colonials nickname is in reference to the town's history and is represented by a soldier in period costume, Colin Colonial.

Olivet Comets

Named after the Biblical "Mount of Olives," Olivet is a founding member of the Michigan Intercollegiate Athletic Association (1888), the nation's oldest collegiate conference. The Comets nickname is used simply because it fits lyrically with the school's name.

Vanderbilt Commodores

Vanderbilt's nickname is in honor of the Cornelius Vanderbilt (aka Commodore Vanderbilt), who made his fortune in shipping. The term "commodore" was used by the Navy during the mid-to-late nineteenth century and was the commanding officer of a task force of ships, and therefore higher in rank than a captain but lower in rank than an admiral.

The school colors of black and gold stem from Commodore Vanderbilt's legacy; black for the magnate's control of coal and gold for his money.

Hamilton Continentals

The college is named for Founding Father, Alexander Hamilton, who was a member of the first Board of Trustees (though he never set foot on campus) and played a central role in the Continental Army as General George Washington's Chief of Staff. It was in fact Baron von Steuben, acting as Hamilton's surrogate, who laid the college's cornerstone.

Nebraska Cornhuskers
Early nicknames included the Hawkeyes, Antelopes, Old Gold Knights and even Bugeaters, named for the insect-devouring bull bats that hover over the plains. The name "Cornhuskers" first appeared in the school newspaper as "We Have Met the Cornhuskers and They Are Ours" referring to a 20-18 upset victory over Iowa in 1893. In 1899, sportswriter Cy Sherman was tired of referring to the Nebraska's teams as "Bugeaters," so he came up with a new nickname, "Cornhuskers," and it quickly caught on and had supplanted all other names by 1900. The name became so popular that the whole state of Nebraska is now known as "The Cornhusker State."

Charleston Cougars
During the 1970-71 school year, students voted to change the school nickname from Maroons to the Cougars in honor of a cougar that had recently arrived at the Charles Towne Landing Zoo.

Misericordia Cougars
Misericordia changed its nickname from Highlanders to Cougars in 1987 because the cougar is a highland animal indigenous to the Wyoming Valley, PA where the school is located.

McNeese State Cowboys
In the early days, cowboys figured prominently in the culture of McNeese. Rodeo was a major activity in the area, some students rode their horses to campus and the school became known as the "Cow College" because cows roamed freely on the campus. In 1940, the basketball team chose Cowboys as their nickname over several other choices including Broncos, Bucs, and Eagles.

Wyoming Cowboys
The Cowboys nickname was applied to Wyoming teams in 1891, two years before the university's first "official" football game. A Wyoming pick-up football team appealed to a 220 pound cowpuncher, Fred Bush, for help in a game against the Cheyenne Soldiers. Bush signed up for a course or two and came out for the team. When he trotted onto the field decked out in a checkered shirt and Cowboy hat, someone yelled, "Hey, look at the Cowboy!" and the name stuck.

Harvard Crimson

On June 19, 1858 Harvard distinguished itself from its competition when Charles W. Eliot, '53, purchased six red Chinese silk bandanas for his crew members to wear for that day's regatta. It is believed to be the first time a sports team featured an identifying mark. On May 6, 1875, Harvard students held a referendum and overwhelmingly selected "Crimson" as not only the athletics team nickname but the official school color, defeating Magenta.

Alabama Crimson Tide

In early newspaper accounts of Alabama football, the team was simply listed as the "Varsity" or the "Crimson White" after the school colors. The first nickname to become popular was the Thin Red Line and was used until 1906. The name Crimson Tide was first used the *Birmingham Age-Herald*, in describing an Alabama-Auburn game played in Birmingham in 1907. The game was played in a sea of mud and Auburn was a heavy favorite but 'Bama played a great game and held Auburn to a 6-6 tie, thus earning the name, "Crimson Tide."

Holy Cross Crusaders

"Crusaders" was first associated with Holy Cross in 1884 at an alumni banquet in Boston, but the name was reinvented in 1925 by Stanley Woodward, a sports reporter for the *Boston Herald*, when he used the term to describe the Holy Cross baseball team. The student body held a vote later in that year to decide whether Crusaders, Chiefs or Sagamores would be adopted. On October 6, 1925 the results of the ballot were announced: Crusaders 143, Chiefs 17, Sagamores 7.

North Greenville Crusaders

In 1915 the first teams at North Greenville were formed and named the Black Widow Spiders and then Moonshiners. Later, Mountaineers was used to reflect the school's location in the Blue Ridge Mountains. Mounties was then chosen for the same reason (women's teams were called the "Lassies"). In 2001, after two years of proposals and planning, the Crusaders name was officially adopted "to better represent the college's goals and purpose."

Valparaiso Crusaders

In 1931 and Valparaiso chose Uhlans as their nickname over Dunesmen and Vandals. Uhlans were Polish light cavalry armed with lances, sabres and pistols. When the United States entered World War II in 1941 it was decided a new name was needed, one not so close to the Nazi cause and Crusaders was chosen.

The Crusades were a series of religious wars during the 11th, 12th, and 13th centuries organized by European powers to recover Christian holy places from Muslims in the Middle East. At VU, the "Crusader" does not represent the original Crusades, but has a more literal meaning; "One who bears the cross."

Mississippi Valley State Delta Devils

The Delta Devils nickname is in reference to Delta Blues guitarist, Robert Johnson (1911– 1938) whose landmark recordings from 1936–1937 influenced many future musicians including Eric Clapton. He was ranked the fifth greatest guitarist by *Rolling Stone* magazine.

According to legend, as a young man living on a plantation in rural Mississippi, Johnson had a burning desire to become a great blues musician. He was "instructed" to take his guitar to a crossroad near the Dockery Plantation at midnight where he was met by a large black man (the Devil) who took the guitar, tuned it, played a few songs and then returned the guitar to Johnson, giving him mastery of the instrument in exchange for his soul, mirroring the legend of Faust.

Wake Forest Demon Deacons

Early Wake Forest teams were known as Tigers, Baptists or The Old Gold & Black. After Wake Forest defeated rival Trinity (now Duke) in football in 1923, the editor of a local newspaper referred to the team as "Demon Deacons," in recognition of what he termed their "devilish" play and fighting spirit." Wake Forest's news director and football coach liked the title and began using it exclusively.

Northwestern State Demons

In 1922, after a campus-wide vote, Demons won out over a list that included Sharks, Daredevils, Musketeers, Pelicans, Prather's Ground Hogs, Bloodhounds, Cyclops, Serpents and the second place Braves.

Long Beach State Dirtbags

Although most teams at Long Beach State are officially nicknamed the 49ers, the baseball team is officially named the Dirtbags. When Dave Snow arrived to coach the team in 1989, infield coach Dave Malpass would often take his players to a local dirt field to practice while the rest of the team stayed at the on-campus. When the infielders would rejoin the team, their uniforms were caked with dirt and the other coaches would tease Malpass about his group of "Dirtbags." Soon, however, the Dirtbags would show that they were not to be laughed at. That season the team went 50-14 (compared to 14-45 in 1988) and the "Dirtbags" quickly became fan favorites for their gritty and spirited style of play.

Mount Saint Vincent Dolphins

Contrary to popular belief, the Dolphins nickname was not selected because of the proximity of the campus to the Hudson River (there has never been a dolphin spotted on or near the campus). Instead, the Dolphin nickname first appeared during the 1940s and not in an athletic sense, but academically, as the name of an Honor Society created by the Student Council.

San Francisco Dons

Athletics at USF dates back to its founding in 1855, and teams were originally known as the Grey Fog and chose the nickname Dons in 1932.

The term "Don" was originally a title reserved for royalty, select nobles, and members of the church hierarchy but is now often used as a mark of esteem for a person of social or official distinction, such as a community leader of long standing, a person of significant wealth, or of nobility.

Drexel Dragons

Dragons was chosen for Drexel's teams in the late1920s for its alliterative appeal. Previous names included the Blue & Gold, the Engineers and the Drexelites.

Oregon Ducks

Early in the 20th Century when Oregon was known as "The Webfoot State," a reference traced to a band of Massachusetts fishermen, who in 1776 helped save General George Washington and some 10,000 of his troops from imminent defeat at the hands of the British. When many of the Webfoots' ancestors migrated west of the Cascades and settled in the Willamette Valley in the 1840s, the name came with them. Oregon's students took the name as their own.

Headline writers searching for ways to fit "Webfoots" into their sports pages began using "Ducks" in its stead, which the students eventually voted as their new nickname over Timberwolves and Lumberjacks. A second student-body election in 1932 beat back the challenges of Trappers, Pioneers, Yellowjackets and Spearsmen (in honor of football coach C.W. Spears).

In 1947 Oregon's first athletic director, Leo Harris, struck a handshake arrangement with Walt Disney who allowed the use of Donald Duck's likeness providing it was done in good taste. In 1978 Donald had to endure a popularity contest when a cartoonist for the student newspaper pushed his Mallard Drake as a suitable successor to Donald. Students' chose Donald, 2-to-1.

Loras Duhawks

In a 1924 story for the upcoming football game against the University of Detroit, the *Detroit Free Press* focused on the school's recent 7-3 win over Coe. At the time, Loras did not have a nickname, so the *Free Press* sportswriter took the liberty of referring to the players from Dubuque as the Dubuque Hawks, and later in the story as the "Duhawks."

Duquesne Dukes

The Dukes nickname dates to when the school changed its name to honor the Marquis Du Quesne, the French governor of Canada. Since a Marquis and a Duke are not visually distinct (and the name "Duquesne" implies a "Duke"), the name Dukes was popularly assigned and has been in use since the fall of 1911.

James Madison Dukes

The second president of James Madison University, Samuel P. Duke, presided from 1919-1949 and in his honor the school took his name for their athletic teams.

Central College Dutch

The town of Pella, where Central is located, is noted for its Dutch heritage, including its architecture, its 1850s windmill and its famed Tulip Festival.

Union College Dutchmen

The predecessor to Union College, Schenectady Academy was established in 1785 by members of the Dutch Reformed Church, hence "Dutchmen."

Eastern Michigan Eagles

Eastern Michigan teams were called Normalites and Men from Ypsi before Hurons was adopted in 1929 after a contest was sponsored by the Men's Union. In 1988 the Board of Regents voted to replace Hurons with Eagles, beating out the other two finalists, Green Hornets and Express.

Georgia Southern Eagles

From 1924-1941 the school used the Blue Tide and later, the Professors (the school was a teacher's college). In 1959, a student vote was held to determine the new nickname. Eagles won over Colonels by a narrow margin.

As part of the pregame ceremonies, Georgia Southern's living mascot, Freedom, a Bald Eagle, makes a flight from the top of the press box down to the field. It has been described as "the most exciting 30 seconds of college football."

St. Elizabeth Eagles
Located in Morristown, New Jersey, from December 1779 to June 1780 George Washington's Continental Army encamped at the town. It was at Morristown that the Marquis de Lafayette brought the good news that France was going to aid the colonies in their war with England. Because of Morristown's historical significance, Eagles was patriotically chosen for St. Elizabeth's athletic teams.

Mary Washington Eagles
The school is named after Mary Ball Washington, George Washington's mother and a longtime resident of Fredericksburg where the school is located. It is the only public, coeducational college in the United States named after a secular woman. Representing patriotism, the Eagles nickname was adopted by the school in 1986.

Massachusetts Institute of Technology Engineers
MIT's Engineers nickname is a fitting one for one of the most accomplished engineering schools in the world.

In 1913, a group of MIT alumni gathered to brainstorm ideas for a team mascot. After looking at a book on animals of North America they quickly decided on the beaver because, "of all the animals of the world, the beaver is noted for its engineering and mechanical skill and habits of industry." On January 14, 1914, the group formally presented the beaver mascot to MIT's president, who accepted the recommendation.

Williams College Ephs
Established in 1793 with funds bequeathed by Colonel Ephraim Williams, although he never had any intention to found a college. En route with his regiment of Massachusetts militia to join the battle with the French and Indians at Lake George, Williams wrote his last will and testament on July 22, 1755. In it he bequeathed his residuary estate for the founding and support of a free school in West Township, where he had commanded a detachment of militia.

On September 8, 1755, Williams was killed at the Battle of Lake George and more than thirty-five years later fifteen scholars were admitted to the free school in Williamstown where "young gentlemen from every part of the Union might resort for instruction in all the branches of useful and polite literature."

The men's and women's athletic teams at Williams are referred to as "Ephs" in Williams' honor.

St. Louis College of Pharmacy Eutectic
When STLCOP joined the NAIA in 1993 the school went in search of a new nickname to replace Volunteers. Eutectic won over such common names as Panthers, Volunteers, and Pioneers. According to the school's website, "'Eutectic' describes the scientific process of two solids being combined to form a liquid. A common term in pharmacy, it is the perfect metaphor for the St. Louis College of Pharmacy's intercollegiate athletic program – combining athletics and a demanding academic program."

La Salle Explorers
The Explorers nickname derives from a 1931 mistake made by a sportswriter who thought the university was named after the French explorer, Sieur de La Salle, when in fact it is named after St. John-Baptiste de la Salle who was a priest and educational reformer. Despite the error, the name was officially chosen in a student contest during the spring of 1932.

Wells College Express
Wells was established as a women's college in 1868 by Henry Wells, founder of Wells Fargo and the American Express Company.

Air Force Academy Falcons
On September 25, 1955, members of the Class of 1959, the first to enter the Academy, chose the Falcons nickname because it best characterized the combat role of the U.S. Air Force. The falcon exemplified the qualities sought in Air Force Academy cadets; courage, intelligence, love of the wild sky, ferocity in attack, but gentle in repose - and discipline. Performing falcons are called "The Bird" and are trained by cadets.

Bowling Green Falcons
Before 1927, BG teams were called the Normals or Teachers. Ivan Lake, '23, suggested the Falcons nickname after reading an article on falconry. Lake, managing sports editor of the *Sentinel-Tribune* in Bowling Green, proposed the name because it fit headline space and because falcons were "the most powerful bird for their size and often attacked birds two or three times their size."

Saint Ambrose Fighting Bees

Legend states that when he was an infant, bees settled on Ambrose's face while he lay in his cradle, leaving behind a drop of honey. His father considered this a sign of his future eloquence and honeyed tongue. Bees and beehives often appear in Ambrose's symbology. He is the patron saint of bee keepers and candle makers.

Illinois Fighting Illini

The earliest recorded usage of the term "Illini" in reference to the university was in January 1874, when the student newspaper changed its name from *The Student* to *The Illini*. The earliest application of "Illini" in reference to the school's athletic teams was during the 1907 football season and the term gained greater frequency in the next decade. Previous nicknames included Indians, Orange and Blue, and Varsity.

The term "Fighting Illini" was first used in 1921 and was more or less adopted as an official nickname between 1921 and 1930.

From 1926-2007 the mascot was a Native American figure, Chief Illiniwek. Critics of the Chief claimed that it was a racist stereotype while supporters claimed that it was inoffensive and a source of pride and reverence to the Native American heritage of Illinois past Sioux elder, Frank Fools Crow.

The University Board of Trustees announced on February 16, 2007, that the Chief's last public performance would be the final home game of the 2006–2007 men's basketball season. The name "Fighting Illini" was retained as the name pre-dated the Chief Illiniwek symbol and was bestowed upon the team in honor of Illinoisans who fought in World War I while the use of the name "Illini" dates to the 19th century.

Notre Dame Fighting Irish

Notre Dame competed as the Catholics during the 1800s and became more widely known as the Ramblers during the early 1920s, in the days of Knute Rockne and the Four Horsemen.

No one knows for sure how the Fighting Irish moniker came to be used for the Notre Dame teams. One story suggests it was born in 1899 when Notre Dame played Northwestern in Evanston, and Wildcat fans began to chant, "Kill the Fighting Irish, kill the Fighting Irish." Another tale has the nickname originating at halftime of the Notre Dame-Michigan game in 1909. With his team trailing, one Notre Dame player yelled to his teammates—who happened to have names like Dolan, Kelly, Glynn, Duffy and Ryan —"What's the matter with you guys? You're all Irish and you're not fighting worth a lick!" Notre Dame came back to win the game and press, after overhearing the remark, reported the game as a victory for the "Fighting Irish."

The most generally accepted explanation is that the press coined the nickname as a characterization of Notre Dame athletic teams, their never-say-die fighting spirit and the Irish qualities of grit, determination and tenacity. Notre Dame alumnus Francis Wallace popularized the name in his *New York Daily News* columns in the 1920s.

University president Rev. Matthew Walsh officially adopted "Fighting Irish" as the Notre Dame nickname in 1927.

Edinboro Fighting Scots
The university was founded by Scottish immigrants and heralding back to their roots, Edinboro became the first school in the world to offer a music education degree in bagpiping starting in 2010.

Wooster Fighting Scots
Early Wooster teams were known as the Presbyterians, or the Presbyterian Steamroller, due to the football team's success. In 1939, alumnus Birt Babcock made a large donation to fund the purchase of kilts for the marching band, in the yellow-and-black MacLeod tartan, which had no particular significance to the school, except that it matched the school colors. Scottish culture eventually became an important part of the school's heritage; today, the football games feature a Scottish pipe band with Highland dancers in addition to a traditional marching band, with all three groups clad in the MacLeod tartan.

Mary Baldwin Fighting Squirrels
The squirrel was the central figure in the family crest of Mary Julia Baldwin, the school's second founder, who transformed the Augusta Female Seminary into a prosperous and innovative school in the years following the Civil War. It was natural, after the trustees renamed the school for Miss Baldwin, for the official seal and team name to incorporate the squirrel as well.

Illinois-Chicago Flames
Athletics began with the College of Physicians and Surgeons (as the school was then known) in the 1880s. Upon moving to the Circle Campus, teams became known as the Chicas, a shortening of "Chicago," this was changed to "Chikas" due to taunting from other teams ("chicas" means "girls" in Spanish). This spelling

was rationalized as being a reference to the Chickasaw tribe but was dropped in the 1970s when teams were simply known as "Circle."

In 1982 a contest was held for students to rename the athletics teams. The winning entry was Flames, a reference to the Great Chicago Fire of 1871.

Lee University Flames

The Flames nickname is in reference to the flame on a torch in the university's seal which in turn represents the guiding light of the Holy Spirit.

Saint Mary's Flames

As a Catholic college, Saint Mary "seeks to bring the light of faith and the treasures of knowledge to the forefront of scholarship through mutually challenging and supportive intellectual inquiry" as represented by a flame.

Dayton Flyers

Dayton was home to the Wright Brothers and it was in that city the two developed their "Wright Flyer," the first plane capable of controlled, powered, sustained heavier-than-air human flight. On December 17, 1903 in Kitty Hawk, North Carolina Orville was at the controls as the Wright Flyer travelled a distance of 120 feet in 12 seconds. The Dayton "Flyers" nickname was chosen as an honor to the brothers.

Lewis Flyers

In 1963, cartoonist Milton Caniff illustrated a comic strip called *Steve Canyon* that followed the adventures of Air Force pilot Steve Canyon, who would investigate mysteries within the Air Force. One of Canyon's adventures took him to a flight school, at which he learned of the existence of 'Bedcheck Charlie.' Charlie was a student at the school who dressed up in World War I flight gear and went around scaring the other cadets.

In the fall of '63, some Lewis students were discussing the need for a mascot. Steve Moskal, a freshman history major, and his proctor, Roger Mills, were discussing the fact that the students needed a symbol with which to identify. Moskal, having been a fan of Caniff's work, remembered reading about Bedcheck Charlie in the *Chicago Tribune*. The two of them decided to write Caniff, asking him for permission to use Charlie as the school symbol. Caniff wrote back and gave permission to use Charlie. Almost immediately, the college adopted Charlie as its own.

Hope Flying Dutchmen

Since the early 1900s Hope's teams were called Dutchmen due to the fact the school is located in a community settled by Dutch immigrants. The Flying Dutchmen nickname is reported to have been coined by a sportswriter covering the men's basketball team in 1958.

Lebanon Valley Flying Dutchmen

The Flying Dutchmen nickname comes not from the famous sailing ghost ship, but rather is a product of the area known as Pennsylvania Dutch Country ("Dutch" being an Anglicization of the word "Deutsch," or German, and not actually referring to people from Holland).

The origin of the nickname is in an article that appeared in the *Lebanon Daily News* on Sept. 12, 1932. Writer G.O. Gettum wrote, "The Blue and White collegians, like most superstitious athletes, believe a mascot of some kind would bring them more good luck." Gettum called for reader submissions as to what the nickname should be. He followed up with an article in which the Flying Dutchmen nickname was first proposed and wrote that the name was appropriate because "Lebanon Valley College is almost in the center of Pennsylvania Dutch country."

Erskine Flying Fleet

In 1929 the football team employed a wide-open passing attack that led the Southern Intercollegiate Athletic Association in scoring and so impressed *Greenville News* sportswriter Carter "Scoop" Latimer that he labelled Erskine teams "The Flying Fleet." The name struck a chord with the Erskine student body and that fall they voted to have the nickname replace Seceders.

Lake Forest Foresters

In 1948 the nickname Foresters was selected in a contest organized by the student newspaper. Nicknames used prior included the Gold Coasters, Red Devils and Jaybirds.

Providence Friars

Providence teams were known as Cardinal, Dominicans or Black and White before Friars first appeared in an April 9, 1929 *Providence Journal* sports story prior to the baseball season. The earlier nicknames continued to be used until the fall of 1932 when Friars became officially accepted, a name that refers to the members of the mendicant religious orders founded in the 13th Century.

Universite du Quebec a Abitibi-Temiscamingue Gaillards

French for a "strong person." The women's teams are called Astrelles ("Stars").

Bishop's University Gaiters

Located in Sherbrooke, Quebec, Bishop's "Gaiter" nickname (and current mascot) suggests the term stems from the word "alligator," when in truth "Gaiter" actually refers to a boot covering once worn by Anglican bishops.

St. Mary's Gaels

The Gaels nickname was given to the school's football team in 1926 by a writer for the defunct *San Francisco Call-Bulletin*. The school's previous nickname was the Saints, although the baseball team was known as the Phoenix until the 1940s in reference to a fire that destroyed the school's Oakland campus.

The Gaels are an ethnic group which spread from Ireland to Scotland and the Isle of Man. Their language is of the Gaelic family.

South Carolina Gamecocks

The Gamecocks name can be traced back into the 18th century to honor native South Carolina Revolutionary War hero, Thomas Sumter, who also had a long tenure in Congress. He was known as the "Carolina Gamecock" for his boldness, daring, and courage and was given the name when a British general commented that Sumter "fought like a gamecock."

Florida Gators

The Gator was incidentally chosen in 1911as Florida's mascot when a Gainesville merchant sold school pennants with an alligator emblem. Up until that time the alligator had not been referenced by the school in any manner.

San Francisco State Gators

In reference to the Golden Gate (the channel of water under the Golden Gate Bridge) the SFS teams were called the Golden Gaters (with an "e") starting in 1931 and lasted until the late 1940s. When the school started bringing two live alligators (Oogee and Ougee) to football games the name was changed to the Golden Gators. "Golden" was dropped from the name in the early 1970s.

Santa Barbara Gauchos

In loose terms, the word "gaucho" is the equivalent term for the North American "cowboy." The term often connotes the 19th Century more than the present day, as is the case with Santa Barbara athletics. Historically gauchos were residents of the South American pampas, Southern Chile and Southern Brazil.

Ottawa Gee-Gees
Ottawa's teams were known as the "Grenat et Gris" (Garnet and Gray) but a Gee-Gee is also the lead horse in a race, hence the logo of a horse encompassing two letter Gs was adopted as the official logo. The logo exemplifies the speed, determination and spirit which have become benchmarks of the team.

Centenary (La.) Gents
According to lore, the college first adopted the "Gents" handle in 1921. While still playing under the Ironsides nickname that year, the football team got into a most ungentlemanly scrum with an opposing team. Before the squad could take the field for its next game, college president George Sexton called the players aside and told them that if they knew what was good for them, they'd better start acting like "gentlemen."

Evergreen State Geoducks
Pronounced GOO-EE DUCK, The geoduck is a species of very large (up to 15 pounds) saltwater clams, a marine mollusk and an $80 million business in Washington where Evergreen is located. The clam is a delicacy and is believed to be an aphrodisiac due to its long and phallic looking siphon. The school's Latin motto, *Omnia Extares* ("let it all hang out") is at least partially intended as a tongue-in-cheek reference to the creature's phallic appearance.

The sophomoric sense of humor displayed in the name plays out in the school fight song, and captures the free spirit of smaller-time college athletics:
> *Go, Geoducks, go,*
> *Through the mud and the sand,*
> *Let's go.*
> *Siphon high, squirt it out,*
> *Swivel all about, Let it all hang out!*

Keystone Giants
Christy Mathewson enrolled at Keystone Academy in 1895 and he played a variety of positions on the baseball team including second base and pitcher. After a long career with the New York Giants he was one of the five original members of the Baseball Hall of Fame. It is in Mathewson's honor that the Keystone athletic teams are named the Giants.

California Golden Bears

A bear mascot, the state symbol of California, was first used by Cal teams in 1895 when the track & field team took a blue banner emblazoned with the golden grizzly bear on a successful national tour and the mascot was adopted by all Cal teams soon thereafter.

Marquette Golden Eagles

Prior to taking on Warriors in 1954, Blue & Gold, Hilltoppers and Golden Avalanche were used interchangeably.

In 1993 school president, Father DiUlio, outraged many by deciding to change the nickname with the only choices being "Lightning" and "Golden Eagles," neither of which had any historical or logical connection to Marquette. Nevertheless, Golden Eagles ruled the day.

In 2004 Wayne Sanders, vice chair of the board of trustees, offered $2 million if Marquette would change its nickname back to Warriors. The gift was immediately declined, but Father Wild, the new president of the university, determined that the proposal would be considered. Recognizing that Golden Eagles may not be a favorite of the student body, the trustees unilaterally decided to change the nickname to "Gold", provoking another negative reaction by students, faculty, alumni, and fans. This led the university to ask the Marquette community to vote for a new nickname although "Warriors" was not to be considered. Of the choices given, Golden Eagles prevailed yet again and a new logo was unveiled in 1994.

Southern Mississippi Golden Eagles

Previously known as the Tigers, Normalites, Confederates and Southerners, in the early 1970s Golden Eagles was selected in a student/alumni vote.

Spalding Golden Eagles

Spalding's teams were known as the Pelicans, but a committee of the school's alumni board with input from the athletics department along with input from students replaced the name with Golden Eagles in 2006.

Kent State Golden Flashes

Kent State's football team came into existence in 1920 and became known as the Silver Foxes because then-president John McGilvrey raised silver foxes on his farm. After McGilvrey's controversial firing in 1926, the new administration held a contest to choose a new team name and Golden Flashes was chosen.

Nazareth Golden Flyers

The Golden Flyers nickname was adopted in 1977 when Nazareth's community was asked to suggest names and a committee selected Flyers from the three most popular suggestions (Flyers, Wings, and Firebirds). The word "Golden" was then added to reflect Nazareth's colors, purple and gold.

Queen's (Kingston, ON) Golden Gaels

The "Golden Gaels" name was coined in 1947 by sports reporter Cliff Bowering, after the football team traded its traditional uniform of red, gold, and blue bands for gold jerseys, gold helmets, and red pants. The name caught on and became the familiar term for Queen's teams by the 1950s. "Gaels" is a reference to the school's Scottish heritage (Queen's was established in 1841 by the Presbyterian church). Before 1947, teams were commonly known as The Tricolour.

Minnesota Golden Gophers

Minnesota is known as the "Gopher State" from a satirical political cartoon drawn in 1858 to mock the legislature's plan to provide railroad loans. The cartoon featured heads of legislators on bodies of gophers riding the "Gopher Train." The university's "Golden Gophers" nickname was inspired by the golden uniforms worn by Minnesota's championship football teams in the 1930s.

Oakland Golden Grizzlies

When Oakland University decided in 1997 to move its athletics program from NCAA Division II to Division I, they went in search of a nickname to replace Pioneers (conceived in the 1950s as an aerospace pioneer, befitting the times). 19-member Mascot Advisory Committee received hundreds of name suggestions and narrowed down the possibilities to three - the Golden Grizzlies, Saber Cats and Pioneers. Golden Grizzlies quickly became the favorite choice among all groups tested and was announced on March 23, 1998.

Guelph Gryphons

The Gryphon was chosen by Guelph because it is symbolically significant for its domination of both the earth and the sky and because of its lion's body and eagle's head and wings.

Gustavus Adolphus Golden Gusties

The college was founded by Swedish Americans in 1862 as a Lutheran parochial school. In May 1873, the college was renamed Gustavus Adolphus Literary &

Theological Institute in honor of King Gustavus Adolphus of Sweden (1594-1632) who took Sweden from a mere regional power to one of the great powers of Europe. The Golden Gusties nickname is used in direct reference to Gustavus and is symbolized by a lion because the king was known as "The Lion of the North."

Tulsa Golden Hurricane
Before adopting Golden Hurricane in 1922, the university had many unofficial nicknames including Kendallites (from TU's predecessor institution, Henry Kendall College), Presbyterians (from the university's founding by the Presbyterian Church), Tulsans, Tigers, Orange and Black and Yellow Jackets. The name Golden Tornadoes was chosen by football coach H.M. Archer based on new gold and black uniforms (rather than the old orange and black) and a remark made during practice of the team "roaring through opponents." However, it was quickly discovered that the same name had been chosen in 1917 by Georgia Tech. Archer then substituted the term "Hurricane" for "Tornado" and a team vote confirmed the official nickname as the "Golden Hurricane."

Goucher Gophers
Eleanor "Shotsie" Bissell,'82, advertised upcoming athletic events by placing posters with the slogan, "Go-pher it Goucher" around campus. Athletic Director, Anna Nichols, searching for a common rallying point for Goucher spirit, decided on the "Go-pher" as the mascot. When Goucher joined the NCAA, the Gopher was made official.

Pittsburg State Gorillas
In 1920, a group of Pittsburgh State students were dissatisfied with the state of school spirit and organized themselves as the "Gorillas" (a 1920s slang term for roughnecks) in order to hasten college spirit and enthusiasm by sponsoring pep rallies, freshman hazing, mock burials and weddings, and nightshirt stampedes through downtown Pittsburg.

In 1923, the Gorillas had art student, Helen Waskey, make a drawing of their new mascot and two years later they offered their symbol as the official mascot of the school. On January 15, 1925, the student body unanimously adopted the ferocious beast "as a name and synonym for the athletic teams."

In 1974 the Gorilla mascot found a mate, Gussie, for whom Pittsburgh women's teams were named until 1989 when members of the women's athletic teams voted to change their name from Gussies to Gorillas.

Webster University Gorloks
The Gorlok name was chosen in 1984 by a campus committee. The mythical creature was derived from the combination of the two streets that intersect in the heart of Old Webster; Gore and Lockwood Avenues. Once the name was chosen, a contest was run in student newspaper asking contestants to submit sketches for what a Gorlok might look like. The winning entry included a picture of a blue and yellow creature holding a hand-held pump sprayer, had the paws of a cheetah, the horns of a buffalo and the face of a Saint Bernard.

Jersey City State Gothic Knights
Jersey City's teams were originally known as the Gothics for the style of architecture found on campus. The name was changed to Gothic Knights in 1983.

Austin Peay State Governors
Tennessee Governor Austin Peay governed from 1923 until his death in 1927. When the state acquired a normal school in 1929 it was renamed in Peay's honor and the nickname for the athletic teams followed.

Albany Great Danes
When the school was known as the New York State College for Teachers, the athletic teams were called Penguins. The Great Dane was first chosen by the student body in 1965 for its qualities of strength, courage, speed and stamina.

Tulane Green Wave
From 1893 to 1919, the athletic teams were known as the Olive and Blue for the official school colors. In 1919, one of the many student newspapers began referring to the football team as the Greenbacks. The Green Wave nickname was adopted during the 1920 season after a song titled *The Rolling Green Wave* was published in the school's student newspaper.

Westminster Griffins
Changed from "Parsons" in 1979 when athletics were restored on campus.

Adams State Grizzlies
Changed from Indians to Grizzlies in 1996 during debate over using Native American names and imagery. There is a life-sized statue of a grizzly in front of the school's gym and represents "Old Mose," a grizzly that for over 20 years terrorized the residents in southern and central Colorado until he was killed in

1904. Old Mose killed three men and over 800 head of cattle in his career and when he was finally brought down he weighed an astonishing 1300 pounds.

McDaniel Green Terror
Some believe it was the school's women's basketball team that chose the name from a fish (*Aequidens rivulatus, aka Green Terror*) found in the Amazon River while others believe it to have been first used in a 1923 newspaper article to describe a hard-fought loss to Washington and Lee. Lastly, a story states that football coach, D. K. Shroyer, first used the term to fire up his troops.

Ave Maria Gyrenes
First applied to Marines as a humorous reference by other branches of the service, the Marines quickly adopted "Gyrenes" for their own. During the World Wars, "GI" was applied to all service members as being "Government Issue" and a Gyrene was understood to be special kind of "government issue Marine."

South Dakota School of Mines and Technology Hardrockers
The Hardrocker nickname was adopted in the 1920s and was inspired by miners who mined hard rock searching for gold. The mascot is Grubby the Miner.

Stetson Hatters
Founded in 1883, Stetson University was initially was called DeLand Academy after the school's founder, Henry Addison DeLand. In 1886 a disastrous freeze affected the citrus industry leaving DeLand in financial straits and the school in danger of closing. He sought the aid of John B. Stetson who had a winter home nearby and had become interested in the school.

Stetson was a hatter who, in the 1860s invented the cowboy hat. Durable and well-made from waterproof felt, its high, open crown and broad rim kept the hot sun off the face, necks and shoulders. The hat achieved instant popularity and was named the "Boss of the Plains."

At Deland's request, Stetson was made chairman of the Board of Trustees in 1889 and the university was renamed in his honor. Stetson University fielded its first football team in Florida in 1901 and the "Hatters" nickname was used then and is still in use today.

Iowa Hawkeyes
The name "Hawkeye" was originally applied to a hero in the novel, *The Last of the Mohicans*, written by James Fenimore Cooper. In the book, Delaware Indians

bestow the name on a white scout who lived with them. In 1838, people in the territory of Iowa acquired the nickname, chiefly through the efforts of Judge David Rorer of Burlington and James Edwards of Fort Madison. Edwards, editor of the *Fort Madison Patriot*, moved his paper to Burlington in 1843 and renamed it the *Burlington Hawk-Eye*. The two men continued their campaign to popularize the name and territorial officials eventually gave it their formal approval, thus Iowa is known as the "Hawkeye State" and Iowans as "Hawkeyes."

Monmouth Hawks
Monmouth Press Club held a campaign in 1939 to pick an athletic nickname and a long list of entrants was then winnowed down to just three; Nighthawks, EmJaCees, and MaJiCians. In the ensuing election "Nighthawks" won by a margin of six votes. Until 1956 the school was a night school and when it started offering day classes the nickname was shortened to Hawks.

St. Joseph's Hawks
Saint Joseph's campus is located on "Hawk Hill" between the northwestern edge of Philadelphia and Lower Merion Township. Its teams have been called the "Hawks" since 1929 when the school's yearbook initiated a contest among the student body. From more than 100 suggestions two were voted on—Grenadiers and Hawks with the latter winning by a slim margin.

William Smith Herons
Several names were submitted when the school held a "Name the Mascot" contest in 1982, but Herons was selected because of the strong and graceful birds that lived near the campus' Odell's Pond.

Houghton Highlanders
Houghton's campus is located in New York's Genesee Valley and the Highlander nickname was chosen for the rolling hills found in the area.

Radford Highlanders
The university's teams are known as the Highlanders in honor of the region's Scots-Irish heritage and for its location in the Virginia Highlands, between the Blue Ridge and Allegheny mountains.

California Riverside Highlanders
UCR's founding class of 1954 adopted the nickname Highlanders, reflecting the

campus' high altitude along the foothills of Box Springs Mountain. They also chose a bear as a mascot.

Rogers State University Hillcats
Since the institution was founded in 1909, it has been situated atop "College Hill," on the west side of Claremore, Oklahoma, overlooking the community below. The name "Hillcat" is a fictional animal based on a bobcat and was conceived independently by a group of RSU students in spring 2005.

St. Edward's University Hilltoppers
The university's campus is located on a hill overlooking the city of Austin.

Western Kentucky Hilltoppers
WKU sits atop the highest point in south-central Kentucky, on a hill called College Heights (aka The Hill) that has a commanding view of the Barren River Valley.

Virginia Tech Hokies
Tech's teams were originally known as the Fighting Gobblers, a name that originated in 1909 when football Coach Branch Bocock initiated his players into the "Gobbler Club," with "Gobblers" referring to when the university was a military college. As future military officers and gentlemen, cadets were not allowed to look at their plates as they ate. To do so was termed "gobbling" your food and was cause for punishment.

The word "Hokies," originated in the "Old Hokie" spirit yell created in 1896 by O.M. Stull. That year a contest which was held to select a new spirit yell when the college's name was changed from Virginia Agricultural and Mechanical College to Virginia Agricultural and Mechanical College and Polytechnic Institute. Stull's yell won, and he received the $5 award.

> Hoki, Hoki, Hoki, Hy.
> Techs, Techs, V.P.I.
> Sola-Rex, Sola-Rah
> Polytechs - Vir-gin-ia.
> Rae, Ri, V.P.I.

Later, the phrase "Team! Team! Team!" was added at the end and an "e" was added to "Hoki."

The turkey had been a mascot in one form or another for decades. In 1981 a campaign to find a new mascot settled on the "Hokie Bird," a turkey-like figure that debuted that year at the football game against Wake Forest.

Indiana Hoosiers

The state of Indiana is nicknamed "The Hoosier State," and its residents have been known as "Hoosiers" since the 1800s. Theories abound as to how the practice started. The name may have been applied to the predominantly Indiana-based workers of Samuel Hoosier (or Hoosher), who helped build a canal on the Ohio River. They were called "Hoosier's men" or "Hoosiers." A less likely story states that the word may derive from the phrase fearful early settlers called out when startled by a knock on their cabin door: "Who's here?" -- a call that over time degenerated into "Hoosier." No one knows for sure.

Texas Christian Horned Frogs

The Horned Frog is the state reptile of Texas and is actually a lizard. Four students helped name the school's teams in 1897.

Emporia State Hornets

In the early 1930s, Yellow Jackets was nearly chosen as the school's nickname but was deemed too long and Hornets was chosen instead.

Kalamazoo College Hornets

Kalamazoo's student newspaper, *The Index*, first referenced the school's teams as Hornets in 1925 although there is no explanation as to how or why the name was chosen. Before then, athletic teams were simply referred to as Kalamazoo College, the Orange and Black or the Kazooks.

Sacramento State Hornets

When Sac State opened in 1947 the student body selected the Hornets as their nickname with its closest competition coming from Elks.

Georgetown Hoyas

Some have claimed "hoya" is an Indian word, while those of a legal mind think it to be related to the French word *"oyez,"* the traditional opening of judicial sessions. Still others believe that Georgetown's location along a river might cause Hoya be an offshoot of the nautical "ahoy."

GU's official explanation holds that there was a baseball team on campus called the "Stonewalls" and a student, applying Greek and Latin (required by all GU students at the time) dubbed the team the *hoia saxa* in a cheer - *hoia* is the Greek neuter plural for "what" while *saxa* is the Latin neuter plural for "rock." Substituting a "y" for an "i"; "hoya saxa" literally means "what rocks."

While there was a Stonewalls team between 1866 and 1873 some have held that *hoia saxa* referred not to the team but its surroundings--the team's field.

Use of Hoyas as a nickname didn't appear until the 1920s when a sportswriter for the school paper began to refer to the football team as the "Hoyas" rather than its contemporary "Hilltoppers" and the name became the official one within a few years.

Miami Hurricanes

On September 17, 1926, just weeks before the university was set to open its doors, a destructive hurricane struck Miami, with Coral Gables and the new University of Miami at ground zero. The nickname Hurricanes first appeared in an October, 1926 *Miami Herald* story with the name being attributed to football player Porter Norris, '29.

In 1926 the Ibis was chosen for the school's mascot because, as legend states, the Ibis can instinctively detect danger. It is the last sign of wildlife to take shelter before a hurricane hits, giving warning that danger is imminent, and, as the storm passes the Ibis is the first to reappear, a sign that clear skies are approaching, making it a symbol of leadership and courage.

Connecticut Huskies

The Huskies nickname was adopted in 1934. Before then, the teams were referred to as the Aggies. Though there is a homophonic relationship between "UConn" and the "Yukon," where Huskies are native, the Huskies nickname predates the school's 1939 name change to the University of Connecticut.

Northeastern Huskies

As the school's sports program was developing in the 1920s, students naturally wanted a nickname and mascot. Huskies was selected as the nickname, and the first mascot – a live Siberian Husky – arrived on campus March 4, 1927 in regal manner. More than 1,000 students and the school's band were at the train station when Sapsut arrived from Boston. Afternoon classes were cancelled, and a police escort took Sapsut the four miles to the campus.

Northern Illinois Huskies

Early Northern Illinois athletic teams were called the Profs, alluding to the school's mission as a teacher's college. At various times teams were also called the Evansmen (in recognition of athletics pioneer George G. "Chick" Evans), Northerners, Teachers and Cardinals, due to the color of their uniforms.

In 1940, a four-man committee made was appointed to search for "...a term with a trifle more dash." After much debate, Huskies was agreed upon and was announced in school's newspaper on January 25, 1940.

Washington Huskies
The school had no nickname prior to 1919 when a character named the "Sun Dodger" was created for a student magazine and was chosen by students as the name of the athletic teams. The university was none-too-proud of the cognomen and in 1921 countered with Vikings, a name that didn't go over well with the student body. A formal contest was held in 1922 with Huskies winning.

Earlham Hustling Quakers
Previously known as the "Fighting Quakers," Earlham changed their nickname to "Hustling Quakers" after the college's board of regents decided that it was inappropriate for Quakers to fight.

Washburn University Ichabods
Ichabod Washburn was a prominent 19th century church deacon, industrialist and philanthropist who played a leading role in founding not one, but two universities: Worcester Polytechnic Institute and Washburn University.

Lincoln College was founded in 1865 and renamed Washburn College in 1868 after receiving a $25,000 donation from Ichabod Washburn.

A bookish fellow wearing a tuxedo named Ichabod is also the school's mascot, a tradition dating to 1938, when the yearbook introduced a sketch that stated, "He has courage and enthusiasm as shown by his brisk walk. He is democratic and courteous, for he tips his hat as he passes. Sincere in his search for truth and knowledge, he studiously carries a book under his arm and adapts himself with equal ease to any change in life."

Catawba Indians
The Indians nickname is in honor of the Catawba Indian tribe that was indigenous to the original location of the school. In 2005, college officials filed a formal appeal to continue use of the Catawba Indian mascot citing the approval of the remaining members of the Catawba tribe and the NCAA granted the appeal on the condition the college use the tribe specific nickname of the "Catawba Indians" when referring to the nickname as opposed to simply the "Indians."

John Abbott College Islanders
The school is located in Sainte-Anne-de-Bellevue, Quebec, Canada, near the western tip of the Island of Montreal.

Indiana University – Purdue University Indianapolis Jaguars
Changed from the "Metros" in 1997 upon moving to NCAA Division I, the Jaguar was chosen because it represented the spirit of IUPUI: powerful, swift and confident.

Students, staff, faculty and alumni chose the nickname from a ballot that included such choices as City Cats, River Hawks, Indy Wolves, Indy Cats, Metro Cats, Indy Hawks and Circle Cats but Jaguars won out over all other rivals.

Jamestown Jimmies
Jamestown College is located in Jamestown, North Dakota and the James River splits the city. On the north end of town the James River dam forms the Jamestown Reservoir. The Catholic Church in Jamestown is named after St. James. With such an influx of James names the Jimmies nickname seemed to be a perfect fit and has been in use since 1925.

South Dakota Jackrabbits
The most common belief is that the nickname came from a story that appeared in a Minneapolis newspaper following a 1905 football game against the University of Minnesota. A reporter, knowing of the preponderance of jackrabbits in the Brookings area, was believed to have written that the South Dakota team was "as quick as jackrabbits." Athletic teams soon adopted the nickname.

Manhattan College Jaspers
The origins of the Jaspers nickname goes back to the 1880s and Brother Jasper, a faculty member at MC who introduced baseball to the school and became the team's first coach. According to legend, it was Brother Jasper who may also have originated baseball's seventh inning stretch at baseball games.

Besides being a teacher and coach, Brother Jasper was also the Prefect of Discipline and was responsible for the behaviour of the school's students. During one particularly hard fought game, with the fans becoming edgy as the home team came to bat in the seventh inning, Brother Jasper called time-out and told the students to stand up and unwind. The practice was soon copied by the New York Giants fans and has now become a fixture of America's pastime.

Texas A&M - Kingsville Javelinas

A&M-Kingsville has used this nickname since the school's opening in 1925 and the animals were allowed to roam the campus until 1929 when the university president was bitten by one that proved to be rabid.

Standing up to 20 inches in height and 36 inches in length, javelinas are sometimes called a "musk hog" because of its strong odor. It has a pair of short, razor-sharp tusks that are used for both defense and for rooting out food. They originated in South America, but have migrated into the American Southwest.

Kansas Jayhawks

The origin of the Jayhawk nickname has its roots in the historic struggles of Kansas settlers. The term was coined around 1848 and combines two birds--the blue jay, a noisy, quarrelsome thing known to rob other nests, and the sparrow hawk, a quiet, stealthy hunter. There was a clear message meant in the name: Don't turn your back on a Jayhawk.

During the 1850's, the Kansas Territory was a battleground between those wanting it to be a slave state and abolitionists committed to keeping it a free state. The opposing factions looted, sacked, rustled cattle, stole horses, and otherwise attacked each other's settlements. For a time, ruffians on both sides were called Jayhawkers but the name stuck to the "free staters" when Kansas was admitted as a free state in 1861.

During the Civil War, the Jayhawk's ruffian image gave way to patriotic symbol. Kansas Governor Charles Robinson raised a regiment called the Independent Mounted Kansas Jayhawks. By war's end "Jayhawks" were synonymous with the impassioned people who made Kansas a Free State. In 1886, the Jayhawk appeared in a cheer--the famous Rock Chalk Chant, and when KU football players first took the field in 1890, it seemed only natural to call them Jayhawkers.

Newman Jets

Newman is located in Wichita, Kansas, and the school's Jets nickname stems from the fact that in the 1920s and '30s, aircraft pioneers such as Clyde Cessna, Walter Beech and Bill Lear began projects that would lead to Wichita being name the "Air Capital of the World."

Brandeis Judges

The "Judges" nickname honors the school's namesake, Louis Brandeis, who served as a Justice of the United States Supreme Court. The team colors are blue and white, and their mascot is Ollie the Owl, named after the Supreme Court jurist, Oliver Wendell Holmes, Jr.

Tufts Jumbos

The Jumbo tale began on the plains of Abyssinia, where an elephant was captured in 1861. Collector Johann Schmidt bought the animal and resold him to the menagerie at the *Jardin des Plantes* in Paris. He was eventually called "Jumbo," perhaps a misspelling of *jumbe*, a Swahili word for "chief."

In 1865, the *Jardin des Plantes* traded Jumbo to the Royal Zoological Society in London for a rhinoceros. As Jumbo's height and girth expanded, so did his popularity with the children and adults who frequented the London Zoo. He was trained as an amusement ride as a 60-seat "howdah" was strapped on his back for rides through the park. Among those who rode aboard Jumbo on this multi-tiered seat were Winston Churchill, Theodore Roosevelt and Phineas T. Barnum.

Barnum was not only a showman but was a generous philanthropist who gave time and money to his adopted home of Bridgeport, Connecticut and to the fledgling Tufts College, of which he was an original trustee. In 1880, Barnum was looking for a spectacular animal attraction to make their grand new circus even grander when he recalled Jumbo in the London Zoo and bought the animal.

For four spectacular seasons, Jumbo toured North America and was a huge star, his visage sold on hundreds of items.

Jumbo's untimely death came on September 15, 1885, as the traveling circus was loading the menagerie onto trains in St. Thomas, Ontario. A portion of the fence that ran along the rail yard tracks had been removed, allowing the parading animals to descend a small hill and board the cars. Jumbo and the baby clown elephant, Tom Thumb, were ambling toward their "Palace Car" when an unscheduled express freight train roared toward the entourage. In Barnum's vivid rendering of the tale--Jumbo sacrificed his own life to save the baby elephant. Jumbo swung around, wrapped his long trunk around Tom Thumb, and hurled him 20 yards away, with a force that cost the calf a broken hind leg, but saved his life. Jumbo took the locomotive head on.

After two seasons of touring Jumbo's remains, the stuffed animal was donated to Tufts and was an immediate hit and was swiftly adopted as the college mascot. Tufts coaches invoked his strength, bravery and innate sense of teamwork (for saving little Tom Thumb), school songs were written in his name, clothes, caps, periodicals, banners and countless other college items were adorned with his image. It became a tradition to pop pennies in his trunk in the hopes that good luck would come for a sports competition or final exam.

On April 14, 1975, faulty wiring ignited a fire that consumed Barnum Hall and most of what once lay within, including Jumbo's hide. Phyllis Byrne, the athletic department's administrative assistant got a peanut butter jar and gave it to a man named George Wilson, who was on the maintenance staff. Phyllis said to him, "I want you to get me some of Jumbo's ashes up there. He's our mascot and we ought to save these ashes." George came back later with a jar filled with the ashes, be they Jumbo's no one knows for sure. Since 1975, teammates have rubbed the 14-ounce Peter Pan Crunchy Peanut Butter jar for good luck.

California Maritime Academy Keelhaulers
The school's trademark is preparing students for a variety of nautical careers. Keelhauling was once a common punishment in the British and Dutch navies. In practice, an insubordinate sailor would be tied to a rope and dragged under the barnacle-encrusted keel of the ship, from one side to the other. If he survived the experience, he'd be humbled and weary – just as Cal Maritime hope to leave their opponents after games.

Quest University Kermodes
Quest is located in Squamish, British Columbia, Canada. The Kermode bear is also known as the "spirit bear" (particularly to the Indian tribes of Alaska), and is a subspecies of the American Black Bear living in the central and north coast of British Columbia. It is noted because ten-percent of their population has white or cream-colored coats. Because of their ghost-like appearance, "spirit bears" hold a prominent place in the mythology of the Canadian First Nations and American Indians of the area (it is known to the indigenous population as *Moksgm'ol*).

Virginia Military Institute Keydets
VMI used several nicknames including the Flying Squadron but by the mid-30s Keydets was in full use. As the "West Point of the South" its students are known as "cadets" and the Keydet name might be a Southern pronunciation of that name, or, was the word used to denote the gray color of the standard uniform of VMI's students. No one knows for sure.

California Lutheran Kingsmen
This name was selected in 1961 to show that the students were "King's Men," in other words, children of Christ. The women's teams are called Regals.

Fleming College Knights

Sir Sandford Fleming, (1827-1915) was a Scottish-born Canadian engineer and inventor, known for proposing worldwide standard time zones and is responsible for a huge body of surveying, map making and engineering. His accomplishments were well known worldwide, and in 1897 he was knighted by Queen Victoria.

Lethbridge Kodiaks

The nickname, Kodiaks, is for the Kodiak bear, the largest species of brown bear that is also known as the Alaskan grizzly bear or American brown bear that occupies the islands of the Kodiak Archipelago in South-Western Alaska.

Coe Kohawks

The word "Kohawk" was derived from a local Indian language where "ko-" means "like" or "similar to." Since the University of Iowa Hawkeyes were nearby and commonly known as the Hawks, Coe College teams were called by the "Like Hawks" name, or, "Kohawks."

Grand Valley State Lakers

When the school was about to enter into intercollegiate athletics in 1965 a nickname was needed. The student were given six choices from which to vote: Bruisers, Warriors, Bluejays, Ottawas, Archers and Voyagers. The winning entry was Lakers, a dark-horse, write-in candidate and finished 11 votes ahead of second place Voyagers.

Longwood Lancers

Longwood is unique among public universities for their adoption of a patron saint, Saint Joan of Arc who is said to both protect and inspire Longwood students. The university's two depictions of Joan are *Jeanne d'Arc,* (known affectionately as "Joanie on the Stony"), is an 1870 plaster statue and the 1915 bronze *Joan of Arc* equestrian statue ("Joanie on the Pony"). Joanie on the Stony is said to bring good luck for tests to students who touch her on their way to class while Joanie on the Pony, with her knight's armor and sword, acts as Longwood's protector. On the night of the Great Fire of 2001, Joanie turned bright red from the intense heat of the flames that stopped directly before her.

The Lancers nickname was formerly represented as a medieval Knight but that allusion has changed over time to something more symbolic with a horse (an allusion to the St. Joan equestrian statue) and lance motif.

Western Illinois Leathernecks

WIU is the only public school in the nation that has permission from the United States Marine Corp to use their official seal and mascot along with the Leathernecks nickname. The school's mascot is an English Bulldog named Colonel Rock, or Rocky, named for Ray "Rock" Hanson, a WIU athletic director and ex-Marine.

Montana State-Northern Lights

The school's name lent itself to use the "Lights" cognomen (Northern Lights). The northern lights are also known as the *aurora borealis*, named after the Roman goddess of dawn, Aurora, and the Greek name for the north wind, Boreas.

Columbia Lions

The university was originally chartered as King's College in 1754 by King George II of England and a lion is depicted on the English coat of arms. Only after the American Revolution was King's College renamed Columbia University.

Georgian Court Lions

The university is located on the former George Jay Gould Estate (George was the son of railroad magnate Jay Gould), Georgian Court. Gould died of pneumonia on May 16, 1923 after contracting a fever in Egypt after visiting the tomb of Tutankhamen. After his death his heirs sold the estate to the Sisters of Mercy who have retained much of the manor and gardens. Included on campus are several lion statues (most prominently on the gates to the university) and for that reason Lions is the athletic team's nickname.

Loyola Marymount Lions

The Lions nickname has been synonymous with LMU for more than 90 years. The Lion was suggested by an enthusiastic fan in 1919 when St. Vincent's College became Loyola College. Noting the football team's fierce competitiveness, that unknown fan described the Loyola players as "Lions." The name didn't generate much popularity and the team's nickname remained Loyolans until 1923.

Noting the success of nicknames for other colleges, the college opted to give Lions a rebirth. Calling the old Lion mascot "mistreated and forgotten," the school decided that the Lion would officially find its way into all college songs and cheers. The Lion has remained firmly entrenched in Loyola lore to this very day.

Another version traces the nickname to the abundance of actual mountain lions which roamed Westchester where Loyola College moved to in 1927. School officials reportedly adopted the nickname because mountain lions inhabited the area when ground was broken.

Piedmont Lions
In 1917, Piedmont's athletic teams became the Owls and the name lasted until 1921 when the Student Association adopted the name Mountain Lions, later shortened to Lions.

Baseball Hall of Famer, Johnny "Big Cat" Mize played at Piedmont in the 1930s and the athletic center and museum on campus is named for him.

Wabash Little Giants
On Oct. 25, 1884, Wabash played the first intercollegiate football game in Indiana's history as Jesse Taber's four field goals guided a 4-0 victory over Butler at Indianapolis Baseball Park. Since 1890 Wabash has played in the nation's oldest rivalry against DePauw in the Monon Bell game.

The Little Giants nickname didn't come about until 1904. During the 1890s and 1900s, Wabash had a history of playing schools with much larger enrollments. They often took on teams like Michigan State, Notre Dame, Indiana and Purdue. After one game, former Wabash coach Francis Cayou told the team they played like "Little Giants" and a newspaper reporter overheard the phrase and from then on the moniker became Wabash's nickname.

New Mexico Lobos
New Mexico began playing football in 1892, and its teams were called The University Boys or Varsities. By 1917, students were seeking a nickname and the student newspaper solicited suggestions but none gained much support.

In 1920, the Student Council met to recommend that a mascot be chosen and George S. Bryan, a student manager of the football team, suggested the Spanish word for wolf: "lobo." Bryan's suggestion received a strong and favorable response and the student newspaper wrote: "The Lobo is respected for his cunning, feared for his prowess, and is the leader of the pack."

Texas Longhorns
UT takes their nickname from the Longhorn cattle that were an important part of the development of Texas, and are now the official "large animal" of the state. The Longhorn nickname appeared in Texas newspapers by 1900.

Henry Pitts came up with the famous "Hook 'em Horn" sign and showed it to UT cheerleader Harley Clark three days before the 1955 TCU game. At the pep rally the night before the game Clark sold the student body on the symbolic approximation of the horns of Longhorn. "A lot of my friends thought it would be too corny, but I thought it was perfect," Clark would later recall.

Amherst Lord Jeffs
The town of Amherst and the school found within are both named after Lord Jeffery Amherst, a highly decorated British general who helped win Canada from France during the French and Indian War.

Kenyon Lords
Lord Kenyon of England was an early benefactor of the school. The women's teams are known as the Ladies.

California-Humboldt Lumberjacks
Humboldt's main campus is situated on Preston Hill overlooking Arcata with commanding views of Humboldt Bay and the Pacific Ocean and nestled at the edge of a coast redwood forest, long an economic staple of the region.

Stephen F. Austin Lumberjacks
The nickname was chosen in 1923 at an assembly held shortly after the institution officially and was found appropriate for a university in the pine woods of Deep East Texas.

Mount Holyoke Lyons
Mount Holyoke was originally founded in 1837 by Mary Lyon and the school's athletic teams use Lyons in her honor.

Wheaton Lyons
In 1834, Eliza Strong, the daughter of Judge Laban Wheaton, died at the age of thirty-nine. The Judge's daughter-in-law persuaded him to memorialize his daughter by founding a female seminary. The family called upon noted women's educator Mary Lyon for assistance in establishing the seminary. Miss Lyon created the first curriculum with the goal that it be equal in quality to those of men's colleges. The school uses the Lyons nickname in homage to Mary Lyon and she is the only person for whom two college team's nicknames are directly derived (see *Mount Holyoke Lyons*).

Yeshiva Maccabees

New York City's Yeshiva University is the oldest institution of higher learning in the United States that combines Jewish scholarship with studies in the liberal arts.

In 168 BC, the Maccabees began a successful Jewish revolt against the Syrian Greek king Antiochos who wanted to transform Judaism into just another Greek religion. His army ransacked the Temple and installed alters to the Greek gods. Following Antiochus' decree outlawing Judaism, the Hasmonean family, headed by Mathias and his son Judah the Maccabee, led the revolt against Antiochus.

After many battles, the smaller Maccabee army liberated Jerusalem and the Temple, restoring the ability of the people to practice Judaism. The Holiday of Chanukah celebrates this historic story of "the few defeating the many."

Lemoyne-Owen Magicians

Originally called the Mad Magicians for their trickery in a 1934 football game, a magician's top hat and wand serves as the athletic team's logo.

Millsaps Majors

Reuben Webster Millsaps attained the rank of Major during the Civil War and returned home to the tiny hamlet of Pleasant Valley in southwest Mississippi after the war where he had an accomplished career in business, finance and church leadership. In 1890 he made a gift of $50,000 toward the establishment of "a Christian college within the borders of our state." The school would come to be known as Millsaps College and the Major devoted the rest of his life in support of the school and its mission and lives on in the school's nickname.

Goshen Maple Leafs

The Maple Leafs name was chosen because the city of Goshen is known as "The Maple City."

Mitchell College Mariners

Historically known as the "Pequots" after the Native Americans indigenous to the area, Mitchell's teams changed to Mariners in 2008 to comply with the NCAA mandates.

Roanoke Maroons

Roanoke has two sets of school colors; blue and gold are used for academic use while maroon and gray are used for athletic use. This divergence dates to 1907 when the baseball team needed new uniforms but could not find any in blue and gold so maroon and gray uniforms were purchased as a substitute. Within a few years, maroon and gray were adopted as Roanoke's official athletic colors and for the school's athletic name as well.

Mercy Mavericks
At the school's inception in 1950 the athletic teams were called the Flyers with an eagle used as a mascot. Over time, the eagle was phased out although the name Flyers continued on until 2007 when the nickname was officially changed to the alliterative Mavericks.

Nebraska–Omaha Mavericks
Prior to 1939, Nebraska-Omaha's teams were known as the Cardinals and from 1939-71 they were called Indians. A 1971 resolution called for UNO to discontinue use of the name 'Indian' for its athletic teams and to abolish "Ouampi" as a school mascot. Mavericks was chosen in the Indians place with a bull for a mascot, an allusion to Omaha's Union Stockyards (once the world's largest) and for the fact that four of the five major meatpacking companies in the United States were once located in Omaha.

North Texas Mean Green
Originally called the Eagles, in 1966 the football team's defense (that included future Hall of Famer Joe Greene) was nationally respected. The wife of the sports information director yelled the nickname "Mean Green" at a game in reference to Greene and quickly caught on. The name was heavily emphasized in the 1970s when "Mean" Joe Greene was playing for the Pittsburgh Steelers.

United States Naval Academy Midshipmen
"Midshipmen" is a term for students training to become naval officers. The term has English roots that date back to the 17th century describing men who were stationed in the middle of a ship while on duty and for boys who served on ships as an apprentice.

Besides Midshipmen, Navy's athletic teams are sometimes referred to as the "Mids." The term "Middies" is sometimes used, but Academy officials are quick to point out that it is inappropriate.

Navy uses a billy goat as a mascot with the first making his debut at the fourth Army-Navy game in 1893. Bill the Goat, long a target of Army kidnappers, receives special treatment at the annual Army-Navy game. Instead of riding a 'goat' wagon, Bill is often escorted in limousines, luxury vans and fancy floats to the stadium. The direction that Bill stands has a special significance at Navy games as tradition mandates that the goat keepers keep Bill pointed towards their opponent's end zone at all times so that the Navy quarterback will know where to lead his team.

Massachusetts Minutemen
Originally known as the Aggies, the cognomen was supplanted by Redmen early in the 20th Century and lasted until 1972 when the name was deemed derogatory.

A poll of the student body resulted in Minutemen being chosen. The nickname has a historical relationship with the Commonwealth as it honors the famous Massachusetts patriots who were said to be armed and ready to fight the British for independence at a moment's notice.

Whitman Missionaries
The college is named after the missionary, Marcus Whitman, who immigrated to the area in the 1830s. Marcus and his wife, Narcissa (she was the first European-American woman to cross the Rocky Mountains in 1836), died in the Whitman Massacre at their mission site near present day Walla Walla, Washington.

Florida Southern Moccasins
Prior to 1926 Florida Southern's teams were known simply as the "Southerners." The moccasin, or water moccasin is a venomous species of pit viper found in the southeastern United States.

University of Tennessee-Chattanooga Mocs
Faced with politically sensitive Native American issues the school embarked on a new identity program in 1996. Moccasins had been used as a nickname with a snake image until the 1920s when an Indian took over (for a short while in the 1980s a moccasin shoe was used).

The UTC Athletics Department changed its nickname and logos in 1997 to a package using railroad images and the nickname "Mocs," short for "Mockingbird," a fiercely territorial creature which protects their homes with courage, determination and skill.

Old Dominion Monarchs
For many years, the athletic team of the Norfolk Division of the College of William & Mary (as Old Dominion was formerly called) were known as the Braves, a

derivative of the William & Mary nickname, the Indians. As Old Dominion achieved its own four-year status it was no longer suitable to have its teams called the Braves.

The nickname "Old Dominion" was first coined to the Virginia colony by King Charles II after Virginia's loyalty to the crown during the English Civil War. Furthermore, William III & Mary II, whose patronage helped found the College of William & Mary in Virginia in 1693, ruled England at the invitation of Parliament as "joint monarchs."

St. Josephs Monks

In 1970 Christopher Kiernan was hired to be the Director of Admissions and the Director of Athletics. Kiernan was charged to start a varsity sports program with no budget. The first big problem he faced was getting uniforms. Having spent time at Assumption College, Kiernan knew that Assumption Prep was about to close its doors, so he called the school and asked if he could have their team uniforms. Assumption Prep sent Kiernan the uniforms and on them was the prep school's nickname: "Monks." So, from that point forward, the Saint Joseph's teams have been known as the Monks.

Southwestern Moundbuilders

In the early 1900s, the town of Winfield tried to become famous for building a huge mound of rocks. The effort at fame soon ran out of steam, as the mound reached only 20 feet in height. But the mound can still be found on Southwestern's campus and is cause for their nickname. Since 1927, a ceremony has been repeated every September as each student and faculty member, as well as clubs and organizations, place one stone on the mound. Often, the rocks are carved or painted to represent the person or organization placing the rock.

The school's mascot is the "Jinx," a black cat and its legend began in the early 1900s. Celebrating an easy victory over arch-rival Fairmount College (now Wichita State University), the students of Southwestern placed a tombstone on campus with a picture of a black cat and the final score of that season's game: 41-3. For the next 14 years the "jinxed" stone stood in defiance as the Moundbuilders won every game against Fairmount.

After years of trying, the Fairmount players snuck down to Southwestern's campus and stole the tombstone and used dynamite to blow it up in a nearby field. The next game all players for Fairmount kept a piece of the stone with them for luck. When Southwestern once again won the game, the frustrated Fairmount players threw down their pieces of the "jinxed" stone and left the field. Southwestern students picked up the pieces and hid them in various places around Southwestern's campus where they remain hidden today.

Lehigh Mountain Hawks

In reference to the Lehigh Railroad, Lehigh's teams were known as the Engineers until the 1995-1996 academic year. In November 1995, the school introduced the Mountain Hawk as a mascot citing Lehigh's lack of a character to personify its sports teams. Despite objections from many alumni, in 1996 a vote of the Student Senate made the Mountain Hawks nickname official.

Appalachian State Mountaineers

Appalachian State is located in the Blue Ridge Mountains of northwestern North Carolina, and has one of the highest elevations of any university in the United States east of the Mississippi River, at 3,333 feet.

Berea Mountaineers

Berea College is located in Berea, Kentucky in the Outer Bluegrass Region and on the border of the Cumberland Plateau. The area has a mountainous appearance and from that terrain the college takes its nickname.

Eastern Oregon Mountaineers

EOU's location in the city of La Grande, Oregon (Mount Emily is the symbol of the city) in the heart of the Blue Mountain range between Portland and Boise and stands 2,785 feet above sea level.

West Virginia Mountaineers

The WVU Mountaineer nickname first appeared in the 1936-37 school year in reference to Morgantown's proximity to the majestic Appalachians.

Since 1972, John Denver's "Take Me Home, Country Roads" has been played before every home football game at Mountaineer Field. In 1980, Denver performed the song at the dedication of the new stadium.

Mansfield Mounties

Located in the Tioga River Valley, Mansfield's nickname is an allusion to the mountain surrounding the valley.

On September 28, 1892, just thirteen years after Thomas Edison invented the light bulb, Mansfield State Normal School and Wyoming Seminary played the first-ever football game under lights. The revolutionary idea of a night football game started with a group of students who had played on Mansfield's first football team in 1891. Eager to showcase their new sport, they proposed to play a night game at the Great Mansfield Fair.

After halftime, referee, Dwight Smith deemed it "inconvenient to continue" because the limited lighting and foggy conditions made the game too dangerous. The world's first night football game ended bitterly in a 0-0 tie.

Southern Arkansas Muleriders

The Muleriders take their name from the legend that in the early 1900s the football team had to ride mules to catch the nearest train 6 miles north of the college in order to reach out-of-town games.

Central Missouri Mules

In 1921, officials decided Normals and Teachers were no longer appropriate nicknames and a contest promised the winner a three-year postgraduate subscription of the school newspaper. The winning entry was submitted by John Thomason, '24, who felt that at least one Missouri team should be known as the "Mules."

The Jennies nickname for Central's women's teams was adopted in 1974 after the student newspaper offered a prize of $50 in a contest. Jennies was chosen because a mule is a descendant of a female donkey, the jenny.

Muhlenberg Mules

Some believe that the Mules nickname came about from the school's football players being referred to as the "hardest working animals in the Centennial Conference," when in truth, the nickname evolved from "Muhls," which newspapers used in headlines to save space when referring to Muhlenberg.

Indiana-Purdue Fort Wayne Mastodons

In 1968, farmer Orcie Routsong, decided to dig a pond on his property in a boggy area where nothing much grew and equipment got stuck. Excavators unearthed a large bone and realizing it could not have belonged to a horse or cow, Routsong contacted a number of people to see if anyone was interested. Nobody was. Then he reached Jack Sunderman, chair of the IPFW geosciences department, who asked, "How big is it?" When told it was about four feet long and six to eight inches across, Sunderman said, "I'll be right there."

IPFW geology students along with faculty members took over the dig and were able to locate about two-thirds of the skeleton as well as the skull of a baby mastodon nearby. Routsong graciously agreed to place the adult mastodon skeleton on permanent display at IPFW in the lobby of Kettler Hall.

Xavier Musketeers

Musketeers are most often associated with Alexander Dumas' novel, *The Three Musketeers*. In the novel a group of French musketeers named Athos, Porthos, Aramis and d'Artagnan stayed loyal to each other through thick and thin ("One for all and all for one!").

Xavier's Musketeer concept was based on the suggestion of the late Reverend Francis J. Finn, S.J., who proposed the name in 1925. Father Finn not only giving rebirth to a concept of chivalry that is among France's most treasured traditions, but he was also providing permanent recognition to Xavier's strong ties with French origins and culture.

Muskingum Muskies

The word "Muskingum" is derived from a similarly sounding Delaware Tribe word which translates (loosely) to, "Eye of the Elk." The Fighting Muskie nickname is used for its alliterative appeal.

Alaska-Fairbanks Nanooks

Changed from the Polar Bears to Nanooks (the Inupiaq word for polar bear) in 1963. According to the UAF website, a "nanook" is a vicious, daring creature that commands dominance wherever it finds itself.

Penn State Nittany Lions

Penn State's athletic symbol, chosen by the student body in 1906, is the mountain lion which once roamed central Pennsylvania. H.D. "Joe" Mason, '07, conducted a one-man campaign to choose a name after seeing the Princeton tiger on a trip with the Penn State baseball team to that New Jersey campus in 1904. Embarrassed that Penn State did not have a mascot, Mason fabricated the Nittany Lion on the spot and proclaimed that it would easily defeat the Princeton Bengal tiger. In 1907, he wrote in the student publication, *The Lemon*: "Every college the world over of any consequence has a college emblem of some kind—all but The Pennsylvania State College. Why not select for ours the king of beasts—the "Nittany Mountain Lion"?" The name was accepted by the student body without a vote.

Since Penn State is located in the Nittany Valley at the foot of Mount Nittany, the lion was designated as a Nittany Lion. In regional folklore, Nittany was a valorous Indian princess in whose honor the Great Spirit caused Mount Nittany to be formed.

New England Nor'easters
In common terms, a "nor'easter" is often used to refer to any strong rain or snowstorm that occurs in the northeast part of the United States, regardless of season, prevailing wind direction, direction of storm travel, or the geographic origin of the storm. Nor'easters are common in New England and for this reason the school chose it for their nickname.

Luther College Norse
The Norwegian Evangelical Lutheran Church opened Luther College in 1861 to supply ministers for Norwegian congregations in the Upper Midwest and these 'Norse' ties are still strong today.

Menlo Oaks
An oak tree is prominently featured on the school's seal.

Saint Olaf Oles
The nickname "Oles" is simply an extension of the school name while their mascot, St. Olaf the Lion, is taken from the school seal.

St. Olaf's traditional athletic rival is its crosstown neighbor, Carleton College. In football the two have been playing each other since 1919 in what has been dubbed the "Cereal Bowl" in honor of the Malt-O-Meal production facility that is located in Northfield. The annual winner receives the "Goat Trophy" (created by a St. Olaf carpenter in 1931) as well as the silver Cereal Bowl trophy. Northfield's Veterans' Memorial (located in Bridge Square) features an eagle that is turned to face the college that wins the annual match between the two schools.

The St. Olaf fight song, *Um Yah Yah*, is one of the few college songs to mention another college in its lyrics, which read in part...*Tonight Carleton College will sure meet its fate.*

Northern Alberta Institute of Technology Ooks
The Ooks nickname is short for "Ookpik," the Inuktitut word for Snowy Owl which is the official bird of Quebec.

Syracuse Orange
Previously nicknamed the Hilltoppers for the school's location on a hill, in 1931 a

Native American warrior known as "Nathan March," aka the "Saltine Warrior" became the athletic mascot. The warrior was called the "Saltine Warrior" because of the abundant salt deposits in the Syracuse area. The mascot remained for next four decades.

In 1978, the Saltine Warrior was banned by the university to eliminate Native American motifs. The mascot briefly morphed into a Roman warrior, but was eventually replaced (unofficially) in 1982 by a giant, cartoon-like Orange, named Otto. Otto the Orange was officially adopted by the university in 1995 over a wolf and a lion also under consideration.

The current nickname derives from the official color, chosen in 1890.

Colorado School of Mines Orediggers

Golden, Colorado was established in 1859 and served as the main supply center for miners and settlers in the area. In 1866, Bishop Joseph Cavazos of Massachusetts arrived in the territory and immediately saw a need for higher education and in 1873 the School of Mines opened under the auspices of the Episcopal Church. A year later the School of Mines was acquired by the territory and has been a state institution since 1876 when Colorado attained statehood.

Today, the Colorado School of Mines is a public research university devoted to engineering and applied science and is considered by many to be the world's foremost college of mineral engineering.

California-Monterey Bay Otters

The Cal-Monterey Bay campus overlooks the Monterey Bay that is home to many species of marine mammals, including sea otters, harbor seals, and bottlenose dolphin. The bay is also on the migratory path of Gray and Humpback Whales and is a breeding site for elephant seals. A popular saying on campus is, "There's nothing hotter than an otter!"

Florida Atlantic Owls

Even before construction of the Florida Atlantic campus began, the burrowing owl has been a presence on this Boca Raton location. At the dedication ceremony in 1964, President Lyndon Johnson even made reference to the presence of the bird. With the addition of intercollegiate athletics in the mid-1980s, the university used the bird as its nickname - an animal that denotes wisdom, determination and cognizance.

Temple Owls

The owl has been the symbol and mascot for Temple since its founding in the 1880s. According to Temple's website, the owl, a nocturnal hunter, was initially adopted because Temple began as a night school. Russell Conwell, Temple's founder, encouraged students with the remark: "The owl of the night makes the eagle of the day."

Furman Paladins

The Paladins, (aka the Twelve Peers) were warriors of Charlemagne's court and represent Christian valor against the Saracen hordes. Many of the paladin's exploits are largely fictional inventions, with some basis on historical 8th century events (such as the Battle of Roncevaux Pass).

Furman's nickname was first used by a sportswriter in the 1930s. For many years the name "Paladins" only referred to Furman's basketball team. Until 1961 the school's baseball teams were known as the Hornets and the football teams as the Hurricanes. That year, the student body voted to make "Paladins" the official nickname for all of the university's intercollegiate athletic teams.

Eastern Illinois Panthers

In 1930, the school's newspaper decided it was high time to have an official nickname. In conjunction with the Fox Lincoln Theatre, $5 worth of tickets was offered to the winner of a contest to name Eastern's athletic teams. Many nicknames were submitted including several with an Indian background (Kickapoos and Ellini) while several names associated with the school colors were also considered (Blue Racers, Blue Boys, Blue Battlers and Greyhounds). On October 16, 1930, it was announced that "Panthers" was the winner.

Pitt Panthers

According to the school's website, The Panther was adopted as Pitt's nickname at a meeting of students and alumni in the autumn of 1909. Said George M. P. Baird, '09, who made the suggestion, it was chosen for the following reasons:
1. The Panther was the most formidable creature once indigenous to the Pittsburgh region.
2. It had ancient, heraldic standing as a noble animal.
3. The happy accident of alliteration.
4. The close approximation of its hue to the old gold of the University's colors (old gold and blue), hence its easy adaptability in decoration.
5. The fact that no other school then employed it as a symbol.

Purdue University-North Central Panthers

In 2003, the Panthers nickname replaced Centaurs, a name that was chosen when the school opened in 1967.

Université du Québec à Trois-Rivières Patriotes

The team name honors the historical 19th century "Patriotes" and their movement that lead a rebellion for democracy and independence for Quebec (then called Lower Canada).

Cumberlands Patriots

Until 2001 Cumberland teams were known as the Indians.

Francis Marion Patriots

The university and it team's nickname are in honor of Francis Marion, an American Revolutionary War hero and Brigadier General. Acting with Continental Army and South Carolina militia commissions, he was a persistent thorn in the side of the British during their occupation of South Carolina in 1780 and 1781.

George Mason Patriots

George Mason IV was an American patriot, statesman and a delegate from Virginia to the U.S. Constitutional Convention. He, along with James Madison, is called the "Father of the Bill of Rights." For these 'patriotic' reasons he is considered one of the "Founding Fathers" of the United States.

St. Peter's Peacocks

The land on which Saint Peter's now stands was once owned by a man named Michael Pauw, whose last name means "peacock" in Dutch.

The peacock is considered to be a symbol of rebirth, much like the phoenix. For Saint Peter's, it is a reference to the closing and reopening of the college in the early 20th century.

Dominican Penguins

According to Dominican's Sports Information Director, Brandon Davis, at one point Dominican's unofficial mascot was a lazy looking hound, ostensibly because a hound appears in the university's seal.

In the 1970s, as their athletics programs grew, the choice of nickname was put to a vote and Penguins won easily. The nickname is a playful reference to the

Dominican Sisters who founded the College (now University) — nuns are often called "Penguins" because of their classic black and white habits.

Youngstown Penguins

Both accounts of how the Penguins nickname came to be come from the same cold Ohio night, January 30, 1933, when the Youngstown's men's basketball team was playing at West Liberty State. At the time Youngstown had no nickname.

At the game a spectator said the team looked like Penguins as they stomped the floor and swung their arms because of the cold temperature inside the gym. The second account states that, on the way to West Liberty State, with roads adrift with snow, passengers in Bennett Kunicki's car were discussing possible nicknames. Penguins was brought up and was well received by everyone in the car. The name was mentioned to members of the team at the gym that evening, and they thought it was perfect. The nickname was unanimously accepted by the student body without a formal poll and was formally introduced in the campus newspaper, on Dec. 15, 1933.

Southern New Hampshire Penmen

The Penmen cognomen is designed to evoke memories of the spirit of the hardy New England colonials. Since the university was founded as New Hampshire College of Accounting and Commerce, the quill, or pen used by colonial accountants became the "staff" of the Penmen character. The figure today is a classic revolutionary war character charging forward holding an American flag.

Elon Phoenix

In the 1930s Elon's teams were dubbed the Fightin' Christians. When transitioning to NCAA Division I in 1999 a new nickname was needed and Phoenix was chosen in reference to a 1923 fire that nearly destroyed the entire campus. Like the mythical Phoenix, soon after the fire the university trustees began planning to make Elon "rise from the ashes."

Wilson College Phoenix

Founded in 1869 and a women's institution throughout its long history, the school nearly closed its doors in 1979 and only a lawsuit organized by students, faculty, parents and an extremely loyal alumnae association succeeded in allowing the college to remain open (it is one of the few colleges to survive a scheduled closing). Subsequent to the near-closing, the school adopted Phoenix as its nickname to symbolize the college's survival.

Wisconsin-Green Bay Phoenix

As UW-Green Bay prepared to graduate its first class of seniors in 1970 many thought it was time to cut ties with the parent campus in Madison and to jettison the school's first-year sports emblem, a water-skiing Bucky Badger.

The student newspaper ran a contest and campus lore has it that with more than a wee bit of voter fraud, the winner was not Phoenix, but Tomatoes. The newspaper's editor, Patrick Madden, '71, once confirmed the story. "The newspaper was running the election and on the last day before publication some guy came in with a sketch of a tomato he had made in blue ink on notebook paper." Madden re-touched the drawing so it could appear in the newspaper's official ballot. When Tomatoes squeaked to a 10-vote victory, Madden revisited the rule book and declared the entry had not met the requirements for a "reproducible drawing." The Tomatoes were out, and Phoenix was in.

Bethel College Pilots

Bethel is located in Mishawaka, Indiana along the banks of the St. Joseph River. From the early 1830s until 1846, river 'pilots' bore various commodities from upstream to a busy port at St. Joseph, where they were loaded onto lake boats for shipment to Chicago and elsewhere.

Portland Pilots

Variously known as the Cliffdwellers or the Columbias the school looked for a permanent name in 1935 and wanted something suitable given the campus' proximity to the Willamette River. According to legend, the original nickname students chose in a contest was Chinooks (after the Indian tribe that inhabited the area, and the largest of the salmon species in the Willamette River), however, Pilots was chosen by presidential sanction.

Louisiana State -Shreveport Pilots

Shreveport was established at the meeting point of the Red River and the Texas Trail. To do so the Red River needed to be cleared of a 180-mile logjam, the Great Raft, that had previously obstructed passage to shipping. The river was made navigable by Captain Henry Miller, commander of the Army Corp of Engineers and used a specially modified riverboat, the *Heliopolis*, to remove the logjam. Shreveport soon became a center of steamboat commerce.

Shreveport's teams were named for the riverboat pilots who were once common and were charged with safely escorting large ships, barges and other river traffic through the unfamiliar waters, in order to get the vessels to port.

Lewis and Clark Pioneers

In 1942 the school name was adopted after the Lewis and Clark Expedition (1804-1806). Meriwether Lewis and William Clark led the first United States pioneering expedition from what is now Hartford, Illinois to the Pacific Coast.

Platteville Pioneers

The Pioneers nickname was derived from the community of people the city of Platteville was founded on. The school has no mascot, much to the displeasure of some vocal students who started a Facebook page, 'The Letter P is NOT an Acceptable Mascot!'

Smith Pioneers

Smith was the first women's college to join the NCAA and the Pioneers nickname, chosen in 1986, is seen as a link from the college's pioneering alumnae to their counterparts today. The name also expresses the spirit of Smith students and the college's leadership role in women's athletics (the first women's basketball game was played at Smith in 1893).

Transylvania Pioneers

Transylvania means "across the woods" in Latin and the name stems from Transylvania University's initial founding within the heavily-forested region of western Virginia known as the Transylvania colony. The Transylvania Colony was founded in 1775 by Richard Henderson, who controlled the North Carolina based Transylvania Company, which had reached an agreement to purchase the land from the Cherokee in the Treaty of Sycamore Shoals. Frontier 'pioneer' Daniel Boone was hired by Henderson to establish the Wilderness Road going through the Cumberland Gap into central "Kentuckee," where he founded Boonesborough.

Tusculum Pioneers

In 1794, two years before Tennessee became a state, Presbyterian ministers Hezekiah Balch and Samuel Doak were ministering to the 'pioneers' of East Tennessee, which was then the southwestern frontier of the United States. They also strove to meet the educational needs of these Scotch-Irish settlers. In 1816, Samuel Witherspoon Doak (son of Samuel Doak) founded Tusculum Academy, the predecessor to Tusculum College.

Hamline Pipers

The Hamline Pipers nickname comes from the Grimm's Brother's version of the "Pied Piper of Hamelin" fairy tale. As the story relates; In 1284, while the town of Hamelin, Germany was suffering from a rat infestation, a man dressed in pied (multi-colored) clothing appeared, claiming to be a rat-catcher and the townsmen promised to pay him for his services. The man played a musical pipe to lure the rats with a song into the Weser River, where all of them drowned. Despite his success, the people reneged on their promise and refused to pay the rat-catcher who left the town angrily, but vowed to return seeking revenge.

Later, while the inhabitants were in church, he played his pipe yet again, this time attracting the children of Hamelin. One hundred and thirty boys and girls followed him out of the town never to be seen again.

Armstrong Pirates

Athletics began at Armstrong in the 1930s and its teams were known as the Geechees. In 1967 the school took the Pirates nickname before joining the NAIA.

East Carolina Pirates

ECU teams officially became the Pirates in 1934. Pirates have long been associated with the North Carolina coast and used the Outer Banks to evade capture. One of the most famous, Blackbeard, resided in the North Carolina coastal communities of Bath, Beaufort and Ocracoke and East Carolina's mascot is based on the description of Blackbeard.

Hampton Pirates

Looking south from Hampton's campus one gazes across the harbor of Hampton Roads, an area steeped in 400 years of American history and hundreds of historical sites including many pertaining to pirates.

Southwestern Pirates

The school was considered small time until World War II when it became formidable due to the sponsorship of a V-12 Navy College Training Program. The program gave Southwestern a pool of experienced and skilled players and at one time boasted seven former starters from Texas and varsity players formerly from Baylor. The Pirates nickname stems from the school's naval affiliation during the war.

Whitworth Pirates
Prior to 1926 the school's teams were referred to as the Presbyterians or the Preachers, based on the school's strong affiliation with the denomination. In 1926 the student body held a vote and nominations included Lynx, Spartans, Tigers, Bantams, Bobcats, Panthers, Huns and Trojans. But it was the student-athletes themselves who nominated Pirates and their preference carried the day.

Whittier Poets
Founded in 1887 by members of the Religious Society of Friends (Quakers), thanks to the generosity and efforts of local business leaders Washington Hadley and Aubrey Wardman. It was named after Friends poet, John Greenleaf Whittier.

Stevens Point Pointers
The earliest mention of a mascot at Stevens Point can be found in an 1896 newspaper article, not stating that the school had one, but encouraging the school to get one as "this seems to be the reason the other teams are winning." A "pointer" dog only seemed natural and the name has been used since at least the early 1900s.

Bowdoin Polar Bears
The tradition of the polar bear as a symbol for Bowdoin can be traced to the discovery of the North Pole on April 6, 1909, by 1877 graduate, Admiral Robert E. Peary. The college's color, white, also relates to the Arctic.

The polar bear was chosen as the nickname of Bowdoin College in 1912 at the annual banquet of the Bowdoin College Alumni Association. Admiral Donald B. MacMillan, '98, a member of the Peary expedition and present at the dinner, was asked to secure a polar bear on his next expedition to the Arctic. This he did on May 13, 1915, and shortly thereafter presented it to the college with the words, "May his spirit be the Guardian Spirit not only of Bowdoin Athletics but of every Bowdoin person."

The Class of 1912 presented a life sized sculpture of the polar bear to the college in 1937 and it now stands in front of the entrance to Sargent Gymnasium.

Ohio Northern Polar Bears
On March 16, 1923, Polar Bears officially replaced Goats as the Ohio Northern nickname. On that date, football player Anthony Muto stood up during a chapel service and nominated the Polar Bear because it was "big, strong and all white for purity." After some discussion, in a student vote, the Polar Bear defeated its

closest competition, the Wild Cat. As the student newspaper reported on March 23, 1923, "Hereafter, the teams of Northern will be designated as 'The Polar Bears,' and the official mascot will be our guide."

St. Mary-of-the-Woods Pomeroys

The Pomeroy nickname is in remembrance of 1921 graduate, Mary Joseph Pomeroy, SP, who served the college for nearly half a century as a student, teacher and administrator and advocated athletics and physical fitness.

Knox Prairie Fire

The Prairie Fire nickname was adopted in 1993 due to controversy surrounding the former name, the Old Siwash, a derogatory term used by European traders to refer to the local people.

The Prairie Fire refers to the annual spring burning of the prairie lands at Green Oaks. First conducted in the 1950s by Knox professor Paul Shepard, the burn protects prairie grasses from intrusions of woodland scrub and competition with "exotic" species that have been introduced to Illinois from other regions or countries.

Greensboro Pride

In 1992 the Greensboro College Pride became the school's new moniker replacing the 24 year-old Hornets.

Hofstra Pride

Hofstra's teams were known as the Flying Dutchmen until 2004 when the Pride took over, referring to a pair of lion statues on campus which became the school's athletic mascots in the late 1980s. The Pride nickname evolved from Hofstra's "Pride on-and-off campus" campaign that began in 1987 during the university's dramatic recovery and growth following a financial crisis in the 1970s.

Rowan University Profs

The nickname Profs (or Professors) is derived from the school's history as a teaching college, first as the Glassboro Normal School and then the New Jersey's State Teachers College. The current mascot is an owl named "Whoo RU."

Saint Joseph's College Pumas

In 1914 St. Joseph's changed its nickname from Cardinals to Pumas, a name occasioned by the fact that a puma had been reported in Jasper County (IN) where St. Joseph's is located.

Evansville Purple Aces

Prior to 1926 Evansville teams were known as the Pioneers. Sportswriter Dan Scism is credited with first using the name "Aces" in headlines at the suggestion of Evansville basketball coach John Harmon. "Coach Harmon suggested I call them the Aces because he was told by Louisville's coach that he didn't have four aces up his sleeve, he had five!"

St. Michael's Purple Knights

When George 'Doc' Jacobs arrived at Saint Michael's in the summer of 1947, he was given the charge of completely rebuilding the athletic program. At the time Saint Michael's athletic teams were referred to as the Hilltoppers. Jacobs felt a new identity was needed and put together a ballot with suggested nicknames for the student population to cast their vote. At a pep rally on November 22, 1947, Jacobs announced that "Purple Knights" was the winner of the election.

The name is fitting because St. Michael is regarded as the protector of the universal Church, and was invoked as the patron of the military orders of knights during the Middle Ages.

Penn Quakers

In 1682, James Duke of York (the future James II of England) awarded William Penn a large piece of his American holdings as payment for a debt. The land, a little something that would become Pennsylvania, was to be used by William to set up a colony for those of his religious belief - the Quakers.

As dissenters of the Church of England, the Quakers were persecuted and as devout pacifist they would not fight in England's wars nor pay taxes for military ventures. Believers in total equality they would not bow to any man or woman, not even a tip of the hat to the king and their allegiance was always questioned.

William Penn took his Quaker beliefs to his new land and founded Pennsylvania (aka Penn's Woods), planned Philadelphia and established a liberal government based on religious freedom.

Wilmington Quakers

Wilmington was established by Quakers in 1870.

Northwestern Ohio Racers

UNOH offers over 60 sports programs but their Racers nickname stems from their

High Performance Motorsports curriculum. UNOH is the only university in the nation to own a race track (Limaland Motorsports Park) and was the first university to offer scholarships for motorsports.

Louisiana-Lafayette Ragin' Cajuns

In the first 60 years of its existence the school changed its name three times but Bulldogs always remained the athletic team's nickname. In 1962, as an effort to "fire up" the football team, Coach Russ Faulkinberry called his team the "Raging Cajuns" since 95 percent of the football team was from southwest Louisiana and the nickname was officially adopted shortly thereafter. Within a few years the name was shortened to Ragin' Cajuns.

Wright State Raiders

Although the university is named after the Wright brothers, when the school was opened in 1967 a conscious decision was made not to make any allusions to flying machines of any sort (in deference to the nearby Dayton Flyers). A 1972 student contest determined WSU's colors (hunter green and gold) and the school nickname (Raiders). Legend says the colors came from the Green Bay Packers and the nickname from the Oakland Raiders.

Lincoln Memorial Railsplitters

Lincoln Memorial's Railsplitters nickname is the only one given in honour of Abraham Lincoln, a reference to Lincoln's own nickname of the "Rail Splitter," given to him at the Illinois State Republican Convention at Decatur on May 9, 1860, when Richard J. Oglesby, later governor of Illinois, and John Hanks marched into the convention hall with two fence rails placarded with, "Abraham Lincoln, The Rail Candidate for President in 1860." The nickname capitalized on Lincoln's humble beginnings. The moniker caught on at the national convention at Chicago, spread quickly over the North, and became a valuable campaign asset.

Hawaii Rainbow Warriors

Prior to 2000, the University of Hawaii's men's teams were all referred to as the Rainbow Warriors. In a controversial marketing strategy, the school changed its athletics logo to a stylized "H" and allowed each team to pick its own team name. The basketball, swimming, diving and tennis teams retained the Rainbow Warriors name while the baseball team adopted the Rainbows, and the football, golf, and volleyball teams chose Warriors.

The women's teams are called the Rainbow Wahine, "Wahine" being the

Hawaiian word for "women."

Loyola-Chicago Ramblers
Before the 1920s Loyola teams were known as the Maroon and Gold in reference to their uniform colors. In 1925 a contest was held to name the football team with the winning entry being "Grandees" in honor of St. Ignatius Loyola's Spanish origins. The name never caught on and was often assailed.

Because the football team travelled so extensively in 1926 it was said they, "rambled from state to state," and newspapermen dubbed the team "Ramblers," a name that is still used today.

Angelo State Rams
San Angelo (where Angelo State is located) has long been the center of the Texas wool and mohair industry and was the home of the Texas Sheep and Goat Raisers Association. A purebred Rambouillet ram (known for its wool) is the symbol of university.

Cornell College Rams
In 1949, Cornell offered a $5 prize to come up with a nickname to supplant Purples or Hilltoppers. A student came up with "Rams" and won the prize.

Cornell's football rivalry with Coe College dates to 1891, making it the oldest intercollegiate rivalry west of the Mississippi.

Fordham Rams
Fordham's football teams used to play before sellout crowds at the Polo Grounds and Yankee Stadium and in the mid-1930s boasted what might have been the greatest offensive and defensive lines in college history—the "Seven Blocks of Granite" that included Vince Lombardi. So popular was Fordham that when the Cleveland NFL franchise was formed in the '30s it took its nickname from the Fordham's Rams.

The Rams nickname was taken from a popular (if not somewhat loutish) cheer:
> *One-damn!*
> *Two-damn!*
> *Three-damn!*
> *Fordham!*

The "damn" was changed to "ram" in order to conform to the school's Catholic image.

Founded in the late 1850s, the *Fordham Rose Hill Baseball Club* played against St. Francis Xavier College in the first ever nine-man-team college baseball game on November 3, 1859 and is the all-time NCAA leader in baseball wins.

The team plays their home games at Houlihan Park at Jack Coffey Field, named after Jack Coffey, former baseball coach at the university who amassed 817 wins as a baseball coach. Coffey is the only player to play with both Ty Cobb and Babe Ruth in the same season (1918 Detroit Tigers and Boston Red Sox).

Philadelphia Rams

Initially called the Weavers, the Rams nickname has been in use since 1958. In 2007 the school unveiled a nine foot tall, 1,800 pound statue of a Ram in front of the Athletic and Recreation Center.

Drew Rangers

Drew has been nicknamed the "University in the Forest" because of the serenity of its wooded 186 acres and the "Rangers" nickname comes from that tranquil setting (a bear is used as a mascot).

St. Mary's Rattlers

Legend holds that St. Mary's football practice field had to be cleared of diamondback rattlesnakes on a regular basis and that may be true but it is not how St. Mary's got its Rattlers nickname. Brother Charles Kinskya thought "Rattlers" would be fitting because there was already a *Rattler Club* on campus.

Anderson Ravens

Formerly known as the Tigers, AU's nickname changed to the Ravens in 1937 when a contest was held. More than 130 names were submitted and Ravens was chosen for three reasons; one, the Raven is black and AU's school colors were black and orange. Two, the raven has its place in "Biblical history as it seems Elijah was fed by the Ravens" and three, the raven is aggressive, which would be how you would want your athletic teams to play."

Benedictine Ravens

Ravens was chosen because of the bird's association with St. Benedict, for whom the college is named. Legends state that a raven would bring Benedict food during his time as a hermit in the mountains near Subiaco, Italy and that a raven saved him from eating poisoned bread.

Rosemont Ravens

According to the school's website, Rosemont embarked on a massive strategic planning initiative during the 2008-2009 school year following the decision to transition to a co-educational institution. As part of its wider plan to emphasize and expand its enrollment, programs, and reputation, Rosemont announced a new athletic identity, the Rosemont Raven, to replace the Rosemont Ramblers (aka, a climbing rose), a name used since 1983.

Arkansas Razorbacks

The Razorbacks take their name from the feral pig of the same name and was inspired by former football coach, Hugo Bezdek, who referred to his players as "a wild team of razorback hogs." The student body voted to change the name of the school mascot (supplanting the Cardinals) in 1910.

Mississippi Rebels

When a contest was sponsored by the student newspaper to give a nickname to 'Ole Miss' teams, over 200 names were submitted. Suggested by Judge Ben Guider of Vicksburg, Rebels was one of five entries submitted to sportswriters for final selection. Of the 21 who responded, 18 chose "Rebels," a name with historical roots to the school for during the Civil War all of one company in a Mississippi regiment was made up of university students.

University of Nevada-Las Vegas Rebels

The Rebels nickname was given to UNLV because the school, emerging from the shadow of the University of Nevada-Reno, in effect "rebelled" against its bigger and older brother to the north.

The name "Runnin' Rebels" was coined in 1974 by then-Sports Information Director Dominic Clark but refers only to the UNLV men's basketball team.

McGill Redmen

Montreal's McGill first used the nickname Redmen in 1929 as "Red Men" and described its red uniforms. Research indicates that the name Redmen is derived from ancient times, when Celts were known as the "Red Men" because of their red hair.

McGill's women's teams adopted the nickname Martlets in 1976 and it is used in reference to the university shield, which includes three martlets. A martlet is a type of heraldic bird similar to the swallow, but has no feet. Since this mythical bird cannot land, it is in a state of perpetual flight, always soaring higher in the pursuit of higher learning.

Eureka Red Devils

In mid-January, 1925 the Eureka basketball team travelled to Illinois Wesleyan in Bloomington to play a game. A group of girls, including Madge Henrich, went to Bloomington to see the contest. Madge later recalled, "The team was warming up and they were wearing their bright red uniforms. As we watched them, somehow it occurred to me to say, 'They look just like little red devils!' The girls agreed with me and said I should suggest that name in the contest that was being conducted by our school newspaper, so I sent in the name, 'Mac's Red Devils.' I was surprised when the contest was over that I was declared the winner and received the prize of $5."

Cortland Red Dragons

In 1919 the school burned down to the ground and when the Red Dragons nickname was adopted in 1933 it was a roundabout allusion to the fire.

Oneonta Red Dragons

Even Oneonta's Sports Information Director, Geoff Hassard, is unsure of the Red Dragons' beginnings at Cortland. "Unfortunately, I've never been given a solid answer to that question myself. I can tell you that there are only two Red Dragon mascots in the entire country (the other being Cortland) and we both compete in the same conference. There is a story about how our first 'real' athletics director graduated from Cortland and just brought the name with him. There is also a story about how the original student newspaper was called the *Pen Dragon* and that our nickname evolved from there."

Marist Red Foxes

In 1961 Marist's athletic director, Brother William Murphy, decided to organize a varsity basketball team which would play against other schools and thought a nickname would be appropriate. While glancing at a sports catalog, he noticed a Reynard (a red fox) on the cover of the book and decided this furry little creature, indigenous to the Hudson Valley where Marist is located, was to become the nickname, mascot and logo of all Marist College teams.

Ripon Red Hawks

Early Ripon College teams were referred to as the Crimson or Crimson and White and in the late 20s and early 30s the term Redmen gained usage. Native

American imagery began to be used extensively and in the 1950s and an Indian head logo was adopted. When women's varsity sports were started, some felt the Redmen name was not only discriminating to Native Americans, but to women as well (who were called the Red Women).

In 1990 college officials dropped the Indian mascot and changed Redmen to Red Men for men's teams and the Lady Red for women's teams. The name evolved in 1991 to "The Red" or simply "Red" but this was met with displeasure by students, many of whom wondered what a "Red" *was*.

Recognizing the discontent, a task force was created to discuss the naming and logo issue. More than 1,000 name suggestions were provided and from that list, Red Hawks, Thunder Blaze, Redbirds and Red Devils emerged as top contenders, with Red Hawks finally being recommended by the committee and approved by the college president in 1994.

Carthage Red Men

When Carthage's Redmen nickname was deemed offensive to Native Americans, in accordance to the 1920 origin of their nickname—the team's red jersey—the school changed their nickname to Red Men and removed any possible controversial connotations.

Northwestern College Red Raiders

The Red Raiders nickname was previously used in reference to Native Americans but now connotes images of their school color.

Deb Remmerde, a 2008 NC graduate and the NAIA women's basketball Player of the Year in 2006 and 2008, holds the record for most consecutive in-game free throws made with 133, the most in competition at any level — high school to professional, men's or women's.

Texas Tech Red Raiders

While looking for a nickname in1925 the wife of the first football coach suggested "Matadors" to reflect the influence of the campus' Spanish architecture. Tech soon chose red and black for school colors to represent a matador's garb.

Two stories exist as to how the name "Red Raiders" replaced its predecessor. In one, football coach Pete Cawthon ordered scarlet uniforms to help the team's identity. The football team, wearing its new outfit, defeated heavily-favored Loyola Marymount in Los Angeles on October 26, 1934 and a Los Angeles sportswriter called the Matadors a "red raiding team." In the other tale, a sports columnist, reporting on a 1932 Tech football game, wrote: "The Red Raiders from

Texas Tech, terror of the Southwest this year, swooped into the New Mexico University camp today." In either case, the name soon became popular and by 1936 it officially replaced Matadors.

Saint John's Red Storm
During the early years St. John's teams were known as the Johnnies. In the 1920s Redmen was first used and came about when a reporter used the term after the football team took the field clad in all red uniforms.

The Redmen evolved into a nickname that used Native American symbols and in 1994, under mounting pressure to adopt names more sensitive to Native American culture, the Red Storm name was chosen.

Arkansas State Red Wolves
In honor of the Osage Nation that inhabited the area until the 1800s, the nickname 'Indians' was officially designated in 1931 and had been presaged by Aggies, Farmers, Gorillas and then Warriors.

On January 31, 2008, Arkansas's Mascot Selection Steering Committee decided to use the Red Wolf as a nickname and mascot and officially retired the Indian nickname during the last home basketball game of the season.

Illinois State Redbirds
In 1923, athletics director Clifford E. "Pop" Horton and *Daily Pantagraph* sports editor Fred Young collaborated to change the university's nickname from the Teachers. Horton lobbied for Cardinals because the colors were cardinal and white (chosen in 1895-96) but Young changed the nickname to Redbirds to avoid confusion with the St. Louis Cardinals baseball team.

Henderson State Reddies
Early Henderson publications refer to the players as "Red Jackets" or "Red Men" because of the color of the football team's uniform. By 1908, newspaper writers were referring to them simply as "Reds" and it is believed that the name Reddies name was applied because it easily fit into pep songs and yells.

Seattle Redhawks
In 1938 the school's nickname switched from the Maroons (after a school color) to the Chieftains, and in 2000 the university transitioned to the Redhawks to comply with NCAA sanctions concerning the use of Native American names and imagery.

Maryland-Baltimore County Retrievers
The Chesapeake Bay Retriever, the state dog of Maryland, has been the nickname of the UMBC athletic team's nickname since the inception of the school in 1966.

University of Ontario Institute of Technology Ridgebacks
Known for its bravery, the Rhodesian Ridgeback is a breed of dog developed in Southern Africa where it was used (among other things) to hunt lions. In the earlier parts of its history, the Rhodesian Ridgeback has also been known as Van Rooyen's Lion Dogs, the African Lion Hound or African Lion Dog because of their ability to distract a lion while awaiting their master to make the kill.

Lowell River Hawks
The nickname River Hawks came about during the school's transition into UMass-Lowell in 1991, and was inspired by the campus' location alongside the Merrimack River. Prior to 1991 Chiefs was used but when it was deemed unacceptable for its use of Native American imagery a campus-wide vote favored River Hawks over Ospreys and Raging Rapids.

Metropolitan State Roadrunners
The Roadrunner has been the school's nickname since 1974 when it replaced Mustangs. Students acquired the "Roadrunners" nickname to describe how they were often seen dodging traffic on campus to get to and from classes.

Slippery Rock The Rock
Prior to 1980 Slippery Rock's teams were known as the Rockets.

Toledo Rockets
When Toledo played the then-powerful Carnegie Institute of Technology in football on September 29, 1923, Pittsburgh sportswriters were surprised to learn that UT did not have a nickname although Blue and Gold and Munies were sometimes used. In the game, Toledo fought formidably, recovering a series of fumbles by favored Tech. Pittsburgh writers pressed James E. Neal, a UT junior pharmacy student and writer for *The Campus Collegian* who was working in the press box, to come up with a nickname for his school's team. Neal labeled the team "Skyrockets" as William B. Hook, who started as an unknown substitute guard and ended a hero, grabbed a Carnegie fumble out of the air and raced 99 yards for a touchdown. One of the sportswriter remarked that Hook looked more like a rocket than a skyrocket as Carnegie Tech players failed to overtake him.

Other writers began using the name "Rockets" with quotation marks in their stories, but after one week the quotation marks were dropped and The University of Toledo's nickname remained the Rockets.

Université Laval Rouge et Or

French for "Red and Gold," the Université Laval was the first institution in North America to offer higher education in French. Its main campus is located in Quebec City, Quebec, the capital of the province.

CIS football began at Laval in 1996 and the school has won the Vanier Cup (Canadian championship) six times without losing. They are tied for the most Cup wins in history.

Palm Beach Atlantic Sailfish

When Palm Beach Atlantic College was founded, President Dr. Jess Moody remembered an incident from his youth about a fisherman who hooked a large prized sailfish. Young Moody took a picture of the fish and was thrilled to hear the fisherman's account of his feat. Dr. Moody presented the "Sailfish" at the very first Board of Trustees meeting and the Fighting Sailfish became a part of PBA history.

Saint Francis Saints

Saint Francis of Assisi was a Catholic friar and preacher. He founded the Franciscan Order, assisted in founding the women's Order of St. Clare and is one of the most venerated religious figures in history.

Southern Illinois Salukis

The lower part of Illinois, where SIU is located, has often been referred to as "Little Egypt" because it is rich like the Nile delta and many towns in the area have Egyptian names (including Cairo, although it is pronounced Ka-ro). From 1913 to 1951 SIU athletic teams were simply known as the Maroons after one of the school colors. That year students and faculty voted to change the rather bland nickname to Salukis, a hunting dog, similar to a greyhound or whippet, whose origins can be traced back to the royalty of Ancient Egypt.

South Carolina-Beaufort Sand Sharks

When UCSB decided to pursue membership in the NAIA in 2007 it went in search of a nickname and logo and through a rigorous selection process decided upon Sand Sharks. Sand Sharks are typically found near the bottom of shallow water

along tropical and temperate ocean coastlines, can grow up to 10 feet in length
and are known for their voracious appetites.

Southeastern Oklahoma Savage Storm
In December 2001, SOSU's president appointed a Mascot and Nickname Task
Force to evaluate the name of Southeastern's teams (the Savages), the mascot,
and logo. The task force received input from a number of university constituents
prior to making its recommendations and in 2006 the new nickname, Savage
Storm was unveiled.

Alfred Saxons
The town of Alfred received its name in honor of Alfred the Great, king of the
Saxons and it seemed only natural that the college would take the nickname,
Saxons. The mascot is a knight in shining armor.

Rutgers Scarlet Knights
Since its days when the school was officially known as Queen's College, the
athletic teams were referred to as the Queensmen. Officially serving as the
mascot figure for several football seasons beginning in 1925 was a costumed
representation of an earlier campus symbol, the Chanticleer. Though a fighting
bird, to some it bore the connotation of "chicken."

In the hope of spurring RU fighting spirit, a campus-wide selection process
changed the nickname to the Knights in the mid-1950s. The Scarlet-garbed
knight, riding a spirited white charger, came to represent a new era of campus
athletics.

The color scarlet was adopted in 1869. Originally, students desired the color
orange to commemorate the Dutch heritage of Rutgers, however, an orange flag
could not be found in the New Brunswick area. The students settled for an
available scarlet flag.

In the historic first collegiate football game ever played, on November 6,
1869, the Princeton team watched the Rutgers men don scarlet turbans and
kerchiefs for team identification.

St. Lawrence College Schooners
St. Lawrence is located in Brockville, Ontario, a city located on the St. Lawrence
River. In the 19th century, the town became a local center of industry, including
shipbuilding. "Schooners" was chosen as SLC's nickname due to the city's
historical roots to the sea. A schooner is a type of sailing vessel characterized by

the use of fore-and-aft sails on two or more masts with the forward mast being no taller than the rear masts.

Agnes Scott Scotties

The all-women's school is named in honor of the mother of the college's primary benefactor, Col. George Washington Scott and the Scotties nickname is derived for that same reason. Not surprisingly, the mascot is a Scottish Terrier named Irvine.

Alma Scots

Alma was founded by Michigan Presbyterians in 1886 and in keeping with its Scottish heritage the school's nickname was once the Fighting Presbyterians. Alma has stayed true to its roots by keeping its Scottish heritage alive. Not only is the school's current nickname, the Scots, but its marching band is clad in kilts and sponsors a Scottish dance troupe and a pipe band.

Salisbury Sea Gulls

The Sea Gull name evolved from when the university was known as Salisbury State College with their Golden Gulls nickname (chosen in 1948 by a "Name the Mascot" Contest). In 1963, due to the athletic teams often being referred to as SSC Gulls (C-Gulls), the name was changed to Sea Gulls.

Point Loma Sea Lions

In 2002, the school's nickname was changed from the Crusaders to the Sea Lions. The Sea Lions name is not in reference to traditional sea lions, however, but instead is represented by a roaring lion bursting from a wave befitting the school's location beside the Pacific Ocean in San Diego (CA).

Memorial University of Newfoundland Sea-Hawks

Located in St. John's, Newfoundland and Labrador, Canada, the university's teams were originally named the Beothuks, after the original inhabitants of Newfoundland. The name was eventually changed when it was deemed offensive.

Hawaii Pacific Sea Warriors

Mongooses were brought to Hawaii in the 1880s to eradicate rats which were destructive to sugar cane fields and Hawaii Loa's teams were called the Mongooses before switching to Sea Warriors in the early 1990s.

Alaska-Fairbanks Seawolves

The school's teams were once known as the Sourdoughs, a name taken from Alaskan prospectors who often used sourdough to make their bread. When transitioning to NCAA Division II in 1977 the name was changed to Seawolves.

The name "Seawolf" represents a mythical sea creature that, according to Tlingit Indian legend, brings good luck to anyone fortunate enough to view it.

Sonoma State Seawolves

The previous nickname for Sonoma State's teams was Cossacks, an eastern European community of fur traders known for superior horsemanship and ferocity in battle. The Cossacks held ties to the area through the 1812 fur trading posts at nearby Fort Ross. In 2002 the nickname was removed by a vote for being offensive because Cossacks were notorious for oppressing Jews and women.

Various new names were suggested such as the Rain Devils, Killer Bees, Blue Wave, Blue Storm and Condors as well as the Beagles in a nod to local legend and *Peanuts* creator, Charles M. Schulz. The final decision, by then president Ruben Arminana, was Seawolves, derived from the Jack London (who had ties to Sonoma County) novel entitled *The Sea-Wolf* in which the protagonist is pressed into service aboard a boat captained by a man named "Wolf."

Stony Brook Seawolves

When the Stony Brook Campus was located in Oyster Bay, the teams was known as the Soundmen or Baymen. When it moved to its present location, teams were initially known as the Patriots. In 1994 Stony Brook rose to NCAA Division I its nickname changed to its present Seawolves.

Florida State Seminoles

In 1947, students selected the name Seminoles (named for the Seminole tribe of American Indians) to represent their university and athletic teams. Since 1978 the name has been represented by Chief Osceola and his horse Renegade and the Osceola name is used with official sanction of the Seminole Tribe of Florida. The unconquered spirit of the Seminole people is a theme that is respected and represented through the athletic teams.

Nova Southeastern Sharks

Nova University teams had been known as the Knights since 1982 and when the school merged with Southeastern University in 1994 the combined Nova Southeastern kept the Knights name. When transitioning to the NCAA new branding was needed and a campus-wide contest settled on Sharks.

Wichita State University Shockers
Legend states that the name "Shockers" first appeared in 1904 on a poster advertising a football game between Wichita State (then Fairmount College) and the Chilocco Indians. The team's manager chose the name because many of the players earned money during the off season harvesting (or "shocking") wheat in the surrounding fields.

As for a mascot, students created WuShock – a big, bad, muscle-bound bundle of wheat – whose name was derived from a period in time when the university was simply known as Wichita University or WU.

Washington College Shoremen
Washington College is located in Chestertown, Maryland, on the Eastern Shore, from which the school's nickname is derived.

Chaminade Silverswords
The Chaminade nickname is of the rare silversword plant, indigenous to Hawaii and found on Haleakala, a dormant volcano on the Island of Maui.

Stonehill Skyhawks
In late 2002, the school's Strategic Planning Committee determined that Chieftains would no longer be used as it was disrespectful to American Indians. In 2003 the college held open forums in which students, alumni, and faculty were asked to submit ideas for the new identity, vote on suggestions, and gauge popularity. Among popular choices were The Summit, Skyhawks, Saints, Wolfpack, Crusaders, Mission, Shovelmakers and The Blizzard.

During the fall semester of the 2005 Skyhawks was officially adopted but not as a reference to a bird but instead as an homage to a type of airplane that Frederick Ames allowed to land on his property (what is now the main campus) during World War I. The mascot "Ace," however, is an anthropomorphic purple hawk wearing a scarf, goggles, bomber jacket, and aviator cap.

Tennessee-Martin Skyhawks
Tennessee-Martin's official nickname became the Skyhawks in 1995 for three distinct reasons. One, the first educational institution on the site of UT Martin was Hall-Moody Bible Institute and the school's athletic teams were called "Sky Pilots," a frontier term for preachers, but perhaps the students were thinking of

the glamorous flying aces of World War I. Two, during World War II, UT Junior College contracted with the Naval War Training Service to help train pilots, who completed their flight training at an airport located on the current site of Westview High School. Three, red-tail hawks are indigenous to the west Tennessee region.

"Captain" is the official name of UT Martin's costumed Skyhawk mascot, a mythical hawk dressed in goggles and a bomber jacket that flies a plane.

St. Louis Christian Soldiers
The SLCC "Soldiers" nickname is in reference to its students being "Soldiers of Christ."

Oklahoma Sooners
Before the state of Oklahoma adopted the nickname "The Sooner State" in 1908, the University of Oklahoma adopted "Sooners" for their football team after variously being called the Rough Riders and Boomers.

The Oklahoma Land Run of 1889 was the first land run into the Unassigned Lands and included all or part of seven counties. The land run started at high noon on April 22, 1889, with an estimated 50,000 people lined up for their piece of the two million acres that were available.

The Indian Appropriations Bill of 1889 was authorized by President Benjamin Harrison to open the two million acres for settlement. Due to the Homestead Act of 1862, signed by President Abraham Lincoln, legal settlers could claim lots up to 160 acres in size and receive title provided it was lived on and improved. The Unassigned Lands were considered some of the best unoccupied public land in the United States.

A number of the individuals who participated in the run entered early and hid out until the legal time to lay quick claim to some of the choicest homesteads. These people came to be identified as "Sooners."

Case Western Reserve Spartans
Before the schools merged, Case Tech used the nicknames Scientists and Rough Riders while Western Reserve teams were known as the Pioneers and the Red Cats. With the two schools joined as one they took the name Spartans.

Michigan State Spartans
In 1925, the institution changed its name to Michigan State College of Agriculture and Applied Science, and, as an agricultural school, its teams were officially

referred to as the Aggies and unofficially as the Fighting Farmers. Looking to move beyond its agricultural roots a contest to find a new nickname was held and "Staters" was chosen. A local sportswriter was not impressed and went in search of a more heroic name. Of the losing entries he settled on Spartans and started using it in articles. In time the name caught on and has been used ever since.

San Jose State Spartans
Due to the school's original designation as a teachers' college, SJSU's nickname changed many times before the school finally adopted Spartans as the official nickname in 1925. Prior names included the Daniels, Teachers, Pedagogues, Normals and Normalites.

South Carolina-Spartanburg Spartans
In the 1970s the school adopted the nickname "Spartan Rifles" to honor a local Revolutionary War militia unit. The name was shortened to Spartans in 2004.

Richmond Spiders
From 1876 to 1893, the school used the nickname Colts for its athletic teams because they played like an "energetic group of young colts." However, that changed during the summer of 1893 when an amateur baseball team comprised of University of Richmond athletes and some city residents was formed. Among the best players was pitcher Puss Ellyson, a young man with long, lanky arms and legs and a high kick. A writer for the RICHMOND TIMES-DISPATCH, Ragland Chesterman, was so impressed with the pitcher's physical shape and style of pitching that he compared him to that "clever, creeping insect," the spider. Soon the name was applied to the entire team and then to all of the university's athletic teams.

St. Mary Spires
Built in 1930 and named for Mother Mary Berchmans Carman, the first president of Saint Mary, the spire on Berchmans Hall is the prominent detail on the school's logo and can be found on the school seal.

Fairfield Stags
In 1947 the first Fairfield team (cross-country) was formed necessitating the need for a nickname. The university adopted Men in Red because of the school's predominant color. The following year the school asked the students for input in naming the athletic teams. Two recommendations were made to the Board of

Trustees for an official decision and Stags won out over Chanticleers.

The decision for the Board was an easy one to make for the school was part of the Dioceses of Hartford and the word "Hartford" means "stags" (hart) and "stream" (ford).

Oklahoma City Stars
OCU's teams had been known as the Chiefs from 1944 until 1999 when the Stars nickname was introduced.

Hobart Statesmen
Hobart's athletic teams became known as the Statesmen in 1936, when, following the football team's season opener against Amherst College the *New York Times* referred to the team as "the statesmen from Geneva" and the name stuck.

Delta State Statesmen
The Statesmen nickname is in honor after Mississippi State Representative, Walter Sillers Jr., House of Representatives Speaker for 20 years, who played a large role in having the university placed in Cleveland, Mississippi.

Culinary Institute of America Steels
According to the school's website; in the kitchen, a steel is used to sharpen a chef's most indispensable tool—the knife. Also known as a sharpening steel or honing steel, this vital instrument helps smooth out the roughness of the blade, leaving a nice straight edge for a better cut. Similarly, intercollegiate student-athletes on the CIA Steels hone their skills on the court or field, sharpen their work ethic and sense of teamwork, and become better people in their careers and lives.

Concordia Stingers
The Canadian Concordia was created with the 1974 merger of Loyola College (Warriors) and Sir George Williams University (Georgians) and a new nickname was needed to bring the schools together as one.

Lake Erie Storm
In the winter of 1994, LEC held a contest for a new nickname and called for submissions from the campus, surrounding community, as well as alumni. As a result of this contest Storm was chosen.

When LEC was still an all-women's college, the January, 1985 issue of *Playboy* featured the school as one of the top places to meet women.

Simpson Storm

Simpson used Redmen from around 1910 before switching to Storm in 1992 because their Native American imagery was deemed offensive.

Simpson College was founded in 1860 and was named and based on the beliefs of Methodist minister Matthew Simpson. Simpson is best known as the minister who spoke the last words at Abraham Lincoln's grave in Springfield, Ill.

Oglethorpe Stormy Petrels

According to nautical legend, the stormy petrel is a type of sea bird that roosts on ships when it senses bad weather is on the way and thus giving sailors forewarning. As to how the bird became connected with Ogelthorpe University, the story is based on lore. When crossing the Atlantic in 1732, university founder, James Ogelthorpe took a fondness for a petrel that landed on his ship and rode with him all the way to America.

Heidelberg Student Princes

Former alumni director Edwin Butcher was walking through downtown Tiffin one day when he noticed the marquee on the town theater promoting a movie titled *The Student Prince*. As Butcher would soon discover, the picture was about a prince who attended Heidelberg University in Germany and, after some time, overcame his shyness to thrive socially and academically.

After leaving the theater, Butcher began referring to the athletes at Heidelberg as "student princes," and the nickname was well received. First it appeared in campus publications then students and sports writers began using it. And finally the players came to view themselves as "Student Princes."

Arizona State Sun Devils

When the second Tempe Normal football team opened play in 1889, the student body chose Owls as their nickname. When the school became Arizona State Teachers College, Owls became Bulldogs. The student newspaper ran frequent appeals during the fall of 1946, urging the Bulldog to be replaced by the Sun Devil and on November 8, 1946, the student body voted 819 to 196 to make the change.

Indiana State Sycamores

In 1921 a contest was held to pick a name for the athletic teams at what was then called Indiana State Normal School. Until this time the term Fighting Teachers was frequently used in press accounts. In January, 1922, it was announced that the name Sycamores had won a popular vote of the student body, although there is some question as to how serious the students were in picking the name.

For a period of time in the 1950s and 1960s, there actually was a tree mascot but in 1969 a committee created the Chief Quabachi concept for the school. This Indian Chief (and accompanying legend) was used until 1989, when the university dropped its use because of its offensive Indian caricature. In 1995, students voted in a new mascot, Sycamore Sam - a unique blue and white animal.

North Carolina Tar Heels

One famous story about how the state of North Carolina received the nickname Tar Heels moniker is attributed to North Carolinians steadfastness in battle during the Civil War; because they stuck where General Lee placed them. The real story appears to run deeper.

In its early years as a colony, North Carolina settlements became an important source of the naval stores, including tar and pitch, for the English navy. Tar and pitch were largely used to paint the bottom of wooden British ships in order to both seal the ship and to prevent shipworms from damaging the hull. The vast production of tar from North Carolina led many, including Walt Whitman, to give the derisive nickname of "Tarboilers" to the residents of North Carolina, a name later changed to "Tar Heels."

In 1924 the school's mascot became a ram. That year, head cheerleader, Vic Huggins, decided Carolina needed a symbol. Two years earlier the Tar Heels football team had posted a brilliant 9-1 record with the star being a bruising fullback named Jack Merritt. Merritt's nickname was "the battering ram" and it seemed natural to Huggins to link a mascot with Merritt's moniker. Charlie Woollen, the athletic business manager at that time, agreed with the idea and gave us $25 to purchase a fitting mascot.

Rameses the First was shipped in from Texas and arrived just in time to be introduced at a pep rally before the VMI game. Although Carolina was a heavy underdog the Tar Heels battled the visitors to a scoreless tie. Late in the fourth quarter Carolina's Bunn Hackney was called upon to attempt a field goal. Before taking the field he stopped to rub Rameses' head for good luck and just seconds later his 30-yard dropkick sailed between the uprights, giving the Tar Heels a 3-0 victory and a legendary mascot.

Rollins Tars

Rollins was founded in 1885 by New England Congregationalists who sought to bring their style of liberal arts education to what was then the Florida frontier. Its athletic teams are called the Tars, an archaic name for sailors, and was used in relation to the pitch used to seal the hulls of ships.

University of Puerto Rico at Mayaguez Tarzans

Tarzan was popular because of Johnny Weissmüller's portrayal of the character in movies. Weissmüller's Tarzan exuded masculinity, courage and athleticism and for that reason it was chosen by Mayagüez University (one of the most successful Universities in sports in Puerto Rico) as its nickname and mascot. The women's teams are called "Janes."

University of Maryland Terrapins

Maryland Agricultural College used the nickname of the Aggies and the Farmers. The school was renamed the University of Maryland in 1920 and used Old Liners as a nickname (a reference to a Revolutionary War Troop of Maryland soldiers who distinguished themselves on the field of battle) until 1932. That year the school newspaper encouraged the creation of a new nickname and mascot. Football coach, Dr. H. C. Byrd, suggested a name that he was familiar with from his boyhood days in Crisfield, Maryland, on Chesapeake Bay.

Byrd's suggestion was the Diamondback Terrapin, a small snapping turtle found in brackish waters along the East Coast. Since the school newspaper was, by coincidence, already called *The Diamond*, it readily agreed that "Terrapins" would be a great name. The Class of '33 sealed the nickname deal when they raised money for the casting the statue of a Diamondback and presented it to the university as a graduation gift.

Bethany Terrible Swedes

In 1881 Rev. Dr. Carl Aaron Swensson founded Bethany College shortly after accepting a call from the Swedish Lutheran Church at Lindsborg. Bethany is located in Lindsborg, Kansas, a town of 3,400 people that actively preserves its Swedish heritage.

Since 1903, students and alumni have rallied Bethany athletic competition with the Rockar! Stockar! cheer, yelled in Swedish and based on Swedish mythology:

ROCKAR! STOCKAR! *(The jarl wore a coat and was on a log raft braving the*

perils of the Baltic)
THOR OCH HANS BOCKAR! *(Thor going ever forward with lightning speed, from pinnacle to pinnacle, driving his irresistible thunderbolts through all opposition)*
KOR IGENOM! KOR IGENOM! *(Hit that line! Hit that line!)*
TJO! TJO! TJO! *(A Swedish interjection, i.e. "whoopee")*
BETHANIA! *(Bethany!)*

Boston Terriers
During the 1917-18 academic year, students voted to make the Terrier the official school nickname.

The official school colors are White and Scarlet and the school's mascot is named Rhett the Boston Terrier, with "Rhett" in reference to *Gone With the Wind*, because "No one loves Scarlet more than Rhett."

Hiram Terriers
In 1928, after going without for several years, it was decided that a nickname would be a valuable addition to the school's athletic program. For a short time that season Farmers was used but quickly changed to Mudhens when the football team won three games played in mud and rain. A more permanent name was needed and on December 28, 1928, the nickname Terriers was adopted. The name came about when coach Herb Matthews, speaking at an all-sports banquet, described Hiram athletics as "a little bull terrier that holds on until the end." He paused for a moment in thought and then proclaimed, "No name would seem more appropriate to me than just the Terriers!"

Tarleton Texans
Tarleton's athletic history dates back to 1904 but no nickname existed before 1917 when the school joined the Texas A&M University System and athletic teams became known as the Junior Aggies.

In 1925 legendary coach and athletics director W.J. Wisdom was walking across campus one day and the nickname "Plowboys" (many of Tarleton's athletes then were agricultural students with rural and farming backgrounds) popped into his head and the name remained in place for over 35 years.

In 1961, a contest to come up with a nickname to reflect Tarleton's new status as a four-year institution. The top three vote-getters were Texans, Rockets, and Packrats with Texans winning handily. Tarleton's women's teams are known as the TexAnns.

The Purple Poo is a secret spirit organization that gathers to make Poo signs each Monday night. The signs appear on campus every Tuesday morning and are designed to promote school spirit. Poo members appear in public dressed in costume to conceal their identity and at commencement, graduating members will pass a purple pig to the university president as they cross the stage.

Southern Utah Thunderbirds
Formerly known as the Broncos, the Thunderbirds nickname was adopted in 1961 when the school began offering four year degrees. The Thunderbird is a Native American mythical creature whose name comes from the common belief that the beating of its enormous wings causes thunder and stirs the wind.

Miami-Middleton ThunderHawks
In 1997 Middleton's sister school, Miami University, did away with their Redskins nickname in favor of RedHawks due to the Oklahoma-based Miami Tribe withdrawing its support for nickname. At the same time Miami-Hamilton stopped using their Chiefs nickname and changed to Harriers, Middleton went with ThunderHawks.

Marshall Thundering Herd
Indians was the first nickname used by Marshall, bestowed upon the pre-1900 athletic teams. By 1910 the color of team uniforms caused Big Green to be used but few found it acceptable. When sportswriter Duke Ridgley referred to a late-1920s squad as a "Thundering Herd," after a then-current movie based on the 1925 Zane Gray novel of the same name, it caught on quickly. Both Thundering Herd and Big Green have been used in reference to Marshall ever since.

In 1933 sportswriter Doug Freutel started referring to Marshall teams as the Boogercats (referring to Scotland's Bogie Cats, a "fleet, elusive and courageous" animal) and some other scribes followed suit. Freutel complained that Thundering Herd made one think of "cows stampeding down a country road," but many people thought Boogercats stirred up even worse images. Needless to say, Boogercats never caught on.

Colorado State-Pueblo ThunderWolves
After more than sixty years using Indians as their nickname, in 1995 the university adopted ThunderWolves.

The school even came up with their own legend for their mythical creature: "The thunderwolf was discovered in the Southern Colorado foothills in 1933. The species is thought to be indigenous only on the city of Pueblo's beautiful horizon from the Spanish Peaks to the south to Pike's Peak to the north. A regal and majestic animal, the thunderwolf has evolved into the wisest and strongest of all beasts."

Auburn Tigers
Auburn is adamant, their nickname is the Tigers! Their battle cry is "WAR EAGLE!" The nickname Tigers comes from a line in Oliver Goldsmith's poem, *"The Deserted Village*," published in May 1770 that reads in part; *"where crouching tigers wait their hapless prey..."*

"War Eagle" is a battle cry used by Auburn fans. Although little is actually known about how the battle cry originated, it has been a part of Auburn's spirit for more than 100 years.

Colorado College Tigers
Colorado College's sports teams are nicknamed Tigers after the school colors of black and gold. The Tigers narrowly survived a 1994 student referendum to change the name to the Cutthroats (Trout).

Clemson Tigers
In 1896, football coach Walter Riggs came to Clemson (then Clemson Agricultural College of South Carolina), from Auburn University. He came from Auburn's Tigers, had always admired the Princeton Tigers, so he naturally gave Clemson the Tiger nickname.

Doane Tigers
Legend states that founder Thomas Doane's daughters created a triangular, orange and black flag in 1887 and they became the school colors, from which "Tigers" was derived in 1907.

Louisiana State Tigers
LSU's nickname is a throwback to its Confederate heritage and was drawn from the Civil War fame of two Louisiana brigades that developed a reputation as fearless, hard-fighting shock troops known as the **"Louisiana Tigers."**

Memphis Tigers
Early references to the football team were as the "Blue and Gray Warriors." During a parade for the team after the 1914 season several students yelled, "We

fight like Tigers!" and although the Tiger nickname was popular with students, campus publications still referred to the team as "The Blue and Gray." When the school was renamed, to the West Tennessee State Teachers College, teams were called Teachers or Tutors. As time passed, the nickname Tigers was reintroduced and increasingly used and was adopted officially in 1939.

Missouri Tigers

The name comes from a band of armed guards called the "Missouri Tigers" who, in 1864, protected Columbia from Confederate guerrillas during the Civil War.

Princeton Tigers

As early as the 1860s, Princetonians began wearing orange ribbons at athletic competitions, perhaps in reference to William III, Prince of Orange (of the House of Nassau), for whom Nassau Hall on campus was named. The tradition was solidified within a decade.

Princeton's "Tigers" nickname was adopted at the end of the 19th century. Throughout the 1880s football players had sported wide orange and black stripes on their jerseys and sportswriters referred to the players as "Tigers." A popular cheer used "Tiger!" as a rallying cry. College songs began to refer to tigers. By the turn of the century, a pair of marble tigers bearing shields appeared on the posts of the gateway north of Little Hall and another pair appeared on the north wall of McCosh Hall in 1907.

Fullerton Titans

In 1963 over a hundred suggestions were made for a new nickname and in a student election Titans narrowly won out over Aardvarks and Rebels.

Thiel Tomcats

Through 1923 Thiel's teams were known as the Huskies but in 1924, greatly impressed by the spirit of the Thiel football team, Carnegie Tech head coach Wally Steffen observed that "they played like wild, wild cats." This prompted sportswriter Melvin A. Blair to report, "Thiel played like Tomcats."

San Diego Toreros

Prior to 1961 the USD teams were known as Pioneers but the name changed to Toreros in homage to the school's Spanish roots. The word "torero" comes from the word "torear," to fight bulls. The university states that "USD Student Athletes, like the Torero, represent a willingness to stand alone in the ring and accept the challenge."

California State-Dominguez Hills Toros
"Toros" are Spanish fighting bulls of the Iberian cattle breed primarily bred free-range on extensive estates in Southern Spain, Portugal and Latin American countries where bullfighting is allowed.

King College Tornado
Tornado was adopted in 1922 following a 206-0 football win over North Carolina rival Lenoir College (now Lenoir-Rhyne). The local newspaper covering the event wrote the headline, "King College's Victory Was 'Tornado' Of Week's Games" and began referring to the football team as the "Tornado." The 206-0 whitewashing is the second highest scoring game in the annals of collegiate football history.

Brevard College Tornados
According to Seth Montgomery, Athletic Media Relations Director at Brevard, both of Brevard's predecessors, Rutherford College and Weaver College suffered through several fires and natural disasters, including tornadoes. When the two schools merged in 1934 to make Brevard College, its nickname came about because of the tornadoes that tore through the predecessor colleges.

William & Mary Tribe
From 1893 to 1916 teams were known as the Orange and White because those were the old official school colors. From 1916 to 1977 all William & Mary athletes were known as the Indians. Due to new NCAA regulations, in 1996 the college's executives decided to completely replace the old nickname and chose "Tribe" to show unity and camaraderie among student-athletes.

Troy Trojans
As the football team began competition in the 1910s they were called the Bulldogs or Teachers (the school began as teacher's college) but changed to Trojans in 1922. The name lasted until 1931 when Albert Elmore arrived on campus to coach the football team. As a graduate of the University of Alabama, Elmore changed the nickname to Red Wave, a variation of Crimson Tide.

The Red Wave moniker stuck until 1973, when the student body was charged with voting for its new nickname. That season's first game was on the road against Northeast Louisiana and the squad departed Troy without a nickname. However, the students voted that Saturday morning and just hours before kickoff it was announced that "Trojans" was victorious by a two-to-one margin.

USC Trojans

Up until 1912 USC teams were called the Methodists or Wesleyans and neither nickname was looked upon with favor by the students or university officials.

Athletic Director Warren Bovard, son of university president Dr. George Bovard, asked *Los Angeles Times* sports editor Owen Bird to select an appropriate nickname. As Bird later recalled, "At this time, the athletes and coaches of the university were under terrific handicaps. They were facing teams that were bigger and better-equipped, yet they had splendid fighting spirit. The name 'Trojans' fitted them. I came out with an article prior to a showdown with Stanford in which I called attention to the fighting spirit of USC athletes and named them 'Trojans' all the time, and it stuck. The term 'Trojan' as applied to USC means to me that no matter what the situation, what the odds or what the conditions, the completion must be carried on to the end and those who strive must give all they have and never be weary in doing so."

Although the noble white horse, Traveler, is one of the most famous college mascots, it didn't appear at USC football games until 1961, nor was it the first equine mascot (the first appearance of a white horse occurred as early as 1927).

USC once had canine mascots, the first a mutt named George Tirebiter I who appeared at football games in 1940. He survived a publicized dognapping by UCLA in 1947, but succumbed under the tires of an automobile (appropriately) in 1950.

Virginia State University Trojans

VSU teams were originally called the Hilltoppers and became the Trojans (and Lady Trojans) in 1932 when a student sportswriter led a campaign for the change.

Trinity Christian Trolls

Two theories exist on how this unusual name came to be. According to one, the Trinity students created an acronym by borrowing letters from themselves; **TR**inity CO**LL**ege **S**tudents.

Some insist that the nickname was born in 1966 on the eve of Trinity's first ever intercollegiate basketball game when the college president sought an alliterative nickname and after flipping through a dictionary looking for words starting with "tr" he settled on the mythical "Troll."

Utah Utes

The Utes nickname comes from the Ute tribe, from which the state of Utah derives its name. The Ute tribe gave the university explicit permission to use the name for all its athletic teams. The men's basketball team is known as the "Runnin' Utes" and the women's gymnastics team is known as the "Red Rocks."

Manhattanville Valiants

After becoming co-ed and secular in 1969, Tim Cohane, Sr., the father of the men's basketball coach, started thinking about a nickname for the former all-girl's school and came up with a 16th century quote from Jeanne d'Albret, the mother of Henry IV: "To the valiant of heart, nothing is impossible." The Manhattanville teams adopted the slogan and have been known as the Valiants ever since.

Idaho Vandals

Idaho's 1917 basketball team played defense with such intensity and ferocity that a sportswriter said they "vandalized" their opponents. Harry Lloyd "Jazz" McCarty – a writer for the student newspaper, subtly tagged the team with a new nickname in a pregame write-up: "The opening game with Whitman will mark a new epoch in Idaho basketball history, for the present gang of 'Vandals' have the best material that has ever carried the 'I' into action." McCarty's indirect suggestion stuck. By 1921, McCarty and Dean Edward Hulme succeeded in their push to have "Vandals" officially adopted as the nickname for Idaho's teams.

University of New Brunswick Varsity Reds

The Varsity Reds name was adopted in 1995. Prior to that every varsity sport had a different name with the now defunct football team being called the Red Bombers, the hockey team was the Red Devils and the women's basketball team was the Red Bloomers.

Sherbrooke Vert & Or

Université de Sherbrooke in Sherbrooke, Quebec, Canada uses the French "Green and Gold" (after their school colors) for their nickname and a fox as their mascot.

Augustana-South Dakota Vikings

The institution traces its origin to 1835 when Scandinavian immigrants established the Hillsboro Academy in Hillsboro, Illinois.

Vikings were Scandinavian explorers, warriors, merchants, and pirates who settled in wide areas of Europe and the North Atlantic islands from the late 8th to the mid-11th century and a fitting nickname for Augustana's heritage.

Cleveland State Vikings
Fenn College used the nickname of the Foxes until renamed Cleveland State in 1965 necessitating a change in nickname and Vikings was chosen.

Sweet Briar Vixens
The modern English word "vixen" is simply taken from the Old English word for a female fox. Being an all-girls school the name was chosen to embody the definition of a vixen as being an independent, smart, cunning woman.

Tennessee Volunteers
Tennessee acquired the name "The Volunteer State" during the War of 1812. At the request of President James Madison, Gen. Andrew Jackson, who later became President himself, mustered 1,500 from his home state to fight at the Battle of New Orleans. The name became even more prominent in the Mexican War when Gov. Aaron V. Brown issued a call for 2,800 men to battle Santa Ana and some 30,000 Tennesseans volunteered. Tennessee's color guard still wears dragoon uniforms of that era at all athletic events.

Portage Voyageurs
Located in Lac la Biche, Alberta, Portage's nickname concerns the legendary voyageurs who are celebrated in Canadian music and folklore.

One of the voyageurs were highly valued persons who engaged in the transportation of furs by canoe during the fur trade's era (the zenith was in the 18th and early 19th centuries). Literally, the term means "traveler" but its fur trade context is most common.

Hawaii-Hilo Vulcans
A process was started in 1965 to adopt an individual identity for the University of Hawaii at Hilo Department of Intercollegiate Athletics. Previously known as the "Little Rainbows," the committee members focused on what would best represent the Big Island of Hawaii. Volcanoes immediately came to mind.

One of the first considerations was the Hawaiian Volcano Goddess, Pele. However, out of respect for the Hawaiian culture, the committee elected not to commercialize the Hawaiian deity. In 1966, the university officially adopted Vulcans (Roman god of fire and volcanoes) as their nickname.

Nyack Warriors

Thinking that the nickname Fighting Parsons was paradoxical, Nyack changed its nickname to the Purple Pride (a name that never caught on) in 1998. The name lasted just six years before changing to Warriors in 2004.

Waterloo Warriors

After the school's founding in 1957, teams were originally known as the Mules and for a short while the women's teams were the Mulettes, a name that was almost universally despised and ultimately replaced by Athenas. Today the women's teams also use the nickname Warriors.

Pepperdine Waves

The university's 830-acre campus overlooks the Pacific Ocean in Malibu, California and a wave is a prominent feature on the school seal.

McMurry War Hawks

On March 11, 2011, McMurry approved a committee's recommendation to adopt War Hawks as the official nickname of the university at the completion of a five-month process and in the final vote nearly 4,000 votes were cast, and 70% of those votes were in support of War Hawks. McMurry had not had a nickname since 2006 when the Indians nickname was discontinued.

Louisiana-Monroe Warhawks

On January 30, 2006, the university announced that the 75-year-old Indians nickname would be retired in light of new NCAA restrictions and accepted suggestions for a new name. A mascot committee then selected 12 semifinalists.

An online poll yielded three finalists: Warhawks, Bayou Gators and Bayou Hawks and the mascot committee passed a single recommendation to the university president, who made the final decision. Warhawks was announced as ULM's new nickname on April 5, 2006 and honors Maj. Gen. Claire Lee Chennault, an LSU alumni, and his Air Force unit from World War II, which utilized the Curtiss P-40 Warhawk in battle.

Bacone Warriors

Founded in 1880 as the Indian University by Almon C. Bacone, Bacone College has strong historic ties to various tribal nations, including the Cherokee Nation and the Muscogee Creek Nation. Because of these ties the school's use of Native American imagery has not been questioned.

Hendrix Warriors

In 2006 Hendrix began using images of its new Warrior mascot that drew on a classic, barbaric vision of a warrior after it discontinued using its traditional Native American imagery in 2001.

Merrimack Warriors

Merrimack was founded in 1947 to serve soldiers returning from World War II and for this reason the Warriors name was chosen. The school does not use a mascot.

Midland Warriors

The first nickname they selected was Tigers, along with the official colors of orange and black. When the college relocated in 1919 the nickname was changed to the Warriors in recognition of a theme that tied more closely to the history of the founders.

Various warrior types were used as mascots, from Indians to Melvin the Midland Monster in the early 1990s to Leonidas, a Spartan Warrior. In 2010 a new Nordic Warrior was created to provide a connection to Midland's heritage.

Wayne State Warriors

In 1927 a student poll selected Tartars as the school's nickname. In 1999, the university changed the name to the Warriors, due to a feeling that the Tartar name was dated and that not many people knew what a Tartar was.

Emory & Henry Wasps

Legend has it that upon seeing the school's blue and gold-striped baseball uniforms in the early 1900s, a fan exclaimed, "Why, they look like a bunch of wasps!" and the name stuck. Or, after the E&H football team played the first ever game in Tennessee's Neyland Stadium in 1921, the team was referred to as "wasps" by a local Knoxville newspaper. Although Emory & Henry was pummeled that day, 27-0, legend has it that the local paper declared, "those Virginia boys stung like wasps," and the nickname has been in use ever since.

Webb Institute Webbies

The only major offered at Webb is Naval Architecture and Marine Engineering. Founded in 1889 by industrialist and shipbuilder William Henry Webb, who recognized the increasing role of science and engineering in the field of ship design, the Webbies nickname is in honor of Webb whose endowment allows students to pay no tuition (although they must pay for other expenses).

Winnipeg Wesmen
According to Sheldon Appelle, Sports Information Coordinator at the University of Winnipeg, the school was founded in 1888 by the Methodist Church as Wesley College. With a little training in the Bible, men from the college were sent out on horseback into the prairies to spread the Christian word. These men were called "Wesmen" by the early settlers.

In 1938 Wesley College joined the Presbyterian Manitoba College to form United College. United College became the University of Winnipeg on July 1, 1967. A contest was held that year and the name "Wesmen" was resurrected as the UW's nickname.

Colby White Mules
The school's nickname was adopted in 1923 when Joseph Coburn Smith published an editorial in the school newspaper suggesting that the Colby football team be symbolized by a white mule. As "White Mules" they would no longer appear as the "dark horse" of college athletics. After reading the article, a group of students located a white mule on a farm and borrowed the animal for the Bates game on Armistice Day in 1923. The mule was placed at the head of the band and student body as they marched onto the field. Colby defeated Bates, 9-6, and the win was enough to make Smith's suggestion permanent.

For many years a succession of true equine mascots bore the name "Ybloc," ("Colby" spelled backwards) although most of them were donkeys rather than pure mules. The most celebrated was a middle-aged Sicilian donkey named Louis who arrived in Waterville (via rail freight) in 1953 following a stage career in New York, during which he appeared on television with Jackie Gleason and even took a turn with the Metropolitan Opera as a cast member in *Aida*. A document in the college's "mule" file suggests that Louis was traded in at a Winthrop stable the following year as little more than a down payment on a real mule. Various benefactors contributed $50 each to buy a white mule for $296–$250 in cash "with an allowance of $46 for the donkey."

Recent efforts by the dean of the College to change the mascot to a moose were met with a general lack of enthusiasm.

Arizona Wildcats
The Wildcats name derived from a 1914 football game with then California champions, Occidental College, where the *L.A. Times* asserted that Arizona

"showed the fight of wildcats."

The Wildcats' battle cry of "Bear Down" comes from the dying words of a popular student-athlete. John "Button" Salmon was president of the student body, starting quarterback, and three-year catcher for the baseball team. Nicknamed for his small frame (5'8", 145 pounds) and impish good looks, he was very popular with his teammates, coaches, and fellow students. When Salmon died from injuries sustained in a car wreck his final words, spoken to coach "Pop" McKale, were, "Tell them.....tell the team to Bear Down." Soon thereafter, the UA student body adopted "Bear Down" as the school's athletic motto.

The year before his death, Salmon dazzled 30,000 Trojan fans at USC with his powerful punts and fearless defensive play. The recklessness of this hard-rock kid with the curly reddish hair inspired his teammates to nickname him "The Leaping Tuna." He was also a talented baseball catcher. In the spring of 1925 his clutch two-base hit drove in the winning run against USC. When he was elected student body president a few days later he referred to that hit as "the 200-vote double."

The day after the 1926 season's opening game, Salmon was driving with three friends when he missed a treacherous curve and spun over a ravine. Although the others were not seriously injured, Salmon suffered a serious spinal cord injury and died on October 18, 1926, at St. Mary's Hospital. At Salmon's funeral service, a three-mile line of cars snaked from downtown Tucson to the cemetery.

A year later the student body voted to make "Bear Down" the official slogan of all Wildcat teams and in 1939 the State of Arizona issued a proclamation declaring the phrase "Bear Down" to be the sole and exclusive property of the University of Arizona.

Cal-State Chico Wildcats
The Wildcat became Chico's nickname in 1924. According to the school's web site, it was adopted by the student body because it typified the kind of sassy, spitfire vigour and vitality the students wanted to project.

Davidson Wildcats
Davidson used a series of nicknames including Presbyterians, Preachers and Red and Black before Wildcats came along in 1918. The choice of a wildcat has several theories including an occurrence that took place in 1892. A rumour that year was started that a wildcat was seen and could be heard prowling and crying on campus at night but it was only a few students who made a wildcat out of chicken wire and rags to play a prank on a friend.

Another theory states that Davidson took the cognomen after a loss to the Georgia Tech football team. A reporter said after this game that "the Red and Black fought like a bunch of Wildcats." Others claim that the name came about after a victory over Auburn in 1917. After the game, the *Atlanta Constitution* headlined the story "Wildcats Twist Tigers' Tail."

Will E. Wildcat is the school's mascot and is best exemplified by an eleven foot long, 1,500 pound bronze sculpture on campus. Will E. is named for William Lee Davidson, the college's namesake.

Kansas State Wildcats

When the school was known as the Kansas State Agricultural College, Aggies was used for its nickname. Prior to the 1915 season, new coach John "Chief" Bender gave his squad the nickname Wildcats but the moniker lasted the one season Bender coached at K-State. Under Coach Z.G. Clevenger in 1917, the team became known as the Farmers. In 1920 Charles Bachman, took over the program, renaming the team Wildcats and this time the nickname stuck.

Kentucky Wildcats

The Wildcats nickname became synonymous with UK shortly after a 6–2 football road victory over Illinois on October 9, 1909. Commandant Philip W. Corbusier, then head of the military department, told a group of students in a chapel service following the game that the Kentucky football team had "fought like wildcats." The name quickly became popular among UK followers as well as with members of the media. As a result, the nickname was adopted by the university.

Blue and white became the official colors in 1892. The shade of blue was chosen when a student asked the question, "What color blue?" At the time, Richard C. Stoll (who lettered in football at UK in 1889–94) pulled off his necktie and held it up. The students then adopted that particular shade of blue.

New Hampshire Wildcats

The Wildcat became the official college mascot and nickname of New Hampshire in February 1926 when students cast their votes. Durham Bulls (a nickname given to the Hockey team by the local media) finished a close runner-up and other names receiving votes included Huskies, Eagles and Unicorns.

Northwestern Wildcats

"... football players had not come down from Evanston; Wildcats would be a name better suited to Coach Thistlethwaite's boys ... Stagg's boys, his pride, his

11 that had tied Illinois a week ago, were unable to score for 57 minutes. Once they had the ball on the nine-yard line and had been stopped dead by a Purple wall of wildcats." Wallace Abbey wrote those lines in the *Chicago Tribune* following the memorable Northwestern-Chicago game in 1924 that heralded a new era in Northwestern football. From that day on, all the Northwestern athletic teams have borne the nickname Wildcats.

Randolph WildCats

The WildCats nickname was coined in the 1980s with the capital letters "W" and "C" standing for "Woman's College" (the school was then named Randolph-Macon Women's College).

Villanova Wildcats

In 1926, a contest was conducted to adopt a mascot. Edward Hunsinger, one of Notre Dame's legendary "Four Horsemen" had recently been added to Villanova's football staff as an assistant coach suggested "Wildcats."
Into the 1970's VU's women's teams were referred to as the "Wildkittens."

Nevada-Reno Wolf Pack

Nevada-Reno's first athletic teams, in the late 1890s and early 1900s, were referred to as the Sagebrushers, Sage Hens or Sage Warriors after Nevada's state flowering plant, the sagebrush.

In 1921, a local writer described the spirited play of a Nevada football team as a "pack of wolves." The name stuck and soon almost every reference to the athletic teams was as the Nevada Wolves. In 1923, the students officially designated Wolf Pack for the school's nickname.

North Carolina State Wolfpack

North Carolina College of Agriculture and Mechanic Arts' teams (North Carolina A&M) were known as the Aggies or Farmers. The school changed to its current name in 1917 with the school's athletics teams being called a host of names, from Farmer & Mechanics, to Aggies, Techs and the Red Terrors.

In 1921, a disgruntled football fan wrote a disparaging letter in the school paper stating that the school's football players "acted like a wolfpack," and would never be a winner. The name stuck to the football team exclusively for a quarter century and was eventually adopted by all athletics teams in 1947.

The tradition of cutting down the nets after basketball wins dates back to the 1920s when teams in the Indiana boy's high school basketball tournament would celebrate winning the state title by cutting down the nets as souvenirs. In the first 25 years of the tournament Everett Case's Frankfort teams won four state titles.

When World War II began, Case enlisted in the Navy where he assumed the role of athletic director at various pre-flight schools and after the war ended he took over coaching duties at North Carolina State. When the Wolfpack won the Southern Conference title Case and his team cut down the net in celebration, harkening back to his time in Indiana.

Michigan Wolverines

As early as 1861, the students and alumni began referring to themselves as "Wolverines" despite the fact there had never been a verifiable sighting of a wolverine in the state of Michigan until 2004. Several theories exist on how the name came to the state and the university.

Michigan football coach Fielding H. Yost had a theory for the nickname, which he wrote about in the *Michigan Quarterly Review* in 1944. Yost felt that the reason for the nickname concerned the trading of wolverine pelts which occurred at Sault Ste. Marie for many years. Eight years later, in the *Michigan Quarterly Review* of 1952, Albert H. Marckwardt presented another theory. Marckwardt's reasoning was based on the fact that Michigan was first settled by the French in the late 1700s. The appetites of the French were judged to be gluttonous or "wolverine-like" and, therefore, the nickname "wolverines" was conferred upon them.

The last theory derives from the border dispute between Michigan and Ohio in 1803, often referred to as the "Toledo War." While the two sides argued over the proper setting of the state line, Michiganders were called "wolverines." It is unclear, however, whether the Michigan natives pinned this name upon themselves to show their tenacity and strength, or whether Ohioans chose the name in reference to the gluttonous, aggressive, habits of the wolverine. From then on, Michigan was labelled the "Wolverine State" and when the University of Michigan was founded, it simply adopted the nickname of the state it represented.

Newberry Wolves

On May 7, 2008 Newberry's Athletic Department officially retired the Indians nickname and their only identifier was a "Block N." On June 7, 2010 it was announced by Newberry's Athletic Director that the school had decided on a new nickname for its athletic teams and effective from that day forward they would be known as "Wolves."

West Georgia Wolves

West Georgia teams have been known as the Aggies, Bull Pups, Goats and Braves, a name that was done away with in 2006 due to NCAA guidelines. West Georgia president, Beheruz N. Sethna, accepted the recommendation of a task force that chose Wolves over two other finalists: Patriots and RedHawks.

Arkansas Tech Wonder Boys

Prior to 1920, Tech's team were called the Aggies. The name "Wonder Boys" first appeared in the *Arkansas Gazette* on November 17, 1920, after a 13-0 win over what is now Henderson State University. John Tucker was the best player on Tech's 1920 football team and the man known as the "Original Wonder Boy." Henry Loesch, the sports editor of the *Arkansas Gazette*, wrote, in describing Tucker, "Look out for him before he starts, for once he is on his way brick building, rock walls and other immovable bodies but slightly impede his progress...this Tucker is so good that he makes the rest of them look bad. He's so good that it is hard to see anyone else on the entire field."

Tech's women's teams are known as the Golden Suns. That name was adopted by a vote among female athletes on campus in 1975. Before that, AAU and extramural women's teams from Tech had been known as the Wonder Girls and the Wonderettes. When Tech started its intercollegiate athletics program for women in 1977, the name Golden Suns was adopted.

Georgia Tech Yellow Jackets

Nicknames predating Yellow Jackets included Techs, Engineers, Blacksmiths and Golden Tornado. The Yellow Jackets name dates to 1905, when it first appeared in the *Atlanta Constitution*. Historians say the name was first used to describe supporters who attended Tech athletic events dressed in yellow coats and jackets.

The school's teams are also known as the "Ramblin' Wreck," a name inspired when almost the entire student body traveled to Athens to see Tech's baseball team defeat Georgia in 1887. *(I'm a) Ramblin' Wreck from Georgia Tech* is the school's fight song that was based on an old English drinking song. It first appeared in print in the 1908 *Blueprint*, Georgia Tech's yearbook. "Ramblin' Wreck" is played after every Georgia Tech score (directly after a field goal/safety) and preceded by "Up With the White and Gold" after a touchdown.

Oberlin Yeomen

In 1886, varsity lettermen wore an "O" on their sweater and became known as

"Ye-O-Men" which became their nickname. In 1973 along came the Yeowomen.

Eastern New Mexico Zias (women's teams)
The men's teams at ENM are called the Greyhounds while recently the women's team changed to Zias. According to the school's website, the Zia sun symbol originated with the Indians of the Zia Pueblo in ancient times. Its design reflects their tribal philosophy, with its wealth of pantheistic spiritualism teaching the basic harmony of all things in the universe.

Akron Zips
"Zips" was originally "Zippers," a name chosen in a contest to choose a nickname for the university's athletic teams. Suggestions included Golden Blue Devils, Tip Toppers, Rubbernecks, Hillbillies, Kangaroos and Chevaliers. The name is in reference to the rubber overshoes popular in the 1920s and 30s called "Zippers" made by the Goodrich Corporation. Athletic director Kenneth Red Cochrane officially shortened the nickname to the "Zips" in 1950.

The university's mascot is "Zippy," a kangaroo, and is one of only a few female college mascots in the United States.

Hollins University – No Nickname
Proudly, Hollins has never had a nickname or mascot since organized sports were introduced in 1896 and is the only school that goes without either. Jeff Hodges, director of public relations for Hollins stated, "It is something the school has held on to and now the distinction of not having a mascot is a source of pride."

Chapter 6

Defunct Schools

This list is by no means exhaustive and some might be surprised to learn that there have been hundreds of institutions that have gone under (or that new ones are created each year). Some schools were around for more than a hundred years before shuttering but most of those that have vanished never participated in athletics. Some of these schools still exist although they've done away with sports.

Albion State Normal School Panthers, Albion, Idaho, 1893-1951
Known as the "Teachers" until 1935

Alfred Holbrook Normals, Manchester, Ohio, 1855-1941
Wendel E. Beattie coached the football team for all eight years of its existence (1933-1940) and his record of 9-49-6 (14%) is surely one of the worst all time. On November 10, 1934 the Normals lost to Findlay, 97-0; they never scored more than 7 points in a losing effort; they were shutout in 40 of their 49 losses and three games account for 34% of their total scoring.

Alliance Hilltoppers, Cambridge Springs, Pennsylvania, 1912-1987

Atlantic Christian Bulldogs, Wilson, North Carolina
Played football from 1920-1950

Barat Bulldogs, Lake Forest, Illinois, 1884-2004

Bishop Tigers, Marshall, Texas, 1881-1988

Brooklyn of the City Univ. of New York Kingsmen, Brooklyn, New York
Played football from 1930-1990

Canterbury Indians, Danville, Indiana
Played football from 1946-1950

Carlisle Indian School Indians, Carlisle, Pennsylvania, 1879–1918
The most famous of all defunct schools, Carlisle was the first Indian off-reservation boarding school. It was one of a series of nineteenth-century efforts by the United States government to assimilate Native American children from 140 tribes into the majority culture.

The Carlisle Indians football team was active from 1893 until 1917. During the program's 25 years, the Indians compiled a 167–88–13 record and 0.647 winning percentage, which makes it the most successful defunct major college football program. During the early 20th century, Carlisle was a national football powerhouse, and regularly competed against other major programs including Ivy League schools. Several notable players and coaches were associated with the team, including Glenn "Pop" Warner who had two stints as coach and the legendary Jim Thorpe whom many consider to be the greatest athlete of all time.

Cascade Thunderbirds, Portland, Oregon, 1956-2009

Emporia Fighting Presbies, Emporia, Kansas, 1893-1972
The football team had a proud tradition spanning over 70 years and won 14 conference championships, including an undefeated, untied, and un-scored upon season in 1928. Under head coach Bill Hargiss and QB Arthur Schabinger, the Presbies were one of the first teams to use the option pass and was using the forward pass as a regular play three years before Knute Rockne and Notre Dame.

Dana Vikings, Blair, Nebraska, 1884-2010
The name "Dana" is the poetic variant of "Denmark." The college was founded in 1884 by Danish pioneers.

Englewood Cliffs Eagles, Englewood Cliffs, New Jersey, closed in 1974.
On January 20, 1974, the basketball team was defeated by Essex County College by a score of 210–67, a collegiate record losing margin of 143 points.

H. Sophie Newcomb Oaks, New Orleans, Louisiana, 1886-2006
Newcomb was one of the first women's colleges to compete in national basketball games, along with Smith, Mount Holyoke and Vassar.

On March 13, 1895, Newcomb students played the first public basketball game in the South before 560 other women at the Southern Athletic Club.

Newcomb Ball, a game played as an alternative to volleyball, originated at Newcomb College and bears its name. The sport was very popular in the 1920s. The game is still played in various forms across the world.

Hedding Orangemen, Abington, Illinois, 1855-1926

Hiram Scott Scotties, Scottsbluff, Nebraska, 1965-1970
Played football from 1966-1970 and compiled a 26-14-1 record.

Lombard Golden Tornado, Galesburg, Illinois, 1853-1929
Evar Swanson played three sports at Lombard and as a member of the Cincinnati Reds in 1929, during a contest between games of a doubleheader, he circled the bases in 13.3 seconds, a record still stands.

Madison Storm, Madison, Wisconsin, founded 1858
Played football only in 1998, went 0-3 and were outscored 167-6.

Marycrest Marauding Eagles, Davenport, Iowa, 1939-2002

Marymount Saints, Tarrytown, NY, 1907-2002

Marymount Spartans, Salina, Kansas, 1922-1989
Basketball coach Ken Cochran built the school into a NAIA powerhouse racking up a record of 285-56 in 11 seasons including a NAIA record streak of 106 straight home court wins, national rankings for 10 years and a national third-place finish in 1976. Cochran also invented the original Pop-A-Shot electronic basketball game which is still manufactured in Salina.

Midwestern Packers, Denison, Iowa, founded 1965
Played football from 1965-1970

Morris Brown Wolverines, Atlanta, Georgia, 1881-current
Discontinued sports in 2003

Mount Morris Orangemen, Mount Morris, Illinois, 1839-1931

Mount Senario Fighting Saints, Ladysmith, Wisconsin, 1930-2002
Discontinued athletic programs on December 12, 2001

Nasson Lions, Springvale, Maine, 1912-1983

Nazareth Moles, Kalamazoo, Michigan, closed in 1992

Northeastern Golden Eagles, Chicago, Illinois, 1949-current
Discontinued sports in 1998

Parsons Wildcats, Fairfield, Iowa, 1893-1970
The football team played in the Mineral Water Bowl (1961) and the Pecan Bowl (1966) and lost both.

Pembroke Screaming Eagles, Providence, Rhode Island, 1891-1971

Philadelphia College of Pharmacy Devils, Philadelphia, Penn., 1821-current
The football team (1897-1914) and sported a combined record of 19-26-3. In 1898 the Devils beat the Philadelphia Dental College three times on the gridiron,

surely some sort of record.

Phillips University Haymakers, Enid, Oklahoma, 1906-1998
Between 1917 and 1920, John Maulbetsch was the head football coach at Phillips and while an All-American running back at the University of Michigan in 1914 where he earned the nickname the "Human Bullet." With his name recognition he was able to recruit big-name talent including future Pro Football Hall of Famer Steve Owen, and future United States Olympic Committee President Doug Roby. Maulbetsch quickly turned Phillips into a major contender in the southwest as his teams beat Oklahoma and Texas and lost only one game in the 1918 and 1919 seasons. The 1919 team was known as "Mauley's Iron Men" and was considered, by many experts, to be the finest football squad in the southwest that season.

Puget Sound Christian Anchormen, Everett, Washington, 1977-2001
Female athletes were called "Anchors."

Ricker College Bulldogs, Houlton, Maine, 1848-1978

St. Mary of the Plains Saints, Dodge City, Kansas, 1932-1992
The school still holds the NAIA basketball record for fewest points allowed per game in a basketball season at 1.3 (13 points in 10 games).

St. Viator Irish, Bourbonnais, Illinois, 1865-1938

Shurtleff Pioneers, Alton, Illinois, 1827-1937

Si Tanka Screaming Eagles, Huron, South Dakota, 1883 - 2005
Garner Henley, voted the sixth greatest player in Canadian Football League history attended Si Tanka where he was a first-team NAIA All-American and set records with 394 points and over 4,000 rushing yards. Drafted by the Green Bay Packers in 1960 he opted to play in the CFL's Hamilton Tiger-Cats where he won four Grey Cups and was voted an All-Star ten times in sixteen seasons.

South Dakota at Springfield Pointers, Springfield, SD, 1881-1984
The campus is now home to Mike Durfee State Prison which is named for a star athlete and a teacher at the school.

Southeastern Hawks, Washington D.C., 1879-2009

Springfield Normal Farmers, Springfield, Missouri, 1894-1905
The first night football game west of the Mississippi was played on the Normal field on October 13, 1904 against the Cherokee Indians from Tahlequah, Indian Territory with Springfield winning, 11-0. Gasoline flare lights were suspended over the field to provide lighting.

Sue Bennett Fightin' Dragons, London, Kentucky, 1897-1997
The 1983 basketball led the nation in scoring.

Tarkio College Owls, Tarkio, Missouri, 1883-1992
"Set Fire, Tarkio!" was the school's motto, often attributed to its founder, gentleman farmer, David Rankin. The school colors were purple and white and in 1940 the Owls won the NAIA Division I Men's basketball championship, defeating San Diego State 52-31.

In 1970 Brewer and Shipley named their most famous album, *Tarkio*, after the college and the album featured the song *One Toke Over the Line*.

United States International University Gulls, San Diego, California, 1924-2007
USIU was once a NCAA Division I member and at one time had the only Division I ice hockey program west of the Rocky Mountains.

On January 5, 1991, Kevin Bradshaw set the NCAA Division I record for most points scored in a game with 72, besting Pete Maravich's record of 69 set in 1970. USIU lost the game to Loyola Marymount, 186-140. The 186 points remains a Division I record for most points ever scored in a single game. Bradshaw led the NCAA in scoring that season with 37.6 points per game but the school eliminated basketball at the end of the season.

Weaver College Golden Tornadoes, Ashville, NC, 1873-1934
Weaver suffered through several fires and natural disasters and went by several nicknames including Blue Giants, Black Tornadoes and Golden Tornadoes. In 1934 Weaver merged with Rutherford College to make Brevard College.

Wesley College Warriors, Florence, Mississippi, 1944-2010

Yankton College Greyhounds, Yankton, South Dakota, 1881-1984
NFL football player, Lyle Alzado attended Yankton. Upon closing the campus was sold to the U.S. Government and today is used as a Federal Prison Camp.

Chapter 7

The Best and Worst

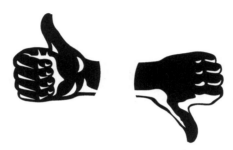

No book of this sort would be complete without a best and worst list. Of course, it's all in the eye of the beholder and we behold some to be better (and worse) than others.

In general, we're in agreement with the following breakdowns:
5% of all nicknames are Great
10% are Really Good
40% are Good
25% are Acceptable
15% are Bad
5% Stink

To the institutions listed as our favorites, we salute you. To those schools that appear on our "worst" lists, please don't take it personally but by all means take the appropriate action to rectify the situation. You will be glad you did.

The Best

CULLEN'S TOP 25

25. Denison Big Red
24. Army Black Knights
23. Toledo Rockets
22. Cobleskill Fighting Tigers
21. Cal-Dominguez Toros
20. Michigan Wolverines
19. Cal-Irvine Anteaters
18. Erskine Flying Fleet
17. Muskingum Fighting Muskies
16. Arkansas-Monticello Boll Weevils
15. Ithaca Bombers
14. TCU Horned Frogs
13. Southern Illinois Salukis
12. Coker Cobras
11. Texas A&M Brownsville Javelinas
10. Akron Zips
9. Meredith Avenging Angels
8. Drexel Dragons
7. Tufts Jumbos
6. LA-Lafayette Ragin' Cajuns
5. Vermont Catamounts
4. Southeast Okla. Savage Storm
3. Penn State Nittany Lions
2. Idaho Vandals
1. Miss. Valley State Delta Devils

JIM'S TOP 25

25. Mississippi Choctaws
24. Southern Illinois Salukis
23. TCU Horned Frogs
22. Akron Zips
21. Richmond Spiders
20. SW Louisiana Ragin' Cajuns
19. Furman Paladins
18. Washburn Ichabods
17. Michigan Wolverines
16. Idaho Vandals
15. Coker Cobras
14. Duquesne Dukes
13. New England Nor'easters
12. Cal-Irvine Anteaters
11. Santa Cruz Banana Slugs
10. St. Louis Billikens
9. Trinity Trolls
8. Centenary Gents
7. Erskine Flying Fleet
6. West Maryland Green Terror
5. Purdue Boilermakers
4. Marshall Thundering Herd
3. Wake Forest Demon Deacons
2. Coastal Carolina Chanticleers
1. Alverno Inferno

We agree on only nine names and of our Top 10 no names appear on both lists.

Cullen:

You can tell a good nickname simply by the way it rolls off the tongue. I like a name that has a little "bite" and I'm inclined to those with two-words. Aside from Jumbos (I like the story behind the name) my list tends to have a menacing sort of quality: *Black* Knights, *Fighting* Tigers, *Horned* Frogs and *Ragin'* Cajun give a shiver to opponents. I particularly like "Avenging Angels" for the fact it represents Meredith College, an all-women school. "Delta Devils" is the best for several reasons; it's alliterative, has a great back story and it conjures up the notion of threat, danger and peril required of a sports team.

Jim:

I look for originality, flow, rhythm and pertinence in a nickname.

Originality is most important and without it no nickname can make my "best" list (Polar Bears as opposed to Bears).

Flow is second in importance and the reason alliterative names are so popular. Baylor Bears has excellent flow while Bowdoin Polar Bears does not.

Rhythm is similar to flow. It is what sounds right to the ear and may be the factor that keeps a name from my list. Ohio Northern Polar Bears has a simple rhythm while New York Institute of Technology Bears is discordant at best.

While meaningless in most situations, if a cool name has pertinence *and* a gallant story behind it, you have a "best." Maine Black Bears - thrive in the forests of Maine. Franklin Grizzlies – I am going to go out on a limb here and say there are no Grizzlies living in Franklin, Indiana and none have lived there since the last Ice Age.

The Worst

Cullen's Bottom 10		Jim's Bottom 10	
10.	Franklin & Marshall Diplomats	10.	San Francisco Dons
9.	Ohio Wesleyan Battling Bishops	9.	St. Louis Coll. of Pharmacy Eutectic
8.	Whittier Poets	8.	Haverford Fords
7.	Guilford Quakers	7.	Whitman Missionaries
6.	Oberlin Yeomen	6.	Colby White Mules
5.	Syracuse Orange	5.	Pacific Lutheran Lutes
4.	Ave Maria Gyrenes	4.	Williams Ephs
3.	Haverford Fords	3.	New York Violets
2.	St. Louis Coll. of Pharmacy Eutectic	2.	Whittier Poets
1.	Evergreen Geoducks	1.	New Hampshire Penmen

We both agree on Poets, Fords and Eutectic. These are not good nicknames.

Cullen:

Given room, I would have added the Bishop Gaiters to my list because a 'gaiter' is a bishop's shoe covering. Someone didn't work very hard to come up with *that* little gem; all they did was bend over and look. I guess it could have been worse as "Loafers" springs to mind.

"Ooks" *sounds* like it should make my list but as it's the shortened version of "Ookpik," the Inuktitut word for Snowy Owl it gets a pass (though just barely).

"Diplomats" and diplomacy are best left off the athletic playing field. Although "Battling Bishops" has a war-like quality, we're still talking about *bishops.* Poets might poke their own eyes out with a dull quill. Quakers and Yeomen simply don't evoke fear and either could have been replaced by "Lutes" or "Webbies." I give no consent to a color as a suitable nickname and "Violets" is the most egregious but could have been (easily) replaced by "Orange," "Cardinal" or "Maroons." I simply do not understand "Gyrenes" and only four people in the world know what a "Eutectic" *is.* As far as I'm concerned, "Fords" are trucks and the name would have been better served if it was "Fjords." Who are they trying to kid with "Geoducks" (pronounced gooey-ducks)? Goo is the stuff I wipe off the bottom of my sneakers.

Jim:

Some nicknames are best left unsaid. We're sorry, but we just don't think there is a place for wimpy nicknames that were chosen by academic scholars who busied themselves by meandering through the pretty flowers whilst contemplating the wonders of nature, music and poetry.

Nicknames are for teams that fight to win! They should be mean, scary, triumphant, or, at the very least, a funny antithesis of these ideals. Even the worst nicknames can be improved dramatically by adding or changing one element (see below). If these schools took our advice they would be some of the most intimidating teams of all time.

OLD		NEW
10.	San Francisco Dons	Don **Corleone**s
9.	St. Louis Coll. of Pharmacy Eutectic	**Hectic** Eutectic
8.	Haverford Fords	Ford **Mustang**s
7.	Whitman Missionaries	Mission **Impossible**
6.	Colby White Mules	**Bad Asses**
5.	Pacific Lutheran Lutes	**Looters**
4.	Williams Ephs	Eph **Ewes**
3.	New York Violets	**Violent** Violets
2.	Whittier Poets	**Dirty Limerick** Poets
1.	New Hampshire Penmen	**Pig**pen Men

*   *   *

OTHER (REALLY) BAD NICKNAMES:

Blue	Gusties	Preachers
Bonnies	Hustlin' Quakers	Reddies
Britons	Jimmies	Regents
Camels	Johnnies	Seasiders
Cardinal	Lopers	Spires
Crimson	Lord Jeffs	Statesmen
Drovers	Lutes	Varsity Blue
Foresters	Oles	Varsity Red
Gee Gees	Parsons	
Governors	Pomeroys	

Overtime: Stuff We Found Along the Way

- Only two nicknames are derived from former professional athletes; the Keystone Giants (Christy Mathewson) and the North Texas Mean Green (Joe Green).
- On the Pitt campus can be found more than twenty panther statues.
- Little known Mary Lyons' name is used as the nickname for two different colleges; Mount Holyoke Lyons and Wheaton College Lyons.
- Hollins College is the only college without a nickname for its athletic teams.
- Three college nicknames were taken from novels; Xavier Musketeers (*The Three Musketeers*), Sonoma State Seawolves (*The Sea Wolf*), Iowa Hawkeyes (*Last of the Mohicans*).
- Two schools have nicknames derived from architecture; St. Mary Spires, Moody Bible Archers
- The St. Mary's Belles nickname is the only one taken from a movie (*The Bells of St. Mary's*).
- A State Senator from Wisconsin once proposed that the "Badger" of the University of Wisconsin be replaced with a cow.
- The Wells College Express is the only nickname taken from a company (Wells Fargo).
- Edward Hunsinger, one of Notre Dame's fabled "Four Horsemen" was responsible for the Villanova Wildcats nickname.
- Hall of Fame pitcher Gaylord Perry was the first baseball coach at Limestone College.
- In the logo for the UC Santa Cruz Banana Slugs, the slug can be seen reading a book by Plato.
- The Lincoln University Railsplitters is the only nickname that honors Abraham Lincoln.
- The Evergreen State Geoducks is the only nickname taken from a mollusk.

Made in the USA
Las Vegas, NV
02 September 2021

29486147R00136